USING 'THE' AND OTHER DETERMINERS

BY KEVIN KIRK

THIS BOOK BELONGS TO

Published by Indgenius Limited
61 Bridge Street, Kington, Herefordshire, HR5 3DJ, UK

This book forms part of the CORE English series, see the website for details: **www.englishbook.shop**

Quantity sales. Special discounts are available on quantity purchases by corporations, associations, libraries, schools and others. Members of the website also qualify for discounts. Please see the website for details.

USING THE AND OTHER DETERMINERS
Written by Kevin Kirk
A CORE English Reference Book
1st Edition
First Published in 2019

ISBN 978-1-9160757-0-2

ACKNOWLEDGEMENTS

This book is dedicated to the memory of Peter Kirk who died, aged 19, from diabetes related complications. Peter helped enormously in the initial stages of the creation of the core series. he compiled the phrasal verb and idiom lists and wrote most of the definitions and examples. He also provided many of the sample sentences in the noun and adjective books.

He is sorely missed.

This book is also dedicated to my lovely daughters, Arienne, Brianna and Paula (Kamonchanok).

REWARD

Is the copy of the book you are holding genuine? Does it have a distinctive watermark on the reference pages? If not it might be an unauthorised copy. This book took 1,000s of hours to produce and just copying it is not only not fair but will force the price up for honest people like you. If you suspect this copy isn't real then please contact us via the website and you can be eligible for a reward.

www.englishbook.shop/copying

Contents

Contents

Contents

Contents

Contents

Contents

Contents

Contents

Contents

Contents

Contents

Contents

Other Determiners continued...

Contents

Other Determiners continued...

ABOUT THIS BOOK

There are so many 'rules' regarding how to use determiners and, in particular, articles that it would be impossible to remember them all.

So, this book takes a different approach in that it acts as a reference book, so if the reader wants to know whether to use an article, say, then they look it up. This is particularly relevant when using 'the', which even experienced and near fluent English learners find daunting. This means that the book is the "missing link" between a dictionary and a grammar book: it covers each of the most commonly used determiners in great detail, including the nuances of their use, and where they fit into the grammatical constructs.

CORE books all follow a similar format in that they focus on one particular word type or part of speech and cover individual examples in depth. In this way you can see:

- A specific corpus (list) of the recommended words of this type that the learner should use in their work.
- How the words are used in terms of their context.
- Where they appear in the sentence.
- What types of words they are co-located with; in many instances, with the exact word they usually accompany.
- The exact meaning(s) of the word/phrase.
- Specific information about the word or phrase with comprehensive descriptions and comments.
- A huge number of examples, giving at least one example of how the word/phrase is used with each usage concept.
- A very comprehensive table of contents so you can find your area of interest quickly and easily.
- A selector (specialised index) so you can find exactly the right word/phrase to use in your writing.
- A website on which you can find answers to your questions and learn in real time.
- An introduction to how the associated website can be used to find contextually correct examples of the word in action.
- A description of the methodology behind CORE English.
- Comprehensive (British English) pronunciation exercises.
- A fairy story that explains what the various parts of speech do, in a whimsical, easily understood way.

WHAT IS CORE ENGLISH?

CORE English is a methodology that was designed to make it easier for English language students to visualize how the language fits together in order to create grammatically correct sentences. In doing so it overturns, or modifies, a certain number of established grammatical 'rules'. It was based on over 7 years of research undertaken at Mahidol University in Thailand and was developed with the help and cooperation of over 2,000 students of varying abilities. The word CORE doesn't represent either an adjective or a noun, but, instead, it represents a verb as it basically cuts out certain sections of a sentence based on the central focus (i.e. the core) in order to study or modify them. In order to demonstrate the methodology in simple terms let us look at a particular sentence construct and how it is being taught at present:

In the afternoon a small number of the more health conscious students will be exercising.

Ok, so let's break that down into the constituent parts of speech:

In	Preposition
the	Definite article
afternoon	Noun
a	Indefinite article
small	Adjective
number	Noun
of	Preposition
the	Definite article
more	Comparative adjective
health	Noun
conscious	Adjective
students	Plural Noun
will	Modal Verb
be	Auxiliary verb
exercising	Present participle of the verb 'exercise'

Imagine being a learner and being confronted with that. When teaching a sentence construct like this you'd normally start with something simpler:

Today the students exercise.

This breaks down into:

Word	Type
Today	Adverb
the	Article/Determiner
students	Noun
exercise	Verb (Intransitive)

Now, what about if we used this same construct with the sentence on the previous page?

Word Cluster	Type
In the afternoon	Adverb
a small number of the	Article/Determiner
more health conscious students	Noun
will be exercising	Verb (Intransitive)

This, in essence, is what CORE is all about. It 'clumps' word clusters into types, which then become interchangeable. So, a beginner can start off with simple constructs and simply substitute more complex structures to add granularity and nuance to what they are trying to say.

Adverb: the above representation is a prepositional phrase, these are used to add granularity to where something appears in time or space. If we use the simple adverb, **today**, it gives us a broad idea of when something is taking place, but we may need to have more details, for example we may want to attend, so we use prepositional phrases. For example: **today** may be represented by the prepositional phrase **in the afternoon** and if we want to add even more granularity we simply add another prepositional phrase to indicate the start time, **from 2 p.m.** and we can also add an end time using another preposition phrase, **to 4 p.m.** So **today** and **in the afternoon from 2 p.m. to 4 p.m.** are interchangeable and can both be regarded as adverbs.

Article/Determiner: articles and determiners are usually regarded as special types of adjectives and, for the most part, are single use words that each have to be learned separately. In CORE they are treated as a special grammatical type and range from single words (like a, an, the, some or any) through to complex clusters consisting of various word types. Each cluster conveys a special meaning so the learner can move from the simple **the** (indicating a specific group) to **a small number of the** (indicating a particular subset of a specific group).

Noun: In most EFL classes we focus on the specific word(s) that attach a description (or label) to something, such that it can be recognised. In CORE this definition is broadened out using adjectives, so that nouns can be represented by noun phrases (as in the example above) or even adding verbs and adverbs so, what we consider to be noun clauses, are treated as simple nouns in terms of sentence construction. So the simple '**students**' could be replaced by the phrase, **more health conscious students** or a noun/adjective clause like **students who want to keep fit.** Grammar 'purists' would say that the noun clause example here is actually a noun (**students**) plus an adjective clause (**who want to keep fit**) but it is essentially interchangeable with a noun; so, in CORE it is regarded as a noun.

Verb: In CORE, verbs are regarded as single entities, so the simple bare infinitive verb **exercise** could be exchanged with a more complex structure, such as **will be exercising**, depending on the context. So all the learner has to do is to choose the action/state and then choose the tense/voice using the context.

To summarize, in CORE grammatical terms the following sentences have the same construct and elements within them and can be freely interchanged.

Today	the	students	exercise
⇕	⇕	⇕	⇕
In the afternoon from 2 p.m to 4 p.m	a small number of the	more health conscious students	will be exercising

TYPE CONSTRUCTS

Some of the grammatical constructs in the methodology are fairly rigid and unchanging, others are infinitely variable. The main constructs are:

Adverbs (variable): single word adverbs basically consist of 4 basic types (plus adjective graduators and conjunctions), which can vary in terms of sentence position. These words are generally used to describe things like methods or positions in time or space. To these single words you must add the extremely variable (and flexible) prepositional phrases, which can add granularity to how, where or when something exists or has been done, how it was done and by how much.

Articles and Determiners (fixed): These constructs follow a predictable pattern, with the exception of some optional adjective graduators, so you can merely study the various definitions and choose the one that best suits your context using the reference book.

Nouns (variable): Nouns are primarily labels and have to be learned in order to recognise objects or entities (they are generally the first things we learn when we learn a language). Nouns are unique to every person and, in general, the larger the number of nouns the person knows the better their range of English. On the other hand we can thrive knowing only a subset of the total inventory of other types of words. In addition you must consider nouns that have been created from verbs (to describe actions or states rather than doing or experiencing them) known as infinitives (usually to describe something that is intended to happen) and gerunds (usually describing something that has happened before or is ongoing).

Verbs (fixed): Verbs are the most structured and rigid grammatical constructs; therefore, in many ways they are the easiest to learn once the constructs are recognised. These constructs and contexts should be studied by looking at all of the choices and associated contextual meanings. This should focus on the way the verbs are used, not on the meaning of the individual verbs, as these can be looked up in a reference book once the use has been determined.

SUB-TYPE CONSTRUCTS

Sub-types are used to vary the meaning inherent in the main type and sentence structures in order to add nuance or to create a better mental 'picture' in the mind of the listener or reader. They can also be used instead of the main constructs to add further detail to something that is already known (pronouns), to create a purely mental (abstract) image of what is being discussed (adjectives) or to get more information (questions).

Adjectives: These can be regarded as an adjunct to nouns. Nouns are how we understand our world, allowing us to visualise, or at least understand, whatever it is being talked about. In other words they refer to factual objects that we know to exist. Adjectives, on the other hand, tend to be based purely on imagination as we all relate to the things described by adjectives in a different way. A simple example is how a colour blind person imagines 'red' to how everyone else imagines it. Because they are imaginative constructs, adjectives, when used alone, describe abstract or relative concepts (like physical, mental or emotional states) and could almost be considered to be imaginative versions of nouns. They can also be used to clarify or add imaginative concepts to noun phrases and also act as standalone abstract references.

Conjunctions: Conjunctions are used to add words, phrases or complete sentences to the text, primarily in order to add clarity. In grammar they have a number of names associated with them (such as markers, conjunctions, conjunctive adverbs or subordinating conjunctives) but they all work in the same way, to add the 'glue' to bind grammatical structures together.

Pronouns: These are a subset of nouns. They are used in the same way as previously known nouns prefaced with **the.**

Infinitives: Infinitives are mainly used to indicate intent (usually after a verb and before a noun) or what something is used for.

Questions: These can be regarded as a subset of verbs as they generally involve verb/subject manipulation and a fairly rigid structure. The majority of question types involve subject/verb inversion (swapping) with so called 'wh' question words used to specify the type of answer that is expected.

MAKING VARIABLES

There are two constructs that are variable. The first are **adverbs**, which provide more details about the action or state, including the dimensional, characteristic or spatial qualities, that the objects and/or players in the sentence are witnessing, enacting or experiencing and the second are **nouns**, which describe the static objects or players in a sentence.

Adverbs: Adverbs add extra information to whatever action has taken place, is taking place or will take place. They are not required in the sentence but they answer questions about things like dates, methods, magnitudes or places. They can also add extra detail to adjectives and to join sentences of equal weight together. They can be in the form of single words, where they answer questions such as the manner in which something is done (how), the place where it was done (where), when it was done (when), the degree of what was done (how much) or the number of times it was done in a given time period (how often).

In order to provide answers to question that require complex answers they can take the form of prepositional phrases in order to answer questions above plus the cause of something, the content of something or the direction of travel. Prepositional phrases can generally be used to replace single word adverbs in order to add more detail - the prepositions reference in this series give examples for each of the prepositions in the corpus - and follow a particular pattern:

Preposition   Noun (phrase/clause)

The structure of the noun can vary, but the principle remains the same, where the preposition itself is used to announce that extra information is being given and then the noun provides the information. The noun can take a number of forms depending on the complexity of the information. For example, using the intransitive verb, go, we can use any of the following to add the information:

I went *there* (simple adverb)

I went *to* the big park (***prepositional*** phrase using a noun phrase)

I went *to* that place we know (using a noun clause)

Finally, if you need to associate an action, rather than a static image, to the extra detail you can add an adverb clause.

I went where I always go (adverb clause)

Nouns: Nouns are the heart of a sentence as they are the objects which do things, have things done to them or are used in order to create the result. They depend on the listener or reader having a mental image of what they are or represent and therefore they tend to be surrounded by extra detail, usually in the form of adjectives, in order to provide an exact picture. For example, we all know people and their mental image is recalled using their name. So, we can say something like 'I saw **Kate** today', where Kate is the noun. Which is fine if we only known one Kate, but what if we know more than one? In that case we can add an adjective to clarify what Kate we have in mind, usually by noting a particular attribute, so our sentence could read 'I saw blond **Kate** today', this is known as a noun phrase and can comprise of a number of preceding adjectives such as in the sentence 'I saw tall, beautiful, blond **Kate** today'.

Another way is to add another noun in order to create a compound noun, in which case our sentence could read 'I saw **Kate Jones** today'. If we don't know, or can't remember her name, then we can use a noun clause, so our previous sentence could be, 'I saw **that tall, beautiful blond girl I told you about** today'. Note that in each instance the sentence remains intact, 'I saw…today', with just the noun changing.

If we want to add further attributes to the noun, in the form of an active description, then we can add an adjective clause, so the sentence could now read 'I saw Kate **who I think is very beautiful** today'. Note that the adjective clause is added after the noun and in both instances the adjectives or adjective clauses are adding abstract characteristics to what is a static mental image.

In addition, rather than going through the tedium of describing Kate in every subsequent mention of her in the conversation, we can use a form of shorthand called a **pronoun.** So the sentence and follow on sentence could read 'I saw Kate today. **She** was going to the library'.

Finally, we often want to specify the noun and to do that we precede it with a determiner. In most grammar books determiners are counted as adjectives but in CORE they are treated as separate grammatical structures in order to make them interchangeable.

In CORE, both adverbs and nouns are treated as single entities so they can be interchanged with other constructs of the same type whilst still retaining the correct grammatical structure.

CREATING SENTENCES

Using the constructs created on the previous pages we can now create a sentence. A simple sentence with a subject and object would look something like this:

Determiner	Noun	Verb	Determiner	Noun	(Adverb)
(null)	Fred	is eating	his	lunch	now

The null determiner in the first column is a place marker as we don't use a written determiner with a proper noun. The adverb is in parentheses as it is optional.

Determiner	Noun	Verb	Determiner	Noun	(Adverb)
The	dogs	drank	their	water	(null)

We can leave out elements without affecting the basic structure, for example with intransitive verbs with no objects but with a prepositional phrase to show how they did it (manner).

Determiner	Noun	Verb	Determiner	Noun	(Adverb)
Our	guests	left	(null)	(null)	in a car

We can see that the sentence can be defined in terms of a pattern and in order to help to visualise that pattern we can use colours, either by underlining each construct or by drawing directly onto a transparent overlay. The colours used in CORE are displayed on the back cover of this book and were chosen to provide the most memorable contrasts between the various constructs.

Sentences in CORE are built outwards starting with the chosen word/cluster type, then their associated support words. This is the exact opposite of the 'traditional' gap fill, where the correct type of word is inserted into a pre-written sentence. Although this looks to be harder it gives the benefit that contextually sensitive sentences can be produced, thus making it easier to 'think' the sentence.

The pattern used above is very simple and is a good starting point but more complex sentence structures can be built using more complex patterns and visualised using colours. The colours can be used to visualise the elements in a sub construct in order to see how complex constructs are formed.

PARSING SENTENCES

In order to help to visualise how a sentence is constructed in terms of its grammatical pattern we can go through it word by word using colours to highlight the words. Note, it is always a good idea to look for infinitives first (to + verb) and highlight them first (in orange) so you don't confuse them with prepositional phrases, then look for conjunctions in order to be able to recognise clauses. For example the following sentence:

The students who passed the exam are invited to receive a certificate from the Dean at 1 p.m.

This breaks down into:

The	*determiner*
students	*plural noun*
who	*conjunction*
passed	*verb*
the	*determiner*
exam	*noun*
are invited	*verb*
to receive	*infinitive*
a	*determiner*
certificate	*noun*
from	*preposition*
the	*determiner*
dean	*noun*
at	*preposition*
1	*determiner*
p.m.	*noun*

If we pull out the clause (prefaced with the conjunction) and the prepositional phrases we get:

The students...are invited to receive a certificate (main sentence)

who passed the exam (adjective clause)

from the dean (prepositional phrase)

If we look at the structure of the main sentence we see:

determiner	noun	verb	infinitive	determiner	noun
The	students	are invited	to receive	a	certificate

As we can see this is similar to our original sentence with the addition of an infinitive to express intent. The adjective clause that follows can be regarded as part of the noun as it helps to enhance it. The structure of the clause is similar to that of a sentence where the determiner and noun have been replaced by the pronoun, **who** (referring to the noun [students] that been mentioned earlier).

conjunction	verb	determiner	noun
who	passed	the	exam

This just leaves the prepositional phrases, which, as we discussed earlier, can be regarded as adverbs. The preposition phrases themselves have a fairly rigid structure usually consisting of:

preposition	determiner	optional adjective(s)	noun
from	the	(faculty)	dean
at	1		p.m.

Questions: Questions follow one of two main forms. The first is where the subject and verb the <u>auxiliary verb and subject are swapped</u> (aka inverted). These can be preceded by nothing, a pronoun, or an adjective or adverb form of a determiner. The main forms are:

<u>Are you</u> going?
Open question usually answered with yes or no

Who <u>are you</u> going to the cinema with?
Pronoun question word answered with a noun

Which movie <u>are you</u> going to see?
Determiner question word answered with a subset of noun choices

Where <u>are you</u> going to see the movie?
Adverb question word answered with a place or time

The other main question form is called a tag question and it usually consists of a sentence followed by (tagged on) a negative form of the verb, with the <u>verb and subject swapped</u>:

The students are seeing the dean, <u>aren't they</u>?

LEARNING WITH CORE

All too often English is taught as an academic subject hedged round with pages of rules that have to be memorised before a sentence can even begin to be constructed.

The philosophy behind CORE is to get straight down to writing grammatically correct sentences simply by plugging in pre-determined, constructs into an existing sentence structure. In other words it is learning by doing.

The way it works is to identify word/phrase clusters as being of a certain grammatical type - such as determiners, verbs, nouns or adverbs - and then substitute them for other words/phrases of the same type that express exactly what is wanting to be said. This was illustrated in the previous section.

In order for it to work the learner will need a fully explained corpus (essentially a detailed list) of sufficient grammatical types/words to cover the overwhelming number of variables. In other words a sufficient breadth to cover over 99% of all situations but not too many to be overwhelming and unwieldy to use. The final corpus used in the methodology uses just over 5,000 words. The biggest group are the nouns of almost 2,000 words, followed by over 1,200 verbs. These words were obtained by scraping documents of all types from around the world with a focus on spoken words (unlike most corpora, which are derived from purely written texts), slang words were then filtered out and, if thought to be important or used enough, included in separate sections (mainly in idiomatic speech in the idioms book). Then the words were categorised into their respective word types, if a word appeared in multiple word types, as many do, their frequency of use in that word type was studied to ascertain whether they warranted inclusion in that word type's corpus. If they were sufficiently commonly used in two or more categories comparisons in their use for each category were included, together with sample sentences, to highlight the differences.

After the sections had been created they were further categorised into use categories to make them easy to find and use. Examples of this are adverbs being categorised into manner, frequency etc or adjectives being categorised into descriptive types, such as positive and negative physical descriptors etc.

These were then written into separate books and their uses were described in detail. The resulting books should be regarded as reference or guidance books rather than 'learning' books. If they were to be categorised they'd fall somewhere between dictionaries and explanatory grammar books. Unlike grammar books they provide copious examples of the word/phrase use in different contexts and some contain exercises to practise self creation based on the principles using the learner's own writing. This allows the learner to create sentences within their own contexts rather than being constrained by those in the grammar book, which they may not understand and would find hard to use in their own work.

In order to parse the word/phrases out of existing sentences the use of colour is recommended. The books themselves are not coloured in order to keep the cost down but the recommended colours are shown on the back cover of this book: the individual book covers are also coloured to reflect the word types being explained. The colour palette was chosen on the basis that they are commonly available in the form of lost cost felt pens and/or coloured pencils and so the methodology can applied at very little cost. The individual colour assignments for each word type were chosen by a focus group who concentrated on the most recognisable resultant patterns once the individual words/phrases had been coloured. This allows the learner to see the grammatical structure of the sentence, particularly common problem types such as prepositions and determiners/articles. Using this method tracing paper can be used to 'lift the word types' from existing sentences by placing it over sentences and then colouring in the words. The resultant pattern can be used to create new grammatically correct sentences without being encumbered by the previous words in the sentence. In this way learners will see that certain sentence structures can be used to express particular grammatical forms (such as statements, questions, travel etc.)

Whilst researching the methodology inherent in CORE particular attention was paid to specific areas of difficulty that students were having in learning how to use English. These specific areas were then studied and simplified by restructuring them. One example of this is how verb tenses are approached; where, instead of saying that continuous/progressive tense consists of a verb plus auxiliary verb it would, instead, consist of a state verb and an adjective.

So 'I am running' is now **I** (pronoun) **am** (state verb stating what follows describes my physical state) **running** (the adjective that describes my physical state). This method simplifies the tense structure as the learner only needs to remember the tense structure of the state verb (a challenge in itself given the various forms of 'be') and then simply append a suitable adjective - with the choice based on the context so the same structure would apply to I am **running**, I am **hot** and I am **tired**, using a present participle, a simple state adjective or a past participle respectively - subsequently guiding the students to use adjectives based on present participles of verbs to talk about ongoing states is far easier than trying to parse tenses. Incidentally, tenses are covered in both the 'conventional' way and using the CORE methodology in the verb books so as not to confuse people who have already grasped the current principles and who merely want to see the nuances of how particular verb tenses are used and what they are used for.

Similarly with determiners, they now contain determiner phrases as well as individual words and they also include words that would 'normally' be regarded as, say, pronouns as determiners. Ask yourself this: if you are a learner you are told a pronoun is used <u>instead</u> of a noun and then you are told to put a 'possessive' pronoun in front of another noun would you be confused? It is far less confusing to regard the possessive pronoun as a determiner - which can be substituted by another determiner if required - than to run though a sort of mental boolean truth table of if A precedes X then it is B. The structure remains the same it is just the nomenclature that is changing.

Another area of difference between current English grammatical text books is in pronunciation. Pronunciation is the key to confidence and it is an important component in the books. It is based on the International Phonetic Alphabet (IPA) and uses the phonemes inherent in 'received' English (previously known as BBC English). This is not because of some sort of cultural imperialism but simply because if the students learn to pronounce all of the received English phonemes correctly then they are more easily understood. Moreover, there are 44 phonemes in received English, which allow more precise enunciation than the 38 in US English (when the early Americans left England they forgot to take most of the diphthongs with them).

Some changes were made in further simplifying the pronunciation of certain words, particularly verb participles, to make them easier to say and understand and an alternate alphabet is proposed. The dedicated pronunciation book covers this important topic in detail; moreover, each book in the CORE reference series features pronunciation for each word/phrase and a common pronunciation exercise. This exercise was carefully designed to include as many of the mouth shape (consonants), tongue position (vowels) and tongue transition (diphthongs) conjunctions as possible so as to provide a good introduction to the spoken language for beginners. It can also be used as a public speaking warm up exercise. Every book contains a short story, in the form of a fairy story, to whimsically introduce learners to the various words types.

Regarding the reference books themselves, each one focuses on the use of a particular word type and covers it in great detail, including copious examples of the word/phrase being used in different circumstances. They also cover such things as the origins of words, differences in pronunciation and spelling between UK and US pronunciation, comparisons of the same word when used in other forms and specific details applicable to that word type (such as collocations used to create phrasal verbs in the verb tables and whether nouns are countable, uncountable or both and whether they are used as verbs). Each word type book has a 'word/phrase/type finder' in place of a conventional index (the table of contents for each book is very comprehensive) so the learner/user can quickly find the right word/phrase/construct to suit their exact requirements. Finally, they also contain information and graphics to assist teachers in the classroom as well as being useful as reference books for individual learners or writers of all types who need to use the language.

In addition there are three books that underpin the reference books and contain an overall view of the language (Glossary), areas where learners make mistakes and a writing book that puts all of the methodology together in a simplified form. Finally, there is a website dedicated to the methodology, which contains discussion, exercises and answers, plus a range of useful tools. It can be found at:

www.englishbook.shop

CORE BOOK SERIES

The CORE reference books currently include:

Writing in English: This book provides a step by step approach to how the various words and word clusters covered in the rest of the reference books are used in practise. It ranges from the formation of simple sentences, incrementally adding phrases and clauses in order to create compound and complex sentence structures. It also provides guidance about paragraph writing and leads on to essay and speech writing and structures. At the end of the book there is the CORE basic corpus, arranged by word type, in order for the learner to be able to recognise and change the words in the samples in order to create their own grammar constructs and a master contents for all of the books. It can also be used as pocket guide to writing with or without the rest of the CORE reference materials and would provide a handy guide to learners involved in formal English classes.

Adjectives: This book covers all aspects of adjective use such as placement, creation of comparatives and superlatives, noun substitution and clauses. It also categorizes common adjectives into useful categories in order for the user to choose the ideal adjective to suit their required meaning. There are also an adjective table, featuring all of the recommended adjectives in alphabetical order, together with sample sentences. These sentences have spaces underneath to allow the various word types to be colour coded according to CORE recommendations and/or add user sentences. There are no definitions under the adjectives in the main text are they are regarded as subjective (imaginary), but they are featured in the adjective selector.

Adverbs: This book covers adverbs in depth including such things as: adverb types, adverb placement, comparisons, and clauses. It also lists all of the recommended adverbs together with their meaning, their types, what prepositional phrase could be used to replace them and examples of their use. There is also a comprehensive adverb selector.

Common Mistakes and Pitfalls: This book covers commonly mistaken words and phrases and covers homophones, homonyms, commonly mistaken word comparisons, misspelled words and misused words. Contractions and abbreviations are also commonly misused and so they too appear in this book.

Articles and Determiners: Determiners and their subset, articles, are commonly misused and misunderstood. In fairness, for non-native speakers they are very difficult to use, with the, in particular, being commonly misused or omitted. This book looks at over 400 common noun types and subjects and studies the 'rules' on how **the** is used and the exceptions to these 'rules'. It also covers other types of determiners, including determiner phrases, that are usually referred to as pronouns or adjectives. There is also a determiner selector. It is a reference book for every non native English writer.

Changing (And Making) Words: This book is mainly about where certain types of words come from and how to convert words to other types of words using prefixes and suffixes, plus a section on the roots of many English words derived from languages like Greek and Latin. It also covers French, Latin, Scandinavian, Anglo Saxon, Greek and other source words and phrases that are commonly found in English today together with both their current meanings and their original meanings. It is ideal for creating new brand or product names.

Idioms: The use of English language idioms is a sign of a good understanding of the language; moreover, they are very commonly used and so a comprehensive reference is required to 'translate' them. This book contains over 4,000 of the most commonly used idioms together with their meanings and sample sentences illustrating their use in different contexts.

Key Verbs: This book covers the most commonly used verbs, which are found in over 80% of every day conversations and writing, and should be the first ones learned and thoroughly understood. To assist in this each verb is covered in depth listing each of its meanings, together with sample sentences. In addition there are examples of how the verb is used as or with a prepositional phrase, as an infinitive, with and in clauses, as a gerund, as a phrasal verb, in the passive voice, in its subjunctive form, in its adverb form, in its noun form and in its adjective form. Additionally, its past and present participles and the simple past are covered, with their respective pronunciation, together with whether it is used as a transitive, an intransitive verb or both. Finally its use in every tense for every person, both in the active and, if applicable (e.g. it is transitive), passive voice. The book also contains exercise sheets for every verb so it can be used in a classroom setting or for self study together with the website.

Nouns: This reference book takes a comprehensive look at the use of nouns using a carefully selected corpus that will cover over 99% of general English needs. It covers all of the different types of nouns including countable and uncountable nouns, recognising and creating nouns from other word types, gender specific nouns, compound nouns, portmanteau words, irregular nouns, common collective nouns, noun phrases and noun clauses. In addition it contains sections on nouns grouped by type, for example those use in specific circumstances and a list of recommended nouns together with their pronunciation, whether they are countable, uncountable or both and whether they are concrete, abstract or both. This section contains 1,892 recommended nouns together with sample sentences and definitions, comprised of 973 countable nouns, 239 uncountable nouns, 654 nouns that are both countable and uncountable, 20 nouns that are only ever used in the plural form and 6 that are only ever used in the singular form.

Numbers, Days, Dates and Time: This book takes a comprehensive look at the use of numbers, days, dates and times in English. It covers such topics as how they are presented (numerically or in words), formats, uses and origins. The book also supplies various numerically based tables covering such things as computer numbering, ASCII, including extended ASCII, and other computer based codes as well as tables showing numbers such as UNICODEs and colour codes. There are also various graphics for use in the classroom.

Question forms and other Miscellany: This book takes an in depth look at question formation and their uses in clauses. It also contains a glossary of English terms plus a wealth of other information such as how to recognise and use conditionals, conjunctions, interjections, euphemisms, anagrams, differences between UK and US English, British understatement, oxymorons, palindromes, metaphors and similes. There is also a section listing all the countries of the world together with links to further information.

Phrasal Verbs: phrasal verbs are commonly used in English and usually have a different meaning to the bare infinitive version of the verb. They may also have more than one meaning depending on the context. This book lists 1,500 of the most commonly used phrasal verbs together with over 2,000 meanings and sample sentences. It also has a phrasal verb selector so you can find exactly the right verb.

Prepositions: Prepositions are the most commonly misunderstood words in English, yet they are very commonly used and thus vital to learn. This book takes a comprehensive look at prepositions; covering such topics as what prepositions are, how prepositions can be used as a more comprehensive form of adverb, using prepositions in speech, answering questions using prepositions, categories of prepositions, the origins of common prepositions and the use of prepositions with pronouns, nouns and noun phrases. There is also a preposition selector to help you to find exactly the right preposition to suit your needs. The use of prepositional phrases as adjectives, using prepositions with noun clauses, how prepositions were derived and a list of the most commonly used compound prepositions including meanings and sample sentences are also included. Finally, it takes a comprehensive look at the currently most used prepositions together with their various meanings (they invariably have more than one meaning) and how they are used in various contexts, together with numerous sample sentences.

The alternative to nouns - Pronouns, Infinitives and Gerunds: This book explores the various types of word forms that can be used instead of nouns to change nouns from passive objects to active (verb based) objects and to avoid repetition. The infinitives section covers the formation and use of infinitives to express such things as intent and their use as adjectives and adverbs. It also covers collocations with adjectives and certain verbs and contains a comprehensive list of the most commonly used infinitives, together with sample sentences. There is also a guide to how infinitives and gerunds, based on the same verbs, are used in various contexts.

The gerunds and present participle section highlights the uses of gerunds and how gerunds and present participles, although appearing to be the same, are different. It includes a section containing the 1,000 most commonly used gerunds and present participles showing how they are used in sample sentences. Finally the pronouns section covers the various types of pronouns and there is a pronoun reference section containing all of the commonly used pronouns in use together with a definition of their use, their pronunciation, their type (indefinite, subject, object etc.) and what verb tense needs to be used with them. There are also numerous sample sentences and each pronoun has a comprehensive comment section outlining all aspects of the use of the pronoun in English.

　　　　　　　　

Pronunciation: Correct pronunciation is the key to confidence when learning English and this book focuses on English pronunciation in its many forms. It takes a very comprehensive look at the subject including subjects such as: a short history of English (why we speak like we do), the IPA symbol charts, creating consonant sounds, consonant/letter tables, creating vowel sounds, mouth parts involved in speech, creating diphthong sounds, vowel letter pronunciations, pronouncing the 'ed' ending of verbs and past participles and vowel and diphthong phoneme uses. The uses section covers how individual phonemes are used in various combinations in English words, each of which is accompanied by a large number of sample words, so the learner can practise the sounds of that phoneme within the word structures, and exceptions (and samples) are included to show where and when the pronunciation differs. In addition there is a British English practise section highlighting why British English sounds different to US English. There is also a long vowel and diphthong association section, including US and UK pronunciation differences, a section on stressing words and syllables and also a comprehensive section on the use of silent letters - including the most common words containing silent letters and the history showing why the letters are silent as well as the exceptions. Finally there is a complete set of IPA flashcards, which can be copied and used in the classroom. The pronunciation audio files are available on the website (see below).

Punctuation and Use of Capitals: This book provides a comprehensive guide to the use of both punctuation and capital letters. Each punctuation symbol is covered in depth together with numerous example sentences. Obsolete and rarely used symbols are also covered as well as intellectual property symbols and planetary and astrological symbols. It also covers the use of codes, such as bar codes, QR codes and Morse code. Greek symbols are also covered, both in their upper and lower case forms, together with their various uses in English. There is even a free font that accompanies this book that includes all of the special characters, including things like Braille, Runes and religious symbols (including the Bahai 9 pointed star) amongst others; with a guide on how to easily insert them into your writing. The use of capital letters sections covers such things as using capitals in sentences and in formal correspondence. There is also a section on the use of certain types of punctuation under special circumstances or to add stress.

The Big Verb Book: This book provides comprehensive verb tables that cover all of the CORE recommended verbs. Each table shows the various uses for the verb and contains the past simple, past participle, third person structures and pronunciation. Common collocations are also included giving a guide to their possible use in phrasal verbs. There is also a guide as to what type of verb it is: transitive, intransitive, both intransitive and intransitive, a state verb or a linking verb. There is also a guide to verbs that also function as nouns. Sample sentences are provided in both the active and, if appropriate, the passive voice.

The irregular and regular verbs are covered separately in the book and the irregular verbs generally have comments appended as their use may be subjective (for example some verbs are irregular in UK English and not in US English and vice versa). This book is a pure reference book in that no explanations are provided as these are covered in the verb tenses and questions book. There is a very comprehensive verb finder at the end of the book so the learner can choose exactly the right verb to suit their needs.

Verb Types and Tenses: This book takes an in depth look at the use of verbs in English. It covers such things as action verbs, state verbs, linking verbs, transitive verbs, intransitive verbs, sense verbs, auxiliary verbs, abstract verbs, modal verbs, moods, functions of verb tenses, subject/verb agreement, intransitive verbs, transitive verbs, forming active and passive verb tense constructions, meanings and uses, active voice versus passive voice, which verbs can be made passive and when to use the passive voice.

The verb tense construction pages allow the learner to choose exactly the right tense to use for any given context by providing every use of that tense together with numerous examples, both in the passive and active voice. There is a tense selector at the back of the book which guides you towards the correct verb tense to use and how to use them.

The worksheets that are included with every tense form are designed to be used in the classroom or as personal development within the context of the learner's experience thus making it easier for them to relate the sentences they produce to their everyday life.

THE WORLD OF THOUGHT

A Fairy Story by Kevin Kirk

Welcome to the world of complete thought. In our world we have an aristocracy, called the pronouns, led by the first person, 'I'. I almost always leads the parade (called sentences in your world) it is present in, unless questions are being asked, in which case I is preceded by its personal bodyguard verb 'am'. 'You' is I's closest confidant and is the second person in the kingdom. Other, less senior, pronouns like he, she and it are the third persons. If I belongs to a group it gets a special status and name, 'we' (the royal we), signifying the group includes the first person.

If I isn't in the group then it is automatically relegated to third position and given the name they. I also has a body double called 'me', as do he (him), she (her), we (us) and they (them) when they are loitering, unprotected, at the end of the parade. 'I' doesn't want 'you' to get above itself so 'you' isn't given a body double and has to share a bodyguard, are, with we and they. The other pronouns have to share a bodyguard, is, with the nouns.

The middle class are called the nouns and their only job is to describe something. The nouns are always trying to achieve a higher status by being recognised by the determiners. The grandest of these is 'the', who, together with its lesser acolytes, 'a' and 'an', have the name 'the articles'. It is considered a great honour for 'the' to walk in front of a noun in the parade marking them out as being special. If 'the' doesn't consider the noun to be worthy (for example 'the' likes rivers and forests but not lakes or cities) then the nouns can hire the lesser (impoverished) pronouns to walk in front of them in the parade as their determiners or even appear instead of them (but I and You are far too grand to do this), giving the impression that they are well known enough not to appear in person. When 'the' makes 'a' or 'an' stand in front of a noun it announces to the world that the noun isn't special at all but is just one of many (the is a bit of a coward and would never do that to a group of nouns – although 'the' will use 'some' to walk in front of uncountable numbers of positive nouns or 'any' in front of ones 'the' considers to be negative or questionable). 'The', being a civil servant, likes to count things - so it often gets numerical determiners to walk in front of plurals. 'The' is very jealous of 'I' and has a yearning to lead the parade. In written parades 'the' is more popular but in spoken parades 'I' is the still the most popular.

Having very little to do, nouns are constantly striving to appear less boring, so they hire make-up artists, beauticians, hairdressers and PR executives, called adjectives, to walk in front of them. Adjectives boast that they can flatter any noun ('we can make any girl beautiful' it says on their website). Nouns can also hire adjectives to make their rival nouns look ugly or stupid.

The world has a police force, called the prepositions, who walk in front of the nouns telling the subjects where to go, what to do and when to do it. As in your world, the little ones are the most authoritarian; always ordering the kingdom's subjects to go <u>to</u> a place, <u>by</u> a certain time, <u>on</u> a certain day and be either <u>in</u> or <u>out</u> of a place <u>at</u> a specific time. On the other hand the big, fat desk sergeants, like around and about, are far more easy-going.

Then there are the working class; the verbs. They are simple folk and like to do a job once and then relax but they are often made to do repetitive jobs. They have their children (called the 'ings'), who are continually running round and their old people (the 'eds') who like to reminisce about things they did in the past. The problem, for these simple verbs, is that the ings and eds keep getting kidnapped and put to work by the nouns and adjectives. The nouns even give the children a middle class name, 'gerund', whereas the adjectives prefer the name participles ('It reminds us of flowers. Beautiful, exciting, fragrant, tropical, colourful, sensual flowers,' said an adjective spokesword). The gerunds are made to dress up as nouns and talk about the work their parents do, so the nouns can pretend they are workers too. Adjectives make the ings stand in line with other adjectives and categorize nouns or to rush round, while being guarded by an auxiliary, continually doing things for the pronouns or nouns. Meanwhile, the eds are made to go on chat shows and talk about the feelings that the nouns or pronouns are experiencing or their great achievements.

The simple verbs tried to get help from the other tenses but the perfects, being young professionals with no ings of their own, had no time to talk about it. Time is not important to them; it's results that count. And the perfect continuous, being teenagers (they still have a bit of 'ing' in them, even though they try to look grown up by adding 'ed' to their name), spend all their time complaining about how long they've been forced to do something for. The simples did approach the newspaper reporters, the passives, who wrote tear-jerking editorials then went off for long, expensive lunches. They are called passives because they don't do any work themselves they just report and comment on things that other people do and spread gossip (usually without saying who did it, in order to avoid being sued).

CORE Reference Book

Intransitive verbs cannot become reporters as they aren't considered acquisitive enough to require any objects (reporters must acquire objects to write about) and usually summon a police word to walk after them to protect them if an object tries to follow them around (the other words mock them by calling them 'phrasal verbs' to indicate they have lost their true meaning).

The politicians, called the adverbs, were also approached but they were more interested in pretending they had a hand in whatever work it was that the verb was doing. You can tell who they are because they always appear in the parades wherever they like (they have even been known to walk in front of I) in order to show themselves off. So when a poor verb has done the work the adverb pops up to say how, when, where or how difficult it was to do, thus trying to claim the credit. Many of them were adjectives before becoming politicians and give themselves the title 'ly' (like 'mp' in your world) after their name to show they no longer have to indulge in grubby trade nor do they have to deal with nouns, except to grade them and they only do that through an adjective. Other, older ones, like today and tomorrow, can trace their ancestors right back to the prepositional phrases, so they don't need 'ly' to gain the respect they need to lead, or trail, a parade.

The lawyers, the conjunctions, weren't a lot of help either. All they do is add clauses (to make things clearer they say) and spend most of their time giving long winded explanations of nouns or appearing for nouns or adverbs. Some politicians are still involved in their previous legal practises and make a very good living as conjunctive adverbs bringing two equal parties together, but they are always shielded from other, lesser, words by ';' and ','. All of the simple tenses suffer, even the 'irregulars', so named because they are regarded as hippies as they like to do things differently, who tried to give their 'eds' different names to try and disguise them but with limited success.

As far as the punctuation are concerned, nobody ever listens to them, in fact everyone stops talking when they show up. They are there to clear up after the parade has passed and they are often misused. However, the periods are armed with a sickle when questions are being asked, or a club when strong statements are being made, in order to act as a rear-guard. Commas simply clean up part way through long parades, especially when fussy, non-defining conjunctions are involved, and inverted commas just highlight what people say. Not many people seem to know what the colon family does, although there are whispers that the weird looking cousin, semi colon, (the one with a permanent leer) is a sort of super comma and people generally change the subject when the perpetually shocked colon appears.

CORE Reference Book

The pronouns and favoured nouns have their own special category of armed verbs working for them, called the auxiliaries, who had been recruited many years ago, mainly from Germany, and who protect the pronouns by walking just behind them in a parade or standing in front of them when potentially hostile questions are being asked.

They also have their sages, the modals, who, despite changing the entire mood of a parade, are considered useful because they can predict the future, assess possibilities or provide reasons why past events are effecting the present.

There are also palace functionaries, called the state verbs, whose job is to provide a link to the adjectives and nouns (a pronoun is far too grand to have direct contact with a mere tradesman like an adjective or a noun) to let people know how or what the pronoun, or favoured noun, is feeling or what they are thinking.

The paralegals, named linking verbs, can be hired by nouns to directly compare themselves with other nouns or even pronouns in order to flatter themselves. Linking verbs, being professionals, rarely exhibit any emotion and tend to just provide a connection between two or more things.

Anyway, I'd love to tell you more about our world but here comes the parade.

Oh dear, 'the' isn't going to like that; being made into a mere object by honouring a simple, unadorned noun like that.

I am leading the parade.

CORE Reference Book

PRONUNCIATION

Read each sentence aloud slowly, pronouncing each word as carefully and properly as you can. Do not pronounce the numbers at the start of each sentence. The underlined parts of the words are the phonemes that correspond to the IPA symbols in the right hand column.

Vowels and Diphthongs	Symbol
1) Each team's dream keeps them lean and mean	iː
2) They mainly aimed to play the same game	eɪ
3) Fred said the dreaded red bed's ahead	e
4) Pretty women hit lit nymph's lips in Italy	ɪ
5) I dried my right eye by Guy's night light	aɪ
6) Oh no Joe don't throw goats at my beau	əʊ
7) After class a sergeant marked father's parked car	ɑː
8) Awed audience applause bored Claudia	ɔː
9) Pulling wool could be good for a full woman	ʊ
10) Whose gruesome true new ewe oozes wooziness	uː
11) Gert hurt germs burning her wormy shirt	ɜː
12) Demure juries sure cure pure manure	ʊə
13) Joyce's moist boys enjoyed choice oysters	ɔɪ
14) Mere seers near here fear tiered deer	ɪə
15) Town clowns frown at brown cows on couches	aʊ
16) A happy cat sat on a plaited mat in Nat's flat	æ
17) Where prayerful bears stare at a mare's hair	eə
18) Father's aggrieved about Italian national cinema	ə
19) Bud loves running up other muddy ruts	ʌ
20) Lots of hot grog rots soggy pods	ɒ

Pronunciation Practise Continued

Consonants	Symbol
1) **P**eter **P**iper **P**icked a **P**eck of **P**ickled **P**epper	p
2) **B**rian's **b**ig **b**rother **b**reeds **b**ad **b**rown **b**ears	b
3) **T**ed **t**ried **T**ony's **t**ame **t**ricks **t**en **t**imes on **T**uesday	t
4) **D**an's **d**usty **d**ogs **d**esperately **d**rink **d**espite **d**ining	d
5) **Ch**urlish **Ch**ur**ch**es ea**ch** **ch**urn **ch**eddar **ch**eese	tʃ
6) **J**ulie conjures up lar**g**e **j**amborees **d**uring **J**une	dʒ
7) **K**evin **K**irk's **c**aterwauling **c**reates **c**onstant **c**onfusion	k
8) **G**ood **G**reeks **g**ive big **g**arish **g**liders **g**uiltily	g
9) **F**our **f**oul **f**ellows **f**looded **F**eltesham **f**en	f
10) **V**iolet's **v**icarious **v**anity **v**eered **v**i**v**idly **v**ertical	v
11) Be**th** **th**inks **th**ings **th**oroughly **th**rough	θ
12) **Th**e te**th**ered bro**th**er bo**th**ered **th**eir mo**th**er	ð
13) **C**itizen **S**am **s**aw **s**everal **c**eremonial **c**edar**s**	s
14) La**z**y **z**oos free**z**e ha**z**ardous **z**ebras	z
15) **Sh**irley **s**ure **sh**ines at **sh**earing gari**sh** **sh**ipshape **sh**eep	ʃ
16) A**z**ure trea**s**ures lei**s**urely plea**s**ures	ʒ
17) **M**any **m**en **m**ove **m**o**m**entous **m**ountains	m
18) **N**ine **n**urses **kn**ew **n**ewts **gn**awed **n**uts	n
19) A phala**nx** of si**ng**ers weari**ng** ri**ng**s sa**ng** so**ng**s	ŋ
20) **H**ubert's **h**ut **h**appily **h**osted **H**arry's **h**armonium	h
21) **L**ucy **l**ikes **l**ooking at **l**ove**l**y **l**i**l**ac **l**ace	l
22) **R**estless **R**hinos **r**oam **R**wanda's **r**oomy fo**r**ests	r
23) **W**ally **w**ore **w**arm **W**ellingtons **wh**en it **w**as **w**et	w
24) **Y**es, Vignette's **y**ellow on**i**on **y**ields **y**ards of **y**ogurt	j
*Note: Rwanda is pronounced /ruˈæn.də/	

WHAT ARE DETERMINERS?

The textbook definition of determiners is that they should be regarded as adjectives; albeit ones with a special function.

However they do differ from adjectives in certain ways that indicate that, although many grammarians disagree, they should really be regarded as separate parts of speech.

Some of these reasons are:

- Whereas most adjectives can take the comparative (-er) or superlative (-est) form, most determiners cannot (for example you cannot have my-er or his-est).

- Determiners are normally required in a sentence (except only under certain special circumstances), whereas adjectives are not. This includes null determiners, where the word is implied but not written or said, for example: I bought ___ milk; where the blank can be represented by words such as no word, **the** *or* **some**.

  Examples:

  I bought __ milk (no word - the milk is my contribution).
  I bought **the** milk (**the** – I bought the milk you asked me to buy).
  I bought **some** milk (**some** – I bought it so you don't need to).

- Determiners can, and often do, have corresponding pronouns but most adjectives do not. Determiners will always preface a noun phrase whereas adjectives will not.

- Determiners express the attributes of the thing being referred to; for example, the possessives **my** and **your** are used without articles and so can be regarded as determiners. So, their main attribute is that they occur together with a noun in order to put that noun (or noun phrase/clause) into context. That is, a determiner may indicate whether the noun is referring to something definite or indefinite or something belonging to or associated with a specified person or thing, or to a particular number or quantity, etc. Adjectives, on the other hand, are used to classify nouns using imaginary and subjective concepts such as the feelings they invoke, how they affect the senses, how they fit into specific classifications and to what they can be compared or measured against.

DETERMINERS IN CORE

In CORE determiners are considered to be an intrinsic part of every sentence. In other words, they are always given a position in the sentence, after the verb and/or the preposition and before the noun or noun phrase. In addition, certain types of determiner are used to preface clauses (such as than or when).

In addition to the recognisable articles (a, a, the, some and any) there are a number of other determiners such as indicative determiners (that, this, these and those), possessive determiners (such as my, your and our), numerical determiners (such as one or ten million), fractional determiners (such as half, quarter, a tenth etc. - where they are are usually used in compound determiners with 'of' e.g. a quarter of), interrogative determiners (such as what, which and whose) and null determiners, indicated in the examples like so: '__'.

Unlike other English grammar texts, CORE also has compound determiners. The main reason to treat these phrases as single entities so they can be interchanged easily with other determiners and they simplify the grammar.

Without doubt, the biggest problem that English language learners have is the complexity of using articles and their relationship to other words types (referred to as pronouns or adjectives) that appear to fulfil the same function. So, if we can simplify things by regarding these constructs as determiners without changing the grammar itself in any way then why not do it? It also gives us the benefit that we can now interchange them when we want to create nuanced meanings. For example, see how different determiners can be used in the same sentence (The types are a null determiner ___ , definite article, possessive determiner, indicative determiner and, finally, a compound determiner):

I saw (__ *or* **the** *or* **my** *or* **those** *or* **a couple of**) cats in my yard.

In many ways this is the core of CORE as it were because we can now apply this methodology and break the language down into 4 types of speech (with sub-types that be introduced in a structured way as the learner progresses).

　　　　

INTRODUCTION TO ARTICLES

The Golden Rule: Singular countable nouns ALWAYS have an article or determiner.

The use of articles is one of the biggest problem areas for English learners, yet they are extremely important for good composition.

Articles, which are a subset of determiners, are used to precede nouns in English and are extremely commonly used; indeed the definite article, 'the', is the most commonly written word in English (The pronoun 'I' is the most commonly spoken word - we love talking about ourselves!). This section was developed in order to demystify the use of articles. In addition to the use of articles it also covers the use of other determiners that are used instead of articles.

When deciding whether to use an article the first decision is whether the noun that ultimately follows the article is generic or non-generic. A generic noun is one that has no gender associated with it. The majority of nouns in English are generic (unlike, say, French where most nouns have a gender associated with them). Bearing this in mind we can create a set of simple rules that work in most cases:

Type of noun	Article	Example
Indefinite Singular Countable with vowel sound	**an**	I have an Iphone
Indefinite Singular Countable with consonant sound	**a**	She has a Windows phone
Indefinite Plural	-	I can see __trees
Indefinite Uncountable	-	I drink __ tea
Definite Generic Plural	-	Trees have __ leaves
Definite Non-Generic Singular	the	I saw **the** mountain
Definite Non-Generic Plural	the	I saw **the** mountains
Definite Non-Generic Uncountable	-	__Talking is important
Definite Non-Generic Countable	the	I liked **the** meal you made

Note, articles (**the, an, an, some** and **any**) are a subset of the wider class of words known as determiners. You will find a comprehensive reference section for all of the most commonly used single word and compound determiners at the end of this book. Meanwhile, one of the most important things that needs to be considered when deciding what article or determiner to use is whether the noun they precede is countable or uncountable. So, countable and uncountable nouns are covered next.

COUNTABLE NOUNS

Countable nouns are easy to categorize in that they are things that can be (and usually are) counted. For example, you can count things like students, people, cars, plates or aircraft. They can take either the singular (dog) or plural (dogs) forms.

The indefinite articles **a** *or* **an**, the definite article **the**, and *quantifying determiners* (such as one or twenty) can be used with countable nouns. For example: ***Two*** buses are coming over **the** hill.

When a countable noun is singular, then a determiner, such as a, an, the *or* one, or a possessive or indicative determiner, would always precede it in the sentence.

Example	Type of determiner
I need **a** drink.	Singular and not specific
Only **one** student failed.	Singular and specific
Has anyone seen **my** bag?	Possessive singular
How much is **that** laptop?	Indicative singular
Can you carry **those** bags?	Indicative plural

When a countable noun is plural, then it generally wouldn't be preceded by an article, unless it is specific in some way (in which case **the** would be used) or it belongs to someone (use a *possessive determiner*) or it is being indicated (use an **indicative determiner**).

Example	Explanation
Beer is stored in _ bottles.	Bottles is the simple plural noun
We all have _ phones.	Phones is the compound plural noun
Where are **the** students?	Students refers to a specific group
These are *my* books.	The books belong to someone
I like **those** paintings.	The paintings that are being indicated

If you want more precision when working with plural countable nouns you can use one of the compound determiners that are covered in depth at the final section of this book.

For example the compound determiner 'a lot of the' can be used to indicate an uncounted number from a *known (counted) group*:

A lot of the *students* are not coming in today as they are sick.

UNCOUNTABLE NOUNS

Uncountable nouns (also known as mass nouns) refer to things that are indivisible, in other words they cannot be easily separated into individual units and counted. They can also refer to things that could be counted but aren't; for example students are generally countable but when referring to them generically (without specifying them or the group they're in) they are treated as uncountable.

Examples of generally recognised uncountable noun types are: **academic subjects** (chemistry, biology, calculus), **aggregations** (advice, information, news), **collectives** (furniture, cutlery, luggage), **abstract concepts** (music, art, beauty), **emotions** (anger, fear, love), **environments** (land, forest, savannah), **exertions** (work, trouble, toil), **fibres** (string, rope, wool), **food** (fruit, meat, fish), **gels** (toothpaste, face cream, lotion), **liquids** (water, juice, milk), **indivisible living things** (algae, grain, grass), **materials** (paper, plastic, metal, wood), **powders** (sugar, salt, sand), **professions** (dentistry, law, medicine), **fatty solids** (soap, fat, cheese), **hardened solids** (concrete, cement, resin), **shades** (light, darkness, murk), **phenomena** (noise, quiet, haze), **sport** (volleyball, soccer, rugby), **substances** (poison, medicine, drugs) or **prohibited or controlled items** (tobacco, cocaine, cannabis, kratom).

Uncountable nouns will not use singular articles (**a** *or* **an**) but they can use the articles **any** (usually in questions or negative answers), **some** (mainly in positive statements) or **the** (to specify the collective).

In order to specify a quantity of an uncountable noun you would use a specifying a unit of measurement, with the noun preceded by the word _of_ (which provides a good way of recognising uncountable nouns in written texts).

The determiners in the examples are in **_bold_**.

Example	Explanation
_**An**_ ounce _of_ flour.	Ounce is the unit of measurement
**The** pile _of_ luggage.	Pile is the quantity of specified group
**Two** teaspoons _of_ sugar.	Teaspoon is the measured quantity
_**A**_ group _of_ students.	The students are unspecified
**That** box _of_ fruit is full.	Box is used as the countable unit.

ARTICLE CHOICE FLOWCHART

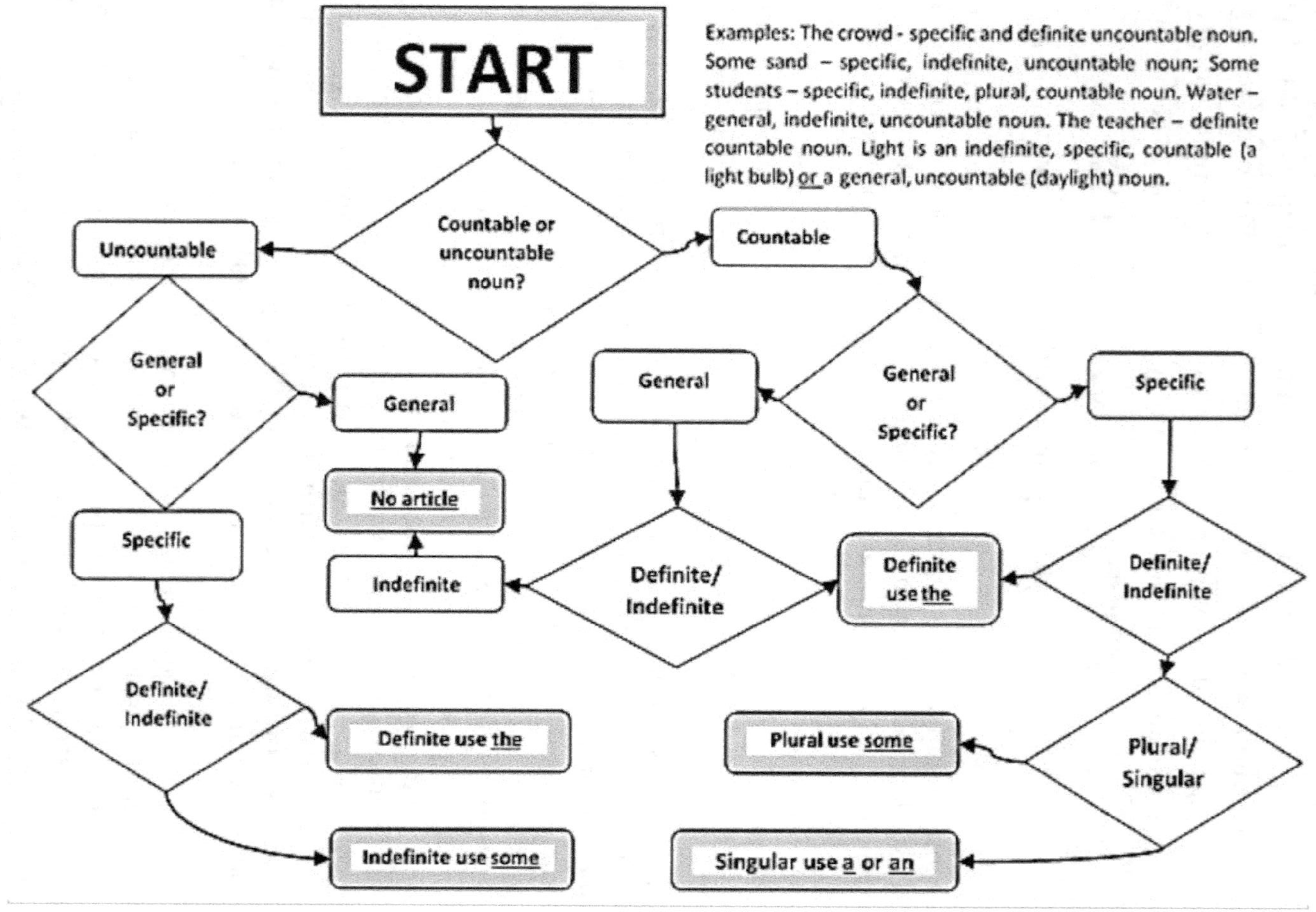

ADJECTIVES -V- DETERMINERS

Determiners are often referred to as adjectives; albeit ones with a special function. However they do differ from adjectives in certain ways that indicate that, although many grammarians disagree, they should really be regarded as separate parts of speech.

For example, whereas most adjectives can take the comparative (-er) or superlative (-est) form, most determiners cannot (for example you cannot have my-er or the-est).

Determiners are normally required in a sentence, whereas adjectives are not. This includes null determiners, where the word is implied but not written or said, for example: I bought   milk, where the blank can be represented by no word, **the** *or* **some**.

Examples:
I bought _ milk (**no word** – meaning that the milk is my contribution)
I bought **the** milk (**the** – I bought the milk that you asked me to buy)
I bought **some** milk (**some** – I bought it so you don't need to)
I bought **no** milk (**no** - I didn't buy the milk, maybe I forgot)
I bought _ it (**no word** - the thing you asked me to get [pronoun])

Note, as milk is uncountable it wouldn't be prefaced with a numerical determiner except if they are quantified with a container (I bought **two bottles of** milk).

Determiners can, and often do, have corresponding pronouns but adjectives do not. Determiners will always preface a noun phrase whereas adjectives will not.

Determiners express the attributes of the thing being referred to; for example, the possessives **my** and **your** are used without articles and so can be regarded as determiners.

So, their main attribute is that they occur together with a noun in order to put that noun (or noun phrase) into context. That is, a determiner may indicate whether the noun is referring to something definite or indefinite or something belonging to a specified person or thing, or to a particular number or quantity, etc.

As a test they can be replaced with the article 'the' in most sentences; whereas, adjectives cannot.

PRONOUNS -V- DETERMINERS

The 'rule' is that they are only regarded as determiners if they precede a noun phrase, whereas if they are on their own they are generally regarded as pronouns, as they are replacing the noun.

In Questions

In questions we use both determiners and pronouns in order to receive a noun in some form (noun, noun phrase or noun clause) in return. Determiners are generally used to find out a sub-set of the following noun; whereas, pronouns are generally used to find out the overall name or description. Study the following examples.

Examples of question words

What music do you like?
In this case **what** is a determiner and it is indicating that the speaker wants to know the name of the sub-set of the following noun (music).

What is that dreadful noise?
In this case **what** is a pronoun and is indicating that the speaker doesn't know the name of what the noise is.

In Statements (indicatives)

When we are talking about something, whether in the singular (**this** or **that**) or as part of a group (**these** or **those**), we generally use the determiner to indicate the attributes of the following noun and we use the pronoun as either a replacement for the noun or as the noun complement.

Examples of indicatives

This hat is too big (**this** is a determiner).
This is a big hat (**this** is a pronoun – noun complement).
This is too big (**this** is a pronoun – noun replacement)
These people are my students (**these** is a determiner).
These are the ones I like (**these** is a pronoun – noun complement).
These are nice (**these** is a pronoun – noun replacement)

　　　　Website: www.englishbook.shop

PRONOUNS -V- DETERMINERS

Some determiners can be mistaken for pronouns and vice-versa - as they are usually the same words. Compound determiners (aka determiner phrases), which are covered later, are not generally used as pronouns but, in some circumstances, particularly if the sentence has been simplified or reduced, they can be. You should consult the reference section later in this book for details.

The most commonly confused ones are possessive pronouns and possessive determiners. The rule is that if they appear before a noun they are determiners, whereas if they appear instead of a noun they are pronouns.

Regarding gender based determiners and pronouns the following table shows the differences in use:

Person	Pronoun	Determiner
1st singular	This car is **mine**.	This is **my** car.
2nd singular	Is that bag **yours**?	Is that **your** bag?
3rd (female)	I think that phone is **hers**.	I think that is **her** phone.
3rd (male)	Is this pen **his**?	Is this **his** pen?
3rd (thing)	Which food bowl is **its**?[1]	Which is **its** food bowl?
1st plural	Which car is **ours**?	Which is **our** car?
2nd plural	Are these children **yours**?	Are these **your** children?
3rd plural	I think that taxi is **theirs**.	I think that is **their** taxi.

[1] Although this is grammatically correct it is regarded as being clumsy, so the determiner version would usually be used.

There are two main areas where pronouns can be used and determiners cannot:

Reflexive pronouns, where the pronoun refers (reflects) back to the pronoun at the beginning. For example, **I** drew this artwork **myself,** where **I** is the pronoun and **myself** is the reflexive pronoun.

Reciprocal pronouns, indicate that both parties will do something for the other and get something back in return. Foe example: They greeted **each other** by waving their hands, where **each other** is the reciprocal pronoun.

NUMERICAL DETERMINERS

Given that the function of a determiner is to define, or to express, proximity, or <u>a relationship</u>, or <u>a quantity</u>, then it must be true that other determiners must exist other than just plain articles.

Numbers, for example, are often used as determiners, with cardinal numbers used for expressing quantities (two apples, five hundred people) and ordinal numbers used to indicate a relationship (first [1st] prize, second [2nd] place).

It is not usual to place another determiner in front of a number being used as a determiner (in which case the second number would be regarded as part of a compound determiner). Moreover, they can be used together with, say, an article to indicate that the group (or place) referred to by the number is somehow unique or special.

For example: the 2nd prize went to… *or* **a three man** team…

Fractional Determiners: Can be be used to show that a quantified subset is in a certain state. For example: I was **half** way there *or* **Half the** time he sat there doing nothing.

If an article or another determiner precedes the number, then the numerical determiner is used to create the compound determiner. In the following examples the articles/preceding determiners are <u>underlined</u> and the numerical determiners are **emboldened**.

For example:

He won <u>first</u> prize.
Ordinal determiner (first)

This is <u>the</u> **first** time I have been here.
Ordinal compound determiner (the first)

<u>One</u> person came to the show.
Cardinal determiner (one)

This is <u>my</u> **one** chance to impress her.
Cardinal compound determiner (my one)

Numerical determiners versus **numerical adjectives** versus **numerical nouns:** they look very similar but they have different meanings.

I sat on step **five** (**noun,** the name of the step is **step five**).
There are **five** steps (**determiner,** the number of steps).
<u>It is a</u> **five** step staircase (**adjective,** one of a type of staircase).

NOUNS -V- DETERMINERS

Possessive nouns can be used instead of determiners in order to show that someone is associated with someone else or something belongs to something else.

Examples:

Sheila's friend (**Noun** describes the person associated with a friend).
Her friend (**Determiner** describing a friend 'belonging' to someone who is known already).
The friend of Sheila (The friend is the focus of the sentence and the association with Sheila is merely clarification).

Recognising possessive nouns

You can recognise them because they are followed by '**s** (for single owners or irregular plural noun owners) or **s'** (for plural owners).

Examples:

Fred<u>'s</u> cat (The cat belonging to the single person Fred).
The student<u>s'</u> study room (The study room for all of the students).
The sheep's field (Irregular plural noun owners).

Using determiners and possessive nouns together

Providing the noun is not a proper noun (for example a name) then it can be preceded by a possessive determiner in order to further clarify the noun.

Example:

<u>My</u> **mother's** house (<u>my</u> is the possessive determiner which defines that the following possessive noun, **mother**, is associated with me).

Using determiners and possessive nouns with adjectives: Adjectives can also be used between the determiner and the possessive noun to provide extra details.

Example:

<u>Their</u> *favourite* **teacher's** class (<u>Their</u> is the possessive determiner, *favourite* is the adjective and **teacher's** is the possessive noun).

USES OF DETERMINERS

Determiners can also be used to put nouns into context by describing abstract nouns, to indicate how many nouns there are, to indicate whether they are definite or indefinite (for example a single specific thing or just one of many from within a group), whether they belong to someone or something and to ask questions about the nouns.

To Describe Abstract (uncountable) Quantities: These determiners help to show the number of instances or the approximate amount of the nouns. These determiners are primarily relative rather than absolute (they don't provide exact numbers but, instead, provide relative quantities). They usually appear first in the determiner order when used in compound determiners.

Examples:

All candidates must fill in an application form.
There aren't **enough** candidates.
Few people took part as it was raining.
Great numbers flocked to the party banner.
Half measures were served as there was a shortage.
Many students are worried about their exams.
No applicants met the entry criteria.

To Describe the (countable) Number of Nouns: These determiners use cardinal numbers to describe exactly how many nouns are being referred to. Examples: one two, three, twenty three etc.

Examples:

You can only really count on **one** person; yourself. (Numerical determiner expressed as a word.)

Only **1** person volunteered (Numerical determiner expressed as a number).

Mains electricity generally has a P.D. of **250** volts. (The determiner is included in the prepositional phrase).

The UK national debt was **£48** billion in mid **2018** (note the currency symbol - Pounds Sterling in this case - precedes the numerical determiner, but in speech it would be stated as "forty eight billion pounds".) The year is expressed as a numerical noun.

USES OF DETERMINERS

To describe a fractional part of a noun: When talking about a described part of a whole, from either of a countable group or an uncountable mass, then a fractional determiner would be used. It would commonly be used within a compound determiner. Note, the difference between the fraction used as a determiner and used as an adverb.

Examples:

Half time is a break in the game (simple determiner).
Half of the mould has gone (compound with an uncountable noun).
He ate **a quarter** of the pie (compound with a countable noun).
The job is only **half** done (adverb as it refers to the extent).

To Highlight Certain Nouns within a Group of Nouns: Those determiners that are used to refer to specific nouns within a greater number of nouns.

Examples:

Another dog is chasing ours.
Each person coming on the trip must bring a coat.
Either way leads to the river.
Neither candidate met our criteria.
Every good boy deserves praise.
Other people go abroad on holiday.

To indicate which noun(s) is/are being referred to: These **indicative** determiners are used to show, point to, or refer to, specific nouns.

Examples:

That car is mine (used to show a single, out of reach thing)
This class is interesting (used to show a single, reachable thing)
Those buildings are huge (used to show multiple, out of reach things)
These scissors are sharp (used to show multiple, reachable things)

To Ask Questions: These **interrogative** (question) determiners are used to ask questions about the nouns that immediately follow them.

Examples:

What day does the event take place on?
Which classroom is the lecture in?
Whose car is parked in the Dean's parking place?

USING A OR AN

A and **an** function as the indefinite forms of articles in the English language. The indefinite form indicates that whatever (or whoever) is being referred to is a countable member of a larger, identifiable, countable group. **An** is used before words starting with a vowel sound, regardless of whether or not the word begins with a vowel. Their main use is to indicate that the following noun is one part of a larger group and it not being claimed (using a possessive pronoun like **my**) or not being specifically referred to or indicated (by using a determiner such as **this**).

The main reason for the difference in use is to do with speech rather than writing (speech was used long before writing was invented) and is because if you use **a** together with a following vowel sound you'll find it awkward as there is a glottal stop (where the airflow through your mouth is constricted) between the article and the following word. As an experiment, try saying "**A** elephant", you'll notice that the transition was awkward; whereas, "**An** elephant" is smoother. Vowels tend to need single mouth shapes (look in the mirror when you voice vowels and you'll see your mouth doesn't move from the shape it had to assume to speak the sound – it is generally your tongue making the transition) whereas consonants have a starting mouth shape and then a transition, as you vocalise the sound, into another mouth shape.

So the easiest way to determine whether **a** or **an** is needed is to voice the words and see if the article flows smoothly into the following word. The words **a** and **an** have the same origins, starting off as the unstressed version of the word **one**, with **an** starting to be used in the 12th century to mean the lone or only. **A** only starting being used (originally with a soft 'n') in the 14th century. In the 16th century it started to be used with words starting with 'h', but only with those words where the 'h' is pronounced (see below).

There are a few words used in English where there is some confusion as to whether to use **a** or **an**, such as:

Examples of exceptional words that are preceded by **a** are:
Ewe (pronounced /juː/) meaning: a female sheep.
User (pronounced /juː.zər/) meaning: someone who uses a product.
Euro (pronounced /jʊə.rəʊ/) meaning: the European currency.

Examples of exceptional words that are preceded by **an** are:

M.P (pronounced /em'piː/) meaning: a member of parliament.
Unknown (pronounced / ʌn'nəʊn/) meaning: not known.
Hour (pronounced / aʊə/) meaning: a period of 60 minutes.

Words in English that were derived from French and start with 'h' (such as hotel – derived from the French word hostel) tend to use an, whereas words that were derived from German and starting with 'h' (such as hut) use 'a' as the 'h' is almost always pronounced. The exception being that with certain dialects, like East London Cockney, where almost all preceding hs are dropped.

Finally **a** and **an** can also be used to represent the number one (an eel – one eel).

In every day speech **a** is pronounced as /ə/ with **an** pronounced as /ən/ (as in g<u>un</u>); the stressed versions, which are used for emphasis, are /eɪ/ (as in m<u>ay</u>) and /æn/ (as in m<u>an</u>), respectively.

Note: **a** and **an** are only used with countable nouns.

COMPOUND DETERMINERS

These tend to be used when describing plural quantities of something or people. They can be composed of prepositions, adjectives, nouns and determiners of various descriptions to indicate certain nuances in meaning In some instances they are suffixed with a determiner, such as the definite article or an indefinite article, and sometimes they are not. For instance consider these two example sentences.

<u>A lot of</u> people came to my party.

<u>A lot of the</u> people who came to my party brought a friend.

In both instances they use the same compound determiner, **a lot of**, and are referring to an unknown number. The first sentence was a generic reference in that it just stated that it was a well-attended party, in the second sentence the emphasis was on the fact that a certain sub group, out of the overall group, were specific in some way (in this case they brought their friends) - **who came to my party** is the defining adjective clause.

SOME

Pronounced /sʌm/, **some** means an amount or number of something which is not stated or known or is a part of something larger. It is generally used instead of **a** or **an** when referring to uncountable nouns.

It is worth noting that the rules below equally apply to **any**one v **some**one, **any**thing v **some**thing and **any**where v **some**where.

Describe unknown quantity: Its most common use is in positive sentences when describing an unknown quantity of something.

Examples:

I would like **some** milk.
I had **some** money left so I bought **some** ice cream.

With countable or uncountable nouns: It can also be used with both countable and uncountable nouns:

Examples:

Countable Nouns - **Some** people in my office are really noisy.
Uncountable Nouns - There was **some** water in the bottom of the boat

When offering something: It is also used when politely offering something to someone where the answer is likely to be yes.

Example: Would you like **some** more cake?

Making requests: Some is used to formulate polite requests, especially where the expectation is that the request will be granted.

Example: Can I borrow **some** money until I get paid?'

Notes and examples

ANY

Pronounced /en.i/, any means the smallest amount or number of something uncountable.

Negative sentences: the most common use of any is in negative sentences:

Examples:

He doesn't have **any** friends.
There isn't **any** fuel left in my car.

In questions involving unknown quantities: Any is used to frame the question, whereas some would most likely be used to answer the question.

Example:

Question: Do you have **any** money?
Answer: I have <u>some</u> money but I'm not sure how much.

In some positive clauses or sentences: Any is used in some positive clauses where those clauses contain the adverbs **hardly, never** or **without,** to change the meaning into either a negative or one where the positive benefit is very small.

Examples:

There is hardly **any** milk left
(There is milk but not much)
You never have **any** money.
(Note: **never** turned the positive into a negative)
I was left without **any** other option.
(Complete lack of choice)

Notes and examples

USING 'THE'

There is only one definite article used in English and that is the word **'the'**. It is used to clearly define or determine people or things that have already been mentioned, or are currently under discussion, or are otherwise presumed to be known, by direct knowledge or previous implication, or being descriptive enough to be recognized by the listener or reader. It is placed before nouns to limit or specify their meaning and when placed before isolated (without a noun) adjectives and participles, it converts them into abstract nouns. It was originally a demonstrative pronoun, being a weakened form of **that**.

It is also used to add extra emphasis to the noun, even proper nouns, and, as such it is often used as the very first part of a noun phrase. Strong pronunciation (indicating emphasis) of **the** is /ði:/ and the weak pronunciation is /ðə/. The strong pronunciation is used to indicate the absolute uniqueness of something.

One of the most important uses of **the** is to draw attention to something that the listener or reader would be expected to know. For example you could say, "I will meet you at **the** coffee shop." In this case the writer/speaker is referring to a coffee shop that both they and the person they are addressing would know about, or at least be expected to know about (for instance if it is the only coffee shop in town).

If the person being addressed is unclear then extra detail needs to be added to clarify exactly what is meant. For example if you are in Bangkok you can say, "Have you seen the King's palace?" with the expectation that the listener would interpret that to mean the one in Bangkok. However if you were in another country (say Spain or Sweden, who also have Kings), or even in another part of Thailand (where the King has another palace) then you would need to qualify that with more detail. In which case, you'd say, "Have you seen the King's palace in Stockholm?"

<u>The</u> is generally used to draw attention to a specific example of something: such as the weather, the wind, the sea etc. or where there are a discrete, easily discernible groups (e.g. islands, bags, etc.)

SPECIFYING NOUNS

In order to ensure that the definite article, **the**, is used, then the sentence containing the noun (noun phrase or noun clause) must be specific enough to be understood completely by the listener, such that they don't need to ask further questions. This is especially true for written work as the readers cannot ask questions in order to clarify the meaning. The question is why would you want to make them specific? The answer to which is because you will then be certain that your listener or, more especially, your reader would know exactly what you are referring to and what you mean. It is no coincidence that the definite article, **the**, is the most commonly used word in written English.

There are various ways in which we can make the noun more specific, the first is to turn it into a compound noun. So for example, you could say "I will meet you…" followed by the prepositional phrase "…in **a** restaurant" would almost certainly prompt the question 'which restaurant?' In which case you would use a compound noun inside the prepositional phrase and the definite article, **the**, to show that there is only one of that name "I will meet you in **the** Al Orjouan restaurant".

If you suspect that the listener or reader needs further clarification you could add a further <u>prepositional phrase</u> "I will meet you in **the** Al Orjouan restaurant *in Riyadh*". If you still feel you need to add clarification, for example if you think they don't know exactly where it is, you can keep adding prepositional phrases "I will meet you <u>in **the** Al Orjouan restaurant *in the Ritz-Carlton hotel* *on Mekkah Road* in Riyadh</u>" You can further clarify it by adding a time and or a date, again using prepositional phrases "I will meet you <u>in **the** Al Orjouan restaurant in the Ritz-Carlton hotel on Mekkah Road in Riyadh *at 12 noon* *on Wednesday*</u>"

You would also use prepositional phrases to specify anything that refers to the noun, or the sentence as a whole, in order to make your meaning clearer and to help justify the use of **the**. Prepositional phrases are your friends – you should learn to love them. ♥

RULES AND EXCEPTIONS

The following pages outline the rules (and exceptions) in using **the**. The most common problems associated with the use of 'the' are the number of exceptions to the rules. So, in this section the exception(s) to the stated rule are underneath each rule together with an explanation (and example) in the following format:

Rule description: describing the general use of the rule.

Example:

An example of the rule in the form of an example sentence or example sentences if more than one rule is described. This/these would be followed by what rule they are examples of (in parentheses).

Exception: describing the deviation (or deviations) from the rule. If there is more than 1 exception then they would be labelled thus: exception 1: exception 2: etc. Each exception would feature its own set of examples.

Example:

Rules and exceptions when using 'the', this/these would be followed by what rule they are examples of (in parentheses).

Null determiners - indicated by underlines ___ - are used where no actual words are written but are placeholders for other determiners.

Notes and examples

This area is for you to copy or create examples of the rule in action

WITH PARTS OF SPEECH

WHOLE GROUPS

The is used to talk about a whole, countable and definable group of people or things.

Examples:

The students are playing football (countable group of people).

The books are in the library (countable group of things).

Exception: If they are uncountable and undefinable then you would use a null determiner (i.e. nothing).

Examples:
___Corn is generally harvested in autumn (Corn is uncountable as it refers to all corn).

The corn was harvested early this year (It is referring to a specific crop of corn – perhaps from the speaker's own farm – so it is countable, or at least quantifiable, and uses **the**).

__Students like parties (Undefined group)

The students <u>in my class</u> don't like parties (group defined by the prepositional phrase <u>in my class</u>).

Notes and examples

PARTS OF A GROUP

The is used when you wish to differentiate a certain member or members of a group from others within the group. It is most commonly used to refer to someone/people or something(s) not present and is generally accompanied by what marks them out as being worthy of special attention. This may take the form of an adjective, which precedes the person or thing being highlighted, or an adjective clause, which follows the person or thing being highlighted.

Examples:

It is **the** <u>most vicious</u> dog in the pack (<u>most vicious</u> is the <u>superlative + adjective</u> phrase that is being used to define the thing - singular).

The students <u>you spoke to</u> are in my class (<u>you spoke to</u> is the <u>adjective clause</u> that marks the persons of interest – plural use).

Exception: If they are referred to by indicating them, by pointing for example or where he/she/it has previously been mentioned, then use **that,** for a singular person or thing, or **those,** for plural people or things.

Examples:

That student is in my class (single person)
Those books are on my desk (previously referenced plural things)

Notes and examples

ONE OF MANY DEFINED THINGS

The is generally used to talk about a particular thing that is part of a group of defined things, in particular if it's the most local one or one that is well known or regularly visited or used.

Example:

Can you take this parcel to **the** post office (local one).

If you are ill you should see **the** doctor (regularly visited)

Exception: If it refers to something that is not defined in terms of geographical area or has not been visited or used before then use **a** or **an**.

Example:

You can buy bread in **a** convenience store (where the store is, is either unknown or is unimportant).

Have you seen **a** doctor about your fever? (Unknown or not visited before).

Note: In US English **a** or **an** are often used instead of **the**; irrespective of locality or previous knowledge.

Notes and examples

TO PROVIDE EMPHASIS

The is used when you want to provide emphasis to something that would normally be just one item within a group. It could be something done by a specific person or group or where the thing or things are very important and therefore specific.

Examples:

The research **the** Mahidol Scientists undertook was ground breaking (It is specific research done by a specific group).

Did you remember to bring **the** map? (Important singular object).

You need to bring pens, a clipboard and **the** survey forms (Important plural objects – the surveying task would be pointless without them).

Exception: If the specified, and important, item being referred to is the property of a person then don't use **the,** use a possessive determiner (like **your** *or* **our**) instead.

Examples:

Have you got **our** tickets? (Plural possessive)

Did you remember **your** passport? (Singular possessive).

Notes and examples

WITH A PREPOSITIONAL PHRASE

When a *noun* has been specified using a <u>prepositional phrase</u> then it will usually be preceded by **the**. This is because the prepositional phrase will focus the noun allowing it to be prefaced with **the**. In other words they are generally complimentary.

Examples:

The *café* <u>in the mall</u> is being refurbished. (Specified subject noun).

All she could think about was **the** *spot* <u>on her nose</u>. (Specified object noun).

Exception: When the noun has certain aspects specified with a prepositional phrase, such as the time or location, but is otherwise unidentified then it would normally be preceded by **a** or **an**.

Examples:

There is **a** *dog* <u>in our street</u> that barks all night. (Unidentified– where the prepositional phrase specifies the area the noun is in but not the noun itself).

Is there **a** *doctor* <u>on the plane</u>? (Question as to whether there is one of the things identified by the *noun* in that particular location).

Notes and examples

IN A PREPOSITIONAL PHRASE

In some instances, if a noun follows a preposition then it will take an article, particularly if another noun follows the preposition, but only if the noun(s) are pointing to something specific, unique or something that needs highlighting. Note that it is unusual if both nouns take the definite article.

Examples:

Fruit of **the** loom (Loom in this instance refers to a specific loom - fruit is a generic reference to all fruit [products] from that loom).

The height of folly (the article in this case turns height into a superlative).

The Shopping Centre in Brent (There is only one shopping centre in Brent).

Note that a sentence like: "**An** injection in **the** buttocks" uses two articles because injection is generic, so it takes an indefinite article, but buttocks are a specific part of the body and are therefore highlighted using a definite article.

Exceptions: If the nouns are proper nouns (i.e. names) then they won't take an article. However, with nobility, the honorific will take the definite article.

Examples: John of Gaunt
William of Orange
The Duke of Westminster (honorific)

Notes and examples

WITH POSSESSIVE NOUNS

Whether a possessive noun is preceded by **the** depends on whether the *possessive noun* (the one followed by 's), rather than the <u>possessed</u> (object) noun, would normally (i.e. when used as a non-possessive noun) be preceded by **the**.

Examples:

The *UK's* <u>energy policy</u> has been criticized (UK is normally preceded by **the** as it refers to a group of countries within a unified kingdom).

Thailand's <u>exports</u> have risen sharply this quarter (Thailand is not preceded by **the** as it refers to a single country).

Exception: If the *possessive noun* is being referred to in general terms then it would be preceded by **a** or **an** rather than **the**.

Example: A *man's* <u>principles</u> define his character (any man).

Notes and examples

WITH NOUN CLAUSES

The would generally be used to preface the noun in a <u>noun clause</u> but would only apply to the noun itself and not the overall clause even though it is treated as a noun.

Examples:

<u>**The** instructions given</u> were wrong. (Subject noun clause).

I understand <u>that **the** class has been cancelled</u>. (Object noun clause).

Exception: If there is no noun in the noun clause then the clause wouldn't be prefaced with **the**.

Examples:

The meeting, <u>that I was supposed to attend</u>, was cancelled. (<u>Noun clause</u> as an appositive).

Her problem was <u>that she didn't eat enough</u>. (<u>Noun clause</u> as a subject complement).

<u>That he wasn't listening</u> was obvious. (<u>Noun clause</u> as the subject).

I heard <u>that he wasn't attending</u> (<u>Noun clause</u> as the object).

Notes and examples

WITH PRONOUNS

The is generally not used with pronouns. Only a few specific determiners are used with pronouns – see the determiner reference section at the end of this book for details.

Example: I love **you**. (**I** = subject pronoun – **you** = object pronoun)

Exceptions: In idiomatic English **the** is sometimes used to describe a change in somebody or to specify a person that has been referred to in vague terms – see the second Q/A example.

Examples:

You are not **the** you I used to know. (Refer to a changed person.)

Question: "She is very beautiful. Who is she?"

Answer: The she you refer to is my wife (To specify an indicated person).

Notes and examples

GENERAL SUPERLATIVES

Superlatives are used to indicate that something is outstanding (for example the best or the worst) and so it follows that a definite article would be used.

Examples:

The best computer
The worst result
The prettiest girl

Exceptions: If <u>comparatives</u> are used instead of superlatives then don't use **the**; instead, use the indefinite article **a** or **an**.

Example: A <u>better</u> solution is to learn to drive.

Notes and examples

SUPERLATIVES DESCRIBING POSSESSED ITEMS

The is used to preface superlatives used to describe personally owned items.

Example: The fastest car I own is my Porsche.

Exception: If you want to emphasise the car itself or the ownership rather that the superlative quality (in this case the speed) then use a possessive determiner, such as '**my**'.

Examples:

The Porsche is my fastest car. (Generic emphasis on fastest car I own – note it is the only one of its kind in my possession so I use '**the**' to indicate its uniqueness even though it is a proper noun).

My Porsche is my fastest car (Placing the emphasis on ownership – it is prefaced with my as it refers to the particular one I own, my wife might have another one).

Notes and examples

WITH COMPARATIVES

In general use comparatives are not prefaced with the as they are usually being used to take a disinterested look at both (or all) of the items or people being compared; therefore, none of the compared items are highlighted or specified.

Examples:

She earns *more than* me. (The comparative, using the determiner *more* and the preposition *than*, is stating that one person's wage is greater than the other's).

This computer is faster than my old one (The comparative, using the simple comparative preposition, than, prefaces the compared item - note the noun phrases could be prefaced with **the** when referring to the items in a disinterested way, where ownership and/or position are not of importance: i.e. **The** computer [previously mentioned or known about] is faster than **the** old one [again previously mentioned or known about]).

Exception 1: When referring specifically to one item within a compared group, in order to draw particular attention to it, then **the** would be used to preface the comparative adjective. Note, it would not be used when doing a direct comparison using '*than*', for example; It is ~~the~~ cheaper *than* my last one.

Examples:

I bought **the** bigger one as it was better value. (The first comparative adjective, the bigger..., is highlighted as it was the one I bought; whereas, the second comparative, better, is being used as a simple adjective as it is not being compared to anything, except in an abstract sense based on the speaker's knowledge or belief. If we wanted to highlight the value aspect then we'd change the verb, was, into a *judgmental verb* and add the reason, commonly with a <u>prepositional phrase</u>: I bought **the** bigger one as it *represented* **the** better value <u>in my opinion).</u>

John is **the** taller of the two brothers ('**the**' changed the comparative adjective into an abstract quality).

Exception 2: The is commonly used to highlight the things being compared to, particularly if there is a group of them.

<u>**Example:** He is taller than **the** other people in his group.</u>

BARE ADJECTIVES

The generally cannot be used to preface descriptive bare adjectives (adjectives acting on their own without being part of a noun phrase), other than participle adjectives (see the next page).

Example: She is ~~the~~ pretty.

Exception: If the adjective appears after the noun, most commonly to highlight what the person or thing is known for, then **the** can be used to preface the adjective. The reason is that it is changes the noun from one of many of that type or name to one that is special in some way.

Examples:

America **the** beautiful (highlighting an exceptional quality of a thing)

Ulf **the** brave (a 9th century Norwegian warrior and leader).

Alexander **the** Great (A legendary Greek leader and conqueror).

Chonglak **the** evil (Used to differentiate them from other Chonglaks).

Notes and examples

PARTICIPLE ADJECTIVES

The can usually be used to preface participle adjectives (adjectives created from verbs) thereby turning them into abstract nouns.

Examples:

The *deceased* wrote the will (*past participle adjective*).

The *living* read the will (*present participle adjective*).

Note that some past participle adjectives are singular (the accused or the deceased); whereas, some are plural (the disabled or the dispossessed). Therefore you should always use the appropriate verb (The accused <u>appears</u> to be innocent - 3rd person singular verb - *or* the disabled <u>appear</u> to be suffering under austerity - 3rd person plural verb).

Exception: Present participle adjectives that describe personal opinions or states, particularly if they are used with linking or state verbs, generally aren't prefaced with **the** (see the note [1] below).

Examples:

The movie was ~~the~~ boring. (Opinion with a state verb).
He is ~~the~~ sweating. (Physical state with a linking verb).

Note [1]. As the language evolves it is becoming increasingly common to see present participle adjectives that describe particular attributes of people or things being prefaced with the (We are the living, you are the dead.)

Notes and examples

GROUP ADJECTIVES

The is used to preface adjectives that describe a certain specific section of a group. The implication is that the listener would know what group is being referred to, so, for example, in the first example below the listener would 'know' that the poor refers to the poor people in society. Note, the people or things are being referred to in abstract terms, so these adjectives become abstract (theoretical) nouns.

Example:

The government wants to do more for **the** poor (which could be written, in full, as: The government wants to do more for **the** poor people in society).

They want to tax **the** rich more (note, the adverb <u>more</u> is not associated with the adjective *rich* but with the verb <u>tax</u>).

Exception: If the adjective refers to a generic group then **the** is not used, particularly if the adjective is followed by a noun. Consider the following examples:

Examples:
More provision needs to be made in railways stations for **the** deaf (<u>the deaf</u> are the specific group that requires special help).

–or–

__Deaf people have problems hearing railway station announcements (the reference represents a generic group in this example; hence, there is no need for a definite article, **the**).

Notes and examples

SPECIFIC SENTENCE PARTS

The is used when discussing specific parts within a previous sentence, made special by aspects such as the type or location. The sentence containing it can be a follow on from a sentence used by the same speaker or in answer to a query by another speaker.

Examples:

Dishes and cups are in the cupboard. **The** salad dish is on the shelf above your head (referring to a specific item from within the general group mentioned in the first sentence by the same speaker).

Question (first speaker): do we have any mugs? (General group) Answer (second speaker) **the** mugs are under the sink. (Specific group as they represent the group previously referred to).

Exception: If they are referred to generically, i.e. as a general grouping and not previously referred to or distinguishable in any way then **the** is not used but any can be used to describe an absence or more can be used to refer to any additional supply.

Examples:

The café doesn't have <u>any</u> cups, they only have __ mugs (<u>any</u> is used to show that it refers to the complete unavailability of those things - the alternative [mugs] is generic so it uses a null).

We weren't sure how many people were coming so we ordered *some* paper plates in case we ran out of __crockery plates (An additional supply prefaced with *some* - note, if the plates they ordered were of the same type they'd use the adjective 'extra' instead of 'paper' and the prepositional phrase 'of crockery plates' would not be needed - *so we ordered some extra plates in case we ran out*).

Notes and examples

FOCUS ON SPECIAL ATTRIBUTES

The is used to reference the noun when talking about its attributes. For example it could be what function(s) the noun performs or what the noun is known for. The **article** is used to preface the <u>noun</u> itself and not the attributes.

Examples:

The <u>heart</u> pumps __blood around **the** body (what function it performs – note the object of the function – blood - is generic so it doesn't generally use **the**, but the body is specific to each individual so it is prefaced with **the**)

The <u>tiger</u> is **the** biggest feline predator (what it known for – the attribute is specific and superlative in this case so it is prefaced with **the**)

Exception: When referring to generic functions or attributes (i.e. functions or things that are not regarded as anything special) then use a or an.

Examples:

A <u>heart</u> is present in all mammals. (Generally statement about the noun).

__ Tigers live in the jungle (with the emphasis on where they live rather than what they are).

Notes and examples

ABSTRACT NOUNS

The is not generally used with abstract nouns (abstract nouns refer to things that cannot be touched or seen – like emotions or feelings).

Examples:

<u>Love</u> makes the world go round (<u>Love</u> is the abstract noun describing a general effect).

Most women are in touch with **their** <u>feelings</u> (using possessive determiner as it only applies to them)

Exception: Where the noun refers to an abstract noun that is targeted towards something or someone specific, or when the abstract noun is a reference to something, then **the** is used.

Examples:

The love I feel for my wife is boundless (targeted at someone).

The feeling I have is that this is going to end in disaster (reference).

Notes and examples

GENERIC NOUNS

The is not generally used with generic nouns. Generic nouns refer to a general group of things of the same type.

Examples: __Cars normally have four wheels *or* __ Tea originated in China. (Cars are countable and tea is uncountable).

Exception: Where a specific type of generic object is mentioned even if it is uncountable then **the** would be used.

Examples:

The car I bought had five wheels (It is countable and specific as it was the one I bought).

The tea you gave me was excellent (It is uncountable but specific as it was the item – presumably in a package - that you gave to me).

Notes and examples

WITH OTHER DETERMINERS

The is usually not used if there is another determiner referring to the same noun in the sentence, such as a possessive determiner.

Example: I think I left ~~the~~ **my** keys at ~~the~~ **your** house. (**my** and **your** are the determiners)

Exception 1: **The** should be used if the thing is specific and there is no previous reference to it/them (such as when the listener is likely to know which keys and which house is being referred to).

Example: I think I left **the** keys at **the** house.

Exception 2: Determiners can precede other determiners when they form part of a compound determiner (see the compound determiner section at the back of this book for more examples).

Example: **The majority of the** time I have nothing to do (The **compound determiner** uses two definite articles; the first [the majority] defines the scope and the second [the time] describes the specific variable).

Notes and examples

IN COMPOUND DETERMINERS

The is used to modify a compound determiner to refer to some specific thing or previously known person or thing in a defined group. This type of determiner is usually used for describing plural or multiple quantities of something. **The** is generally used in compound determiners to preface concrete nouns. The compound determiner in the examples is <u>underlined</u>.

Examples:

<u>All of the</u> students passed the exam (concrete, countable noun).

<u>Lots of the</u> water leaked from the bucket (concrete, uncountable noun)

Exception: The is generally not used when the noun is abstract; **a** or **an** are generally used instead.

Example: My paperwork is in <u>a bit of a</u> mess (Note the use of the compound determiner).

Notes and examples

WITH PROPER NOUNS

Use with countable nouns: If an object or person can be described using any noun other than a proper noun (i.e. someone's name) then it can be defined as the one being described by using **the.**

Example: **The** cat sat on **the** mat. (There is one defined cat sitting on one defined mat)

Exception: It is possible to use **the** when preceding a proper noun, such as someone's name or a place, in order to stress that the person, or place, is exceptional in some way. The article, **the**, would be stressed in speech (using ði:)

Example: You are not **the** John Smith, the famous actor, are you? (This means that this particular John Smith is different to other John Smiths as he is famous).

Notes and examples

WITH SUBSEQUENT SENTENCES

Going from 'a' to 'the' in subsequent sentences. When referring to an indefinite person or thing use 'a' in the first sentence; subsequent references would use the definite article 'the' in order to confirm that the same (now defined) person or thing is still being talked about. Further mentions may be replaced by a pronoun.

Example: <u>**A**</u>[1] woman was seen in the vicinity of the robbery. <u>**The**</u>[2] woman was described as being in her twenties and tall with long blond hair. <u>**She**</u>[3] looked very furtive, according to eye witnesses.

[1] = first mention. [2] = second mention referring back to original. [3] = replaced by the pronoun <u>she</u>.

Exception: If the person or thing is referred to more than once in the same sentence then **the** may be replaced by a pronoun.

Example: <u>A</u> woman was seen in the vicinity of the robbery, <u>she</u> was described as being in her twenties, tall with long blond hair.

Notes and examples

DISCUSSING PARTS OF SPEECH

The is used to talk about a specific part or parts of speech in order to highlight them or to specifically group them together to prove a point; for example, in grammar lessons (or in CORE English!).

Example: The adjective generally precedes **the** noun in **the** sentence.

Exception: If they are referred to generically, i.e. as a general grouping, then **the** is not used.

Example: __Adjectives normally precede __nouns in __sentences (adjectives, nouns and sentences are all generic terms).

Notes and examples

BARE VERSUS SPECIFIED NOUNS

Singular nouns can be prefaced with **the**, but only when they are known about or previously mentioned; instead, they'd be prefaced with another determiner, such as an indefinite article, **a** or **an**, or a possessive or indicative determiner.

Examples:

The book (previously mentioned book)

A book (indefinite article – one of many).

My book (possessive - the one belonging to me).

That book (indicative – the one I mentioned before or I am now pointing to).

Exception: If the noun is prefaced with an adjective, thus becoming a noun phrase, it doesn't have to be known about or referred to already and can be preceded by **the** because the adjective has specified it (made it special). Other ways to specify the noun are to make it into a compound noun or add a prepositional phrase or an adjective clause.

Example:

The *red* book is heavy (*adjective*).

The *prepositions book* is very good (*compound noun*).

The book *on the table* (*prepositional phrase*).

The book is the one *that I just read (adjective clause).*

Notes and examples

APPOSITIVES

An appositive is a noun that appears next to another noun to which it refers in order to give an alternative name or description to the first noun, for example: **My wife, Thippanat,** works in a bank. Where **my wife** is the first noun (prefaced with the personal pronoun **my**) and **Thippanat** adds a name to the first noun. Appositives are generally enclosed within commas. In most instances the appositive would not be preceded by **the** as they are often either proper nouns (names) or one of many (using **a** or **an**).

Example:

The teacher, Kevin, has written a book (proper noun appositive – with the focus on the only teacher using **the**).

Kevin, **a** teacher, took the class (one of many teachers, using a proper noun as the focus).

Exception: The should be used if you are referring to someone specific, like the only person involved, or the main person involved, in something.

Examples:

Dr. Clark, **the** psychiatrist, attended the case meeting (a specific person from within a group is involved).

Silapakorn, **the** lead researcher, submitted the paper to the journal (the main person involved).

Notes and examples

PREFACING PREPOSITIONS

The is not used to preface prepositions in a normal sentence.

Example: I saw ~~the~~ through her scheme.

Exception 1: The can be used when it is referring to an abstract reference - for example when the <u>prepositional phrase</u> is being treated as an adjective. In the first example the abstract reference is enclosed in inverted commas to show that it is being treated as an adjective, in the second it uses dashes between each word.

Examples:

Where is **the** '<u>to whom it may concern</u>' letter in this computer.

He gave **the** <u>on-my-honour</u> speech that he uses when people question his honesty.

Notes and examples

PLACES, AREAS AND FEATURES

PLACES CONNECTED TO TRAVEL

The is generally used with nouns used in travel and tourism as they refer to a specific place or event.

Examples:

The hotel was next to **the** beach. (The hotel we stayed in/The beach we relaxed on).

The festival takes place on the first Sunday in August (the festival I am describing).

[1] **The** resort is on [2] **the** coast of Albania near [3] **the** ancient Roman city of Buthrotum. ([1] The resort we are highlighting, [2] the only coast Albania has, [3] the specific Roman city)

The weekend break was great fun. (the one we went on)

Exception: When the travel has not yet been finalised, in other words when describing the type of place or type of holiday, then **a** or **an** are used.

Examples:

We want to stay in **a** resort in Corfu.

I looked on the Internet for **a** suitable golfing holiday.

Notes and examples

TEMPORARY ACCOMMODATION

The is generally used when referring directly to a hotel, guesthouse or resort, etc. This would apply whether the place is named or not as long as it refers to the place where the speaker stayed, is staying or will stay, as it is specific to them.

Examples:

I am going back to **the** guesthouse (the one I am staying in)

We stayed at **the** Oriental Plaza (named hotel without the word hotel).

The Ang Sang resort was very peaceful (The one where we stayed).

Exception: If the place is not specified, because, for example they haven't actually found or booked it yet, then use **a** or **an.**

Examples:

I must find **an** hotel to spend the night (note the use of an as the 'h' is usually silent in speech, in written English it is usually 'A hotel').

I leased **a** long term apartment while I worked here (one of many and not specified as it was the concept of how the person lived that was being emphasised rather than the place itself).

Notes and examples

TOURIST ATTRACTIONS

The is generally used when referring to tourist attractions and facilities as they tend to be specific, even if they are generally regarded as uncountable.

Examples:

The beach is very clean (countable).

The sea was very blue (uncountable).

I went swimming in **the** lake (**the** is used even though the name of the lake wasn't specified, as it is assumed that the listener would know which one, for example if it was the one close to the resort they were staying in)

Exception: If they are referred to using a proper noun only (without a noun specifying what they are) then no determiner is used. Consider the two examples shown below:

Examples:

Khao Yai is very beautiful (no specifying noun).

The Khao Yai <u>forest</u> is very beautiful (with a <u>specifying noun</u>)

Notes and examples

EDUCATIONAL BUILDINGS

The is generally used when referring to educational buildings, mainly because they are specific to a particular institution and, in most cases there is only one of them in that place. This would apply whether or not the building was named and whether they are singular or plural.

Examples:

I will study in **the** library (no name but the only one there).

The lecture is in **the** Nelson Mandela lecture theatre (named).

There was a small fire in **the** classroom (the one I was in).

The classrooms are in **that** building (plural subject referring to a whole group and a singular indicated object).

Exception: When referring to one of many then use **a** or **an**. When referring to more than one use a numeric determiner, when the quantity is known, or **any** (in questions) or **some** if the quantity is not known.

Examples:

Is there **a** free classroom I can use? (One of many – this could be written as "Are there **any** free classrooms" if the use of that classroom is not being specified).

There are **three** free classrooms (plural with a known quantity).

There are **some** free classrooms (plural with an unknown quantity).

Notes and examples

GOVERNMENT BUILDINGS

The is used to refer to specific government buildings. If the building is named after someone then the word 'building' is appended to the end of the name to form a specialised compound noun ; otherwise, the building is generally specified with a prepositional phrase.

Examples:

The Ronald Reagan building (named after a President).

The National Library <u>of Congress </u>(A <u>prepositional phrase</u> is used to refer to what the building is associated with).

The Houses <u>of Parliament</u>. (Building's use defined with a <u>prepositional phrase</u>).

Exception 1: Where the reference is to a proper compound noun then **the** is not used.

Examples:

Portcullis house

Lunar House

Exception 2: When the building occupies a whole street then **the** is not used as the building the department or ministry is housed in is not being referred to directly - a <u>null</u> __ is used instead.   However, if a specific address is being used (such as referring to a single address from the many that the department occupies) then **the** would be used.

Example:

It has been referred to __ Great Smith street (whole street occupied by a ministry).

The ministry's address is Victoria Street, London (building address). **The** Victoria street office deals with international trade (specific address of a specific function).

Exception 3: When an area is associated with the government it is usually named using a proper noun so it would be prefaced with a null.

Examples

__ Whitehall is the area of London associated with Government.

We meeting will take place on __ Capitol hill. (Area of Washington associated with congress).

Those decisions are taken by __ Bangkok (refers to the fact that the government is based in Bangkok and so Bangkok is being used as a metaphor for central government).

PUBLIC BUILDINGS

The would normally be used to preface a public building (which the public has access to) if it has a specified function, or it has a range of functions, or it is historic.

Examples:

The town hall is where the town council sits. (Specified function).

The corn exchange in Cambridge is now used as a music venue. (Historic building).

Exception 1: By tradition some historic public buildings are not prefaced with **the** even if they are expected to be.

Examples: __Guildhall in London is the ceremonial and administrative centre of the City of London and its Corporation. (Note, when referring to an event taking place there then it would be prefaced with **the** as part of the *prepositional phrase* describing the place - I attended a function *at **the** guildhall*).

Exception 2: If a public building is being referred to in a general sense (for example describing the function of all such places) then **a** or **an** would be used to preface it.

Example: A guildhall is either **a** town hall or **a** building historically used by guilds for meetings and other purposes.

Notes and examples

PUBLIC SERVICE BUILDINGS

Public service buildings are places where the general public go to access services provided by government agencies or agencies that are run for or on behalf of the government. These include places such as post offices, libraries, licensing centres, specialist clinics, benefit agencies, job centres and advice bureaus.

They would generally be prefaced with **the** as the speakers are talking about the specific place that is pertinent to them, even if other such places are nearby, or in a way that highlights the place's function that the speaker has knowledge of as they have previously used the service(s) there.

Examples:

I need to go to **the** post office to send this parcel (either the post office that they'd normally use or one of any such post offices in the vicinity).

She went to **the** driving test centre yesterday to try and get a driving license (the only one in the area).

I picked up this brilliant book about using the and other determiners at **the** library (referring to the place in terms of its function).

Exception: Where advice about what place to visit to access a particular service is being given or commented on then a, an or any can be used.

Examples:

You should visit **a** drop in clinic to check out that rash (**a** is being used here to indicate any one of the places of that type - **a** is commonly used where the speaker hasn't been to the place or used the services, they just know that such a place exists. If they have used the service they would generally use **the** instead).

You can transfer money overseas at **any** post office (using any to say that that service is available at all such places).

Notes and examples

PRISONS

Prisons and other correctional facilities are generally named after a person, the closest town or the area they are located in; therefore, they'd normally be prefaced with a null determiner. If the prison is well known it would only be referred to with the name without the word prison.

Examples:

He was incarcerated in __ Wandsworth prison (the word prison is used to differentiate it from the surrounding district with the same name - in London the word prison is often dropped).
Al Capone was an inmate at __ Alcatraz (famous prison therefore there is no need to use the word prison).

Note: In general, someone who has been sentenced would be 'in' prison (null determiner) ; whereas, a visitor would be 'at' the prison (using the). In the second example 'at' is used because Alcatraz refers to a particular and known regime as well as a prison. In the UK if someone is remanded (not having been convicted in a trial but deemed a flight risk or a risk to the public) they would be 'remanded to' a named prison (prefaced with a null determiner) or 'remanded in custody' if the prison is not named.

Exception 1: If a prison is entitled with a particular regime then **the** would generally be used, with the place name appended as a prepositional phrase.

Example: The United States Penitentiary, Administrative Maximum Facility (ADX) at Florence, Colorado is better known as a 'supermax' prison.

Exception 2: If the word prison is used to refer to a type of punishment a null determiner would be used.

Example: __ Prison is too good for child molesters.

Exception 3: If the prison doesn't exist yet or it is being referred to as an abstract place then a or an would be used.

Examples:

They are going to build **a** prison outside the town (the place doesn't exist yet).
I think there is **a** prison somewhere around here (abstract reference).

PUBLIC UTILITY STRUCTURES

Public utilities are life enhancing facilities and services that are enjoyed by everyone. These include such things as piped water, sewerage handling, treatment and disposal, electricity and waste handling. The fixed structures or systems that support these facilities are generally prefaced with **the** as they are generally large, complex or prominent.

Examples:

The sewerage works is being expanded to meet the needs of the growing population.

The power station in Battersea has been turned into a public art facility (specified with a prepositional phrase giving the location).

The water system in London was originally supplied by private companies called undertakings before being nationalised and renamed the Metropolitan Water Board.

Exception: Single structures within the system are often prefaced with **a** or **an**, particularly if they are not yet in use or are named. If they are specified with a prepositional phrase they would usually be prefaced with **the.**

Examples:

They are building **a** recycling centre next year (projected facility).

The town of Gaffney has **a** water tower shaped like a peach (unnamed).

The water tower *in Gaffney* is called **the** Peachoid. (Specified with a *prepositional phrase* - note the structure's name is prefaced with **the,** even though it is a proper noun, as the name is being used to categorise it as the only one of its kind).

Some unkind people say **the** Gaffney peach looks like an enormous pair of buttocks sitting on a barstool (specified with the name of the town used as an adjective).

Notes and examples

LEGAL AND LAW ENFORCEMENT

Buildings associated with law enforcement and the legal system are generally preceded by **the**, primarily because they tend to be the only one of their kind serving a specific area. In the case of courts they are generally a source of civic pride and often occupy a prominent position in the community. The police as a group and the head of the law enforcement agency are generally prefaced with **the** as they represent a specific concept.

Examples:

She reported the crime at **the** police station.

The Sheriff's office is responsibility for investigating illegal activities in the area.

The US Marshal's office supplies protection to judges.

He appeared in **the** magistrate's court after being caught shoplifting.

He was referred to **the** county court as his crime was considered to be too serious to be dealt with locally.

The police took over two hours to attend the violent burglary.

The Sheriff is giving a press conference regarding the progress of the investigation today.

The FBI is the US's premier law enforcement agency.

The police force keeps our community safe.

As Charles Dickens said "**The** law is an ass".

The legal system of a country is usually based on common law - where something is allowed unless is it is prohibited - or Napoleonic law - where it is prohibited unless it is specifically allowed.

Exception 1: When referring to the legal system as an abstract concept without drawing attention to any specific aspect then a null determiner would be used.

Examples:

Silence in __ court.

You will end up in __ court if you keep spraying graffiti everywhere ___ Law enforcement is there to help keep you safe.

Exception 2: When referring to a type of place without specifying any particular building then **a** or **an** would be used.

Examples:

Cases regarding debts are usually heard in **a** small claims court.

There is **a** police station in every town.

INDUSTRIAL BUILDINGS

The is not generally used when referring to industrial buildings like factories, warehouses, foundries, plants, refineries or workshops as they are generally regarded as generic and mundane and the activities taking place inside are of far more interest.

Examples:

The Company has **a** factory in Taiwan.

Exception: When the activity taking place in the building is being highlighted then **the** would be used, as it is specific to those activities.

Examples:

Most of the products are made in **the** factory in Taiwan. (Note that using **the** in this context generally implies that the factory in Taiwan is owned by - or has very close ties to - the company, if it isn't then **a** would be used instead, "Most of the products are made in **a** factory in Taiwan", meaning that someone else owns the factory and produces the products for the company on a sub-contractual basis).

Notes and examples

INDUSTRIAL COMPLEXES

The is usually used to describe areas within an industrial building or complex as they are named after their specific function. For example, below are some <u>function areas</u> found in a steel works.

Examples: The iron come from **the** <u>blast furnace</u> and is turned into steel in **the** <u>BOS plant</u> before moving on to **the** <u>slabbing mill</u> and finally **the** <u>rolling mill</u> where it turned into strips.

Exception: While the plants or functional areas are specific and thereby prefaced with **<u>the</u>**, the individual parts within the plant are not generally specific if there are more than one of them, so they would be prefaced with a, an, a numerical determiner or many.

Examples:

There is **a** cyanide hardening bath in the gear plant (unspecific singular)

There are **two** large oxygen tanks next to the BOS plant (numerically determined plural).

There are **many** coking ovens in the coking plant (uncounted plural).

Notes and examples

MILITARY BASES

The is not generally used when referring to military bases.

Examples:

When I was in the Air Force I was stationed at __ RAF Locking, __ RAF Siggiewi and __ RAF Boddington (Air force bases).

He was stationed at __ Fort Dix (Army Base).

The new Wren was stationed at __ Portsmouth (Navy base)

Exception: The is used to refer to a base that is comprised of a single structure, usually with a single purpose.

Examples:

The Citadel (a gun battery protecting an important point).

The Arsenal (where weapons or ammunition are made or stored).

 Notes and examples

BUILDINGS IN MILITARY BASES

The is used to refer to areas or buildings within military bases, because the reference is usually towards the functions performed there or the type of weapons housed there.

Examples:

The armoury is where the small arms are stored and repaired on **the** army base.

The submarine base is next to **the** main docks in **the** base shipyard.

Exception: When personnel stationed at a particular military base refer to an area they would use the possessive determiner, **our**, to describe the area or building.

Examples:

Our guardroom is next to the main gate.

Our runway needed to be repaired after the accident.

Notes and examples

RELIGIOUS BUILDINGS

Religious buildings tend to be prefaced with **the** as they are specific and their final noun generally refers to the religious practises that take place there. The building would also be prefaced with **the** if it refers to a place that is known or shared by both the speaker and the listener.

Examples:

The Al-Aqsa Mosque is next to **the** ancient Jewish Temple in Jerusalem. (Mosque is a house of worship for Muslims and the Temple was a house of worship for Jews).

How do you get to **the** Buddhist temple? (Known building).

Exception 1: When the building's name is prefaced with the name of the town where it is situated then it wouldn't be prefaced with the.

Examples:

__ Canterbury Cathedral
__ Abbots Ripton Church

Exception 2: When referring to a religious building in a generic way, such as where the name isn't important but the activity that takes place is, then use **a** or **an** to refer to a single building. If a number of them exist then either a numerical determiner (where the number of them is known) or **many** (if the number isn't known) are used.

Examples:

Don't wear shorts when visiting **a** Thai temple (any one of many).
There are **three** Gurdwaras in this part of Leicester (number is known).
There are **many** Hindu Temples in India (number not known).

The word 'Mosque' was derived from the Arabic word 'Masjid' meaning the meeting place (reference to the generic name rather than a specific building).

Exception 3: If the attendance at a place of worship is being referred to, it is usual (particularly in the US) to preface the word with a null determiner.

Examples:

Where does he attend __ Mosque? (Where is his preferred mosque?)
Does she attend __ church regularly? (Any church).

POINTS ON THE GLOBE

Points on the globe and geographical areas are preceded with **the**.

Examples:

The equator, the Antarctic, **the** North Pole (all points on the globe.

The Middle East, **the** West (geographical areas).

The tropics, **the** Polar Regions (areas or bands).

Exceptions: Continents are not preceded by **the**.

Examples: __ Asia, __ Africa, __ Europe

Notes and examples

NAMES OF COUNTRIES

The names of countries are not preceded by the definite article.

Examples: England, France, Germany.

Exception: If the countries are comprised of a group of some things (like islands or states) or the words republic or Kingdom - to signify the method of governance - appears in the name then **the** would be used.

Examples:

The United States of America (group of states in a federal structure)

The United Kingdom of Great Britain (group of countries under one monarch).

The Philippines (country made up from a group of islands).

The People's Republic of China (republic).

The Kingdom of Thailand (Kingdom).

Notes and examples

NAMES OF CITIES

The is not used with the names of cities.

Examples: London, Rome, Paris.

Exception 1: If the word city or town appears before the name then use **the**. The reason is that it refers to as being specific either as a special place or a place of interest. For example, **the** city of London refers to the financial area of London (a place of interest) and **the** town of Goiás refers to a UNESCO world heritage site (a special place).

Examples: The city of Troy (city), the town of Buthrotum (town).

Exception 2: When referring to how a place has changed in UK English **the** is often used to preface the name.

Example: This is not **the** Liverpool I grew up in, it has changed so much (idiomatic use).

Notes and examples

LARGE BODIES OF WATER

The names of oceans and seas are preceded by the word **the**.

Examples:

The gulf stream runs north in **the** Atlantic Ocean.
The water in **the** Mediterranean Sea circulates anticlockwise.

Exception 1: Lakes and bays are **not** preceded by **the**, except when they are in a group (**The** great lakes).

Examples:

__ Lake Ontario is one of the great lakes.
__ Subic Bay used to be a huge US naval base.

Exception 2: When referring to a specific large body of water of any type in a general way, usually without naming it, then **the** would be used.

Examples:

He goes swimming in **the** lake every day.
The boat capsized and the passengers were swept into **the** sea.
The ocean contains millions of different life forms.

Exception 3: When the word is used as an adjective or a compound noun then it would be preceded by a or an.

They went on **a** <u>sea</u> cruise. (As an <u>adjective</u>).
He bought **a** *lake*side cottage for his retirement. (*Part* of a compound noun)

Notes and examples

RIVERS, STREAMS AND CREEKS

The names of rivers are generally preceded by **the**. The name of the river can be followed by the noun 'river' or not - it is generally up to the writer's personal choice. In some instances the word 'river' can precede the name of the river. When talking about a river in a general sense, where the emphasis is on the activity rather than the river itself, **the** would be used without the name.

Examples:

The river Thames flows through London (The noun 'river' preceding the name).

The Chao Phrya river often floods Bangkok. (Name of river with the accompanying noun 'river')

The Nile is thought to be the longest river in the world. (Name of river without the accompanying noun 'river')

I lay down beside **the** river and studied the clouds (talking about the activity with the place [the river] specified inside a prepositional phrase).

Exception: When discussing rivers in general terms then **a** or **an** would be used.

Example: Most early cities were sited next to **a** river.

Streams, creeks, brooks, ditches and springs are generally too small or insignificant to be named and would usually be preceded by **a** or **an.**

Examples:

A stream runs along the bottom of my garden.
I love listening to the sound of **a** babbling brook.

Exception: If the minor water course/source is considered important then it would be prefaced with **the.**

Example: The source of the river Thames is considered by the UK environment agency to be **the** Trewsbury Mead spring.

Notes and examples

STATES

States (either stand alone or as part of a federation or republic) are not preceded with **the**.

Examples: Florida, Colorado, California

Exceptions: If a place is declared as a state but isn't generally (or legally) recognized as such then it could be referred to as the state of… An example of this is the state of Jefferson, which existed for a brief period in 1941 and comprised of parts of Northern California and Southern Oregon.

Examples: The state of Jefferson, **the** state of Franklin (1783-1787).

Note: The expression **the state of …** is commonly used in English to refer to the current condition of something (Look at **the state of** this room, get it tidied up now! *or* The president will give **the State of** the Union address today).

Notes and examples

AREAS WITHIN OTHER AREAS

Areas that are contained within other areas are generally prefaced with **the**. The area being discussed would be prefaced with **the** but the area that they are part of may or not be depending if it is named using a proper noun.

Examples:

The geothermal areas of Yellowstone include several geyser basins. (The discussed are are the geothermal areas; whereas, the area they are within, Yellowstone park, is not specified with **the** as it is named with a compound proper noun).

The best farmland in England is in **the** fens. (Both the areas under discussion, the best farmland, and the larger area, the fens, are prefaced with **the** as the word 'fens' is not a proper noun; instead, it is a descriptive noun - it originates from the Germanic word, *fanjam*, meaning swamp or marsh - so the noun is describing an area that was previously swampland).

Exception: When describing the area in a generic or abstract way then **the** would not be used and the noun would be prefaced with a null determiner).

Examples:

__ Farmland is used to grow food (Generic reference to all farmland irrespective of the area it is found in).

__ Fen Farmland is very fertile (Abstract reference with the speaker giving their own opinion which may or may not be accurate. Note, the previously used noun, fen, is now being used as an adjective).

Notes and examples

PLACES IN AN AREA

The would be used to refer to a place within a known area or where the area has previously been referred to.

Examples:

I am sitting in **the** *student* café <u>on campus</u>. (The place where the speaker is and specified using a <u>prepositional phrase</u> and an *adjective*).

I am sitting in **the** café <u>that I told you about</u> (Place that had been previously referred to and specified using an <u>adjective clause</u>).

Exception: If the place isn't likely to be known by the reader or listener - particularly if it isn't important to know it - then **a** or **an** would be used.

Example: I am sitting inside **a** café. (An unspecified place in an unspecified area - you don't need me to specify it as it is a generic type and the implication of what I am doing there [drinking coffee, relaxing, nibbling snacks etc...] is more important).

Notes and examples

FEATURES IN A SPECIFIC PLACE

The is used to refer to some feature, fixture or fitting in a place where someone is or is referring to. **The** would also be used if the feature has been specified, usually by using a specifying prepositional phrase.

Examples:

Can you please close **the** window? (The only one in this room or the only one that is open).

Can you switch off **the** lights when you leave? (The lights in this room. If referring to the lights in a building use the compound determiner **all of the** – Can you switch off **all of the** lights when you leave?).

You can put the groceries on **the** table. (The table in this room).

Can you *switch* **the** light <u>over the cooker</u> *on*? (Feature specified using a <u>prepositional phrase</u> - as a specified noun within a *phrasal verb*).

Exception: If there are more than one feature and none of them were specified – in other words the action could refer to any of them - then **a** or **an** would be used.

Example:

We need some air in here can you open **a** window? (One of many windows in that room).

It's getting dark in here, can you switch **a** light on? (Any one of the lights in that room).

Notes and examples

NAMES OF ISLANDS

The names of islands are not normally prefaced with **the.**

Examples: __Staten island *or* __Pitcairn island

Exception 1: If the islands form part of a group of islands then **the** is used.

Examples: The Aleutian Islands or **the** Shetlands

Exception 2: If the island is known for something specific or is distinctive for some reason then use **the.**

Note, an **isle** (pronounced /aɪl/) is generally regarded as a small island.

Examples:

The Island of Jamaica (it is the main island of Jamaica and is distinctive as the country occupies the whole island).

The Isle of Man (It is an island that is distinct from the rest of the British Isles as it has its own system of government).

Notes and examples

MOUNTAINS AND VOLCANOES

The names of mountains are generally not prefaced with **the**.

Examples: __Mount Everest (mountain), __Mount Etna (volcano)

Exception 1: If the mountain is specific in some way then **the** is used.

Example: The Matterhorn is one of the highest peaks in Europe.

Exception 2: If you are describing a range of mountains then use **the**.

Examples: The Alps, **the** Himalayas.

Notes and examples

AREAS OF NATURAL BEAUTY

These are noted for being of significant landscape value and feature beautiful natural features. They may or may not be designated as national parks but usually feature some form of official protection.

The is sometimes used to refer to places or areas of natural beauty when they consist of a collection of features such as hills or lakes.

Examples:

The Chilterns *or* The Cotswolds (hills)

The Lake District (lakes)

Exception: If the description uses a proper noun, such as areas named after local towns, a feature connected to a community or a whole political or geographical area, then **the** is not used.

Examples:

Arnside and Silverdale (towns).

Chichester harbour (harbour connected with a community).

Cornwall (a county – whole political area).

Notes and examples

SITES OF SCIENTIFIC INTEREST

These are specifically designated conservation areas mainly due to having scientific, archaeological or botanical value. They include national nature reserves, Ramsar sites, Special Protection Areas, and Special Areas of Conservation.

The is not generally used to describe them as they commonly use proper nouns to describe them and they tend to be fairly small areas consisting of one main feature.

Examples:

Alder Carr (wet valley).
Aversley Wood (woodland).

Exception: When they consist of a collection of either similar or varying features they would use **the**.

Examples:

The Barnack Hills & Holes (Hills, grazing land and hollows).
The Castor flood meadows (A group of meadows next to a river).

Notes and examples

STREETS, ROADS AND AVENUES

The names of streets, roads, lanes or avenues are generally not prefaced with **the**.

Examples: First Street, Watling road, Pig lane, 5th avenue

Exception 1: If the street or road is specific in some way, usually by being prefaced with an adjective, then **the** is used.

Examples:

The high street (usually the main street in town).
The Great North Road (the major road going north).

Exception 2: If a roadway is locally known as being special, for example it is very expensive to buy a property there, then it would be prefaced with **the** even if it is not specified with an adjective.

Example: She lives on **the** avenue.

Notes and examples

DESERTS, FORESTS, GULFS AND PENINSULAS

The names of deserts, forests, gulfs, peninsulas and isthmuses (narrow pieces of land connecting two larger pieces of land) are prefaced with **the**.

Examples: The Sahara Desert, **the** Persian Gulf, **the** Forest of Dean, **the** Iberian Peninsula, **the** Auckland isthmus

Exception: Promontories (high pieces of land that jut into a body of water) are generally not preceded by **the**, particularly if they are named after somebody.

Example: Wilson's Promontory

Notes and examples

AIRPORTS AND STATIONS

Articles are not used to preface names of airports or railway stations.

Examples: __Heathrow airport *or* __Waterloo railway station

Exception: The can be used with airport or railway station provided that it is not preceded by a name (i.e. Suvarnabhumi Airport) and where the reader (or listener) is likely to know which airport is being referred to.

Examples: I will pick you up at **the** airport or I will arrive at **the** railway station at 9 p.m.

Notes and examples

FAMOUS BUILDINGS, STATUES OR STRUCTURES

The is generally used to preface well-known or unique buildings, statues or structures.

Examples:

The Empire State building (well-known building)
The Angel of the north (well-known statue)
The Taj Mahal (unique building)
The London Eye (a well known structure in London)

Exception: The wouldn't be used if the name of the building or structure contained a person's name, even it is well known or you intend to, say, meet someone there, unless the location was specified.

Examples:

__ Trump tower (no location given).
The Trump tower in New York (specific location).

Notes and examples

AGRICULTURAL BUILDINGS

Agricultural buildings are not generally prefaced with **the** as they are generally generic, so use **a** or **an** for a singular noun, or a null determiner (no word) if generic references to a type are being used.

Examples:

We store the hay in **a** barn (singular reference).

__Cowsheds are where cows are milked (plural genetic reference).

Exception: The would be used when referring to a specific building, usually with a defining adjective, or to the only one on a farm.

Examples:

The hay is in **the** <u>hay</u> barn (specific building prefaced with an <u>adjective</u>).

Put the tractor in **the** barn (only one on the farm).

Notes and examples

PARKS AND RECREATIONAL FACILITIES

The is generally used to preface the names of known (to both participants in the conversation) parks or recreational facilities when specifying it in relation to an activity or event or to draw attention to some specific feature. You would also use **the** if the location of the place was being specified or it is being named (but the name itself does not use **the**).

Examples:

I went jogging in **the** park (activity in a known place, probably because it is the only one in the place or area).

The <u>new</u> Whitbury new town leisure centre is opening this week (<u>specific feature</u>).

The park is called __ Hyde Park (being named - with null determiner in front of the park's name).

Exception: The generally wouldn't be used if the park or the facility is being referred to directly by name. Note the word, park, is capitalised in this instance as it forms part of a <u>compound proper noun</u>.

Examples:

I went jogging in __ <u>Lumpini Park</u>.
__Whitbury new town leisure centre is that way.

Notes and examples

COMMERCIAL PROPERTY

Commercial property is regarded as being different to commercial buildings in that commercial property refers to all buildings that are let in order to make a profit. These range from homes, through offices and shops to factories and shopping malls. **The** is generally not used for properties within a portfolio, nor for property companies, as they tend to be prefaced with proper nouns.

Examples:

__Alexandre Tower (residential).

__Portcullis House (government building).

__Bluewater Mall (Shopping mall),

__Llanwern steelworks (Industrial property).

Exception: The does get used to refer to specific property investment funds.

Examples:

The Threadneedle fund

The SWIP fund

Notes and examples

INDIVIDUAL SHOPS OR STORES

The is generally used to refer to the shop by its function, or what it sells, rather than by its name.

Examples:

I bought a newspaper at **the** newsagent.

The fishmonger in my town is very good.

There were no steaks at **the** butcher's (note the use of a possessive noun with no object – see the description below).

Exception: If the name of the shop is being referred to then **the** is not generally used, use **a, an** or a null determiner instead. The exception to this is if the shop being referred to is a specific one in a chain of such shops. You can also refer to the shop using a possessive noun with the following noun (usually shop [UK] or store [US]) being assumed rather that spoken/written: over time the inverted comma is generally dropped and the plural name becomes the group name.

Examples:

She buys her books at __ Barnes and Noble (null determiner).

I usually buy my milk at **the** 7/11 (it is a specific one in a chain of such shops – usually because it one that is known by both the speaker and the listener or it is the most local one or it is the only one in town – **a** or **an** could be used instead to refer to an unspecified shop "I buy my milk at **a** 7/11").

I bought a book at __ W.H. Smith's (Using a possessive noun).

Notes and examples

DEPARTMENTS IN A STORE

The is used to refer to specific departments in a department store. Note that departments may be referred to as departments, sections, concessions, stands, booths, halls or by their function.

Examples:

I bought some cheese in **the** food hall.

Go through **the** ladies' shoe section to get to **the** cafeteria.

Exception: The name of the department store itself is generally not prefaced with **the** as it is a proper noun; however, if it features an indirect reference it would use **the**.

Examples:

Sears (originally founded by Richard Warren Sears).

Harrods (derived from the possessive noun as part of Harrod's stores limited – the original name).

The house of Frazer (Indirect reference as part of the name).

Notes and examples

SHOPPING MALLS

Shopping malls differ from department stores in that the latter are usually single premises (which may or may not have car parking) with individual departments selling ranges of goods and all owned by a single owner; whereas, malls would be large building, commonly with large car parks, in which individual shops/stores, usually owned by different owners, sell a variety of goods. Their names are usually preceded by **the** as the actual name is either used as an adjective, it is used as an indirect reference or it forms part of a compound noun.

Examples:

The Bluewater shopping complex (adjective).

The mall at Bang Khae (indirect reference).

The New China Shopping Mall (compound noun).

Exception: If the mall's name doesn't feature its function, for example it is just a proper noun, then it wouldn't be prefaced with **the.**

Examples:

__ Centralworld (Bangkok)

__ Centro Mayor (Bogota)

Notes and examples

STORES IN SHOPPING MALLS

Stores in a shopping mall differ from departments in a department store in that they are individual units, usually with separate ownership, as opposed to parts of a whole (unless the store itself is part of a chain of stores), and normally go by a name comprising of a proper noun. Therefore they are not generally preceded by **the**.

Examples:

McDonalds

Robinsons

Exception: Where there is only one store of that type or name in the mall, or it is the only one performing a specific function, then **the** is used to refer to it by its function rather than its name.

Examples:

The computer shop at the mall (Only shop selling computers in the known mall)

The Burger King at Bluewater (Only one of this name in the mall – note it is being made specific using the prepositional phrase <u>at Bluewater</u> to differentiate it from other Burger Kings.).

Notes and examples

MARKETS

A market, also known as a marketplace or a public market, is a place where people come together to meet and trade or barter goods. They are generally not fixed in that the stall are often dismantled after a day's trading or they comprise of a series of booths rather than discrete shops. As they tend to be specific, and generally unique, in a town they would normally be prefaced with **the**.

Examples:

I am going to **the** market later, do you need anything?

I bought an interesting lamp at **the** flea market (a market where second hand goods are sold).

I park in **the**[1] cattle market during the week as **the**[2] market is only active at the weekend. ([1] referring to a specific market, [2] referring to the market that had been mentioned previously).

Exception: When talking about markets in a general sense, for example asking about availability, then use **a** or **an**.

Example: Does this town have **a** market?

Notes and examples

PLACES TO LIVE (RESIDENTIAL)

Places of residence are generally regarded as personal property, even though they may only be rented or leased, as they are under the personal control of an individual, a family or a group. Therefore they would generally be prefaced with a possessive pronoun or possessive noun rather than **the**. **A** or **an** can be used to preface a residence if it hasn't been obtained yet.

Examples:

You can come over to **my** house if you like (possessive pronoun).

We are all meeting at **Sheila's** condo (possessive noun).

I am looking for **a** new apartment (not obtained yet).

Exception: When the place of residence is being used as a point of reference when giving directions or when talking about times/time-frames or availability for instance, then **the** would be used.

Examples:

Turn left by **the** house on the corner (as a reference)

The house was built in 1948 (time)

It was **the** last apartment left empty (availability)

Notes and examples

HOTELS AND RESTAURANTS

The is generally used to preface the names of hotels, pubs (public houses – bars) or restaurants.

Examples:

The Savoy (hotel)
The King's Head (pub)
The Star of India (restaurant)

Exception 1: The is not used when the establishment contains the name of a person.

Examples:

__Brown's hotel
__Fred's diner (restaurant)

Notes and examples

ENTERTAINMENT VENUES

The is generally used when referring to places of entertainment as they tend to be specific. Places that use generic references are prefaced with **the** to show that they of a specific type of place or type of entertainment.

Examples:

He first met his wife at **the** nightclub. (Specific type of place).
Do you want to go to **the** circus? (Non-permanent specific place).
I went to **the** movies yesterday (Specific type of entertainment).

Exception: If the place is named using a possessive noun then it will not be prefaced with **the**, unless it might be mistaken for another one of the same name or under the same ownership, in which case it will be followed by a <u>prepositional phrase </u>to specify it.

Examples:

I went to Julie's nightclub last night. (Only a single one exists).
I went to **the** Julie's nightclub <u>in Coventry</u> last night. (One of many)

Notes and examples

                    Website: www.englishbook.shop

PUBLIC TRANSPORT HUBS

Public transport facilities are usually specific, even though they may be one of many, as they are specific stopping and boarding points for the transportation itself so they would generally prefaced with **the.**

Examples:

You can catch a number 9 bus at **the** bus stop (**the** is used as it refers to the nearest one which is specific. Note the bus itself, even though it is referred to specifically by number, is usually prefaced with **a.** This is because the number refers to the route it plies, not the number of the bus itself – in UK English you can use <u>the number 9 bus</u> instead when you want to draw the listener's attention to the exact bus number they need to take to get to their destination).

The bus station is in the middle of the city (there is only one bus station).

Exception: If a generic reference is being made, for example describing a place where you can find that type of transport, then **a** or **an** are used. **Many** (uncounted number) or a numerical determiner (known number) are used to describe the number of such places in the town

Examples: Note the use of different nouns in the first 2 examples:

You can get a taxi at **a** taxi rank (UK English).

You can get a cab at **a** taxi stand (US English).

There are **many** taxi ranks in the city centre (unknown number).

Notes and examples

MEDICAL ESTABLISHMENTS

The tends to be used when referring to medical establishments in a formal way. Consider the first three examples below, which all refer to the same hospital. If you refer to a hospital visited previously then you would also use **the** as it was a specific hospital, even if it wasn't named or defined previously.

Examples:

The Royal Hospital of St Bartholomew (Formal name).

St Bartholomew's Hospital (Official name).

Barts (Nickname in common use).

He went to **the** hospital when he cut his arm (the visited one).

Exception: When referring to them in a generic or non-defined way then use either no word (null determiner) or **a/an**. Note: in the UK it is common to say **the** hospital even when referring to it in a generic way as it is most likely the only hospital in town.

Examples:

You need to go to __ Hospital (null determiner as hospital is generic).

She went to **an** obstetrics clinic yesterday (one of many).

How did she get on at **the** obstetrics clinic yesterday? (Referring to the specific clinic - although it was not named it is specified as it's the one she went to - note, **get on** is a UK idiom meaning what was the outcome?).

Notes and examples

MEDICAL DEPARTMENTS

The is usually used to refer to departments in a hospital or medical establishment, even if it is just a single room or area, as they are distinct, with different functions and therefore specific.

Examples:

She is on **the** maternity ward (a ward is where patients sleep, rest and recuperate. It can refer to a single large room with many patients or single rooms, one per patient, but connected to a certain department).

I sent him to **the** X-ray department.

Exception: When referring to them in a generic way, for example when talking about the function **and** the place, rather than just the place, then use no word (null determiner).

Examples:

I need to transfer you to _ oncology (both the place and the function)

I transferred him to **the** oncology department (Specific place)

Notes and examples

NATURAL ENVIRONMENTS

Environments tend to be very specific, particularly when used as the subject of a sentence, therefore they are usually preceded by **the. The** would also be used to highlight a particular environment, such as when it has special properties that wouldn't be possible or feasible in another environment or conveys a deeper meaning such as an inference to something, like a possible crime or mystery. You would also use **the** when discussing a desired environment. Plural environments will usually be preceded by **the.**

Examples:

The forest was dark and forbidding. (A specific [scary] forest).

The cattle ranged freely on **the** savannah. (Particular environment).

He went into **the** forest and was never seen again. (Deeper meaning).

I would love a house in **the** forest. (Desired Environment).

The seas around the island teem with fish. (Plural environments).

Exception 1: When making a general reference to an environment use **a** or **an.**

Examples: According to the map there is **a** forest near here.

Exception 2: When making a general reference to environments, such as those belonging to a certain place, then no article is used (underlined blanks below). However, if the environments have a special significance they are generally specified with **the.**

Example:

The countryside, which is outside the city and built areas, features __forests,   tundra and   lakes. (General reference to environment types).

The lakes <u>outside the city</u> are very polluted (Specific properties of environments that are specified with a <u>prepositional phrase</u>).

Notes and examples

MANMADE ENVIRONMENTS

The is generally used to preface nouns used to describe a manmade environment as it refers to somewhere specific. Note, in the second example the dwelling places are prefaced with <u>a</u> or <u>an</u> as they are general descriptions of a type of dwelling.

Examples:

There was a march in **the** city centre. (The city the speaker is in, or has previously talked about *or* it is the country's capital).

He has <u>a</u> house in **the** suburbs and <u>an</u> apartment in **the** city.

Exception: When referring to a manmade environment in a general sense, then **a** or **an,** - or a possessive determiner when a community is being referred to - are generally used.

Examples:

I live in **a** town (General).

There is **a** 1,000 year old church in <u>our</u> village. (One of a number of 1,000 old churches, with this one <u>possessed by the speaker's village</u>).

Notes and examples

NOTABLE PLACES

Public areas are often named after some important event, a particular date (when some important even took place), a reference to another place or a person and so they will not be prefaced with **the.**

Examples:

28 May Street is located in the Nəsimi Raion area of Baku. (Named after the date of the establishment of Azerbaijan Soviet Socialist Republic).

Trafalgar Square is in the centre of London. (Named after the battle of Trafalgar).

Tiananmen Square in Beijing is named after the Tiananmen - Gate of Heavenly Peace – which is nearby. (Reference to another place).

Kim Il-sung Square is in Pyongyang, North Korea (Named after an outstanding national figure).

Exception: When something notable takes place in the place the name would become an <u>adjective</u> and would be prefaced with **the.**

Example: The <u>Tiananmen Square</u> protests took place in 1989.

Notes and examples

GEOGRAPHICAL ANOMALIES

Geographical anomalies are generally prefaced with **the** as they are unique.

Examples:

The Kentucky Bend doesn't touch the rest of Kentucky as it rests within an oxbow formed by the Mississippi.

The only way to reach **the** Northwest angle in Alaska by car is to drive through Canada.

Exception: If the anomaly is an island or a small peninsula/promontory (commonly named 'point' something) then it isn't prefaced with **the**.

Examples:

__Liberty Island, on which the statue of Liberty stands, is technically in New York but is surrounded by New Jersey.

__ Point Roberts is part of Washington State, USA but exists within Vancouver, Canada.

Notes and examples

AREAS USED AS A REFERENCE

The is generally used to preface particular areas, the main reason being that when mentioning them the speaker is allowing the listener to get some idea of where some event has or will happen or where some phenomena is.

Examples:

There is a free concert in **the** market square tonight. (Note, the place is assumed to be known to the listener).

The demonstration took place in **the** Place de la Concorde in Paris. (Named place with the word 'place' first).

Exception: If the area is named (and prefaced) using a proper known then **the** wouldn't be used; however, if the name is prefaced with an area description (usually followed by 'of') then **the** would be used. Study the following two examples.

Examples:

The concert is in Hyde <u>Park</u>. (The <u>area description</u> is at the end).

The tour was through **the** <u>National Park</u> of Abruzzo. (Starts with the <u>area description</u>).

Notes and examples

LARGE DISCRETE OBJECTS

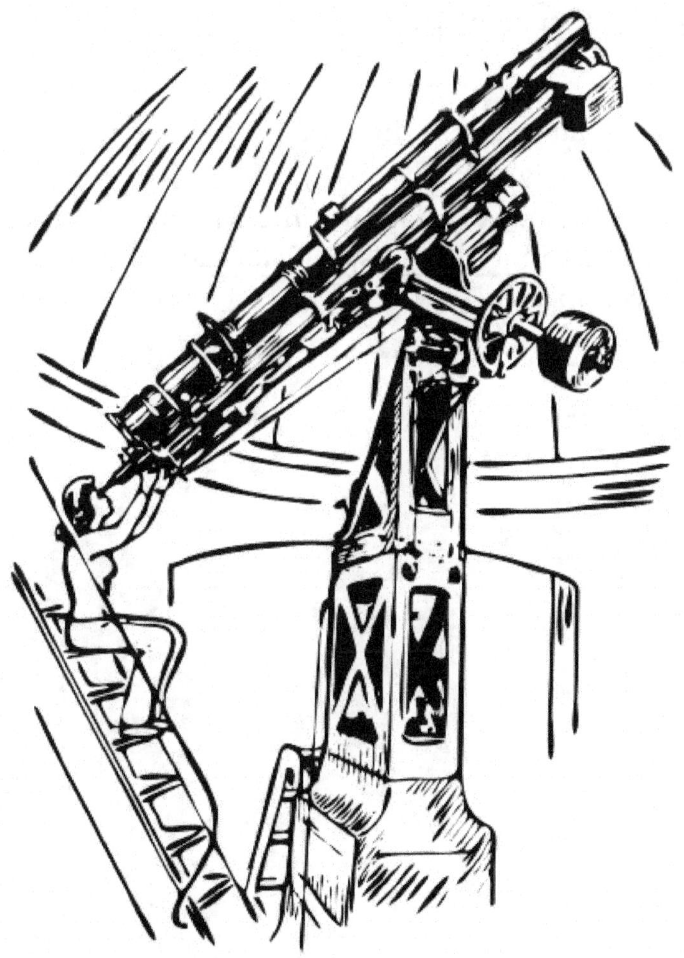

ONLY THING IN A PLACE

The is used to refer to something that either only exists in one place or is the only thing of its type at a particular place.

Examples:

I went to **the** Indian Zest restaurant to eat (Only one place with this name and/or description).

We went to **the** restaurant near **the** harbour (only one in that specific place).

Exception: If there are more than one of this type in the place then use **a** or **an**, although the place itself is usually referred to using <u>the</u> as it only refers to that area/place.

Examples:

We ate at **a** restaurant near <u>the</u> harbour (one of many at a specific place).

We stopped to eat at **a** restaurant in a village we passed through (unspecified restaurant in an unspecified location).

Notes and examples

FIXED MACHINES

Fixed machines are usually fairly large and fixed in place. Whether **the** is used to preface a fixed machine depends on whether it is specific. For example, it is the only one in the place with the specific attributes, it has a specific function that other machines cannot fulfil, it is named or it is the one that will be used to do a particular job.

Examples:

The 500 ton press is largest we have (the only one in the place with those attributes).

The laser is used to engrave anilox rollers. (The only one that can fulfil this function).

The Heidelberg printer is our best machine (Named machine).

The gas furnace will be used as it's the only one big enough for this job (The one to be used for a particular job).

Exception: If a machine is not special in some way or its function is not being discussed, even if it is being named, then **the** wouldn't normally be used.

Examples:

Have we got a paper guillotine? (Not a special guillotine but any guillotine).

We have **a** BCS flexo carton printer. (Function not being discussed).

Notes and examples

PLANT

Plant can refer to a particular place where manufacturing takes place or it can refer, usually in conjunction with the word machinery – 'plant and machinery', to "equipment used to help an entity to trade such as trucks, tools, office furniture, computers, ladders, etc." In the latter context, where trade equipment is taken as a whole as an (uncountable) group, it would be prefaced with **the** when being discussed as a particular group of assets. The place of production would also be prefaced with **the** and if the piece of plant is named it is usually prefaced with **the.**

Examples:

The <u>plant</u> and machinery is being treated separately by the liquidator that the other assets (whole asset group).

The plant is being rebuilt as it is not efficient any more (place).

The central air conditioning system has stopped working (named piece of integrated plant).

The excavator has broken down (stand alone piece of equipment).

Exception: If the plant is being referred to in abstract sense then it would be prefaced with a <u>null determiner</u>.

Example: You need to be careful as __ heavy plant is in use in this quarry.

Notes and examples

PRODUCTION MACHINES

Whether **the** is used to preface the name or type of a production machine depends on whether it is special in some way; for example, regarding its size, function, uniqueness, being the only one of its type with that name or, possibly, cost, in which case it would be prefaced with **the**. The thing to remember is that they represent something that is special in some way to that particular manufacturing company, but not necessarily to any other company. **The** is also used to refer to a group of machines of the same type.

Examples:

The company's tunnel kiln is over 100 metres long (size).

The oven is used to solder computer motherboards (function).

The extruder is the only one of its kind in the state (unique).

The Lake Erie 5,000 ton press is installed in our metalworking department (the only one with that name in the company).

We purchased **the** cheapest moulding machine we could find (being specified by its cost).

One of **the** annealing ovens caught fire today (to refer to a specific machine out of a specified group of similar machines).

Exception: If the discussion about the machine is taking place in fairly close proximity to the machine in question then **this** (for something within touching distance) or **that** (for something that can be seen but is away from the speaking and is being pointed at) would be used.

Examples: This machine produces paperclips and **that** machine puts them into boxes.

Notes and examples

STATUES

Statues are almost always unique, even when referring to multiple statues, and so they'd be specified using the even if they are not named.

Examples:

The statue of Nelson Mandela in Parliament Square, London is made of bronze. (Singular).

The terracotta warriors are famous throughout the world. (Plural).

Exception 1: If the statue doesn't exist yet then **a** or **an** would normally be used.

Example: The city government in Washington DC was considering erecting **a** statue of Marion Barry.

Exception 2: When talking about statues in a generic sense even if they are named, particularly when referring to multiple statues, without referring to any one in particular, a <u>null determiner</u> is used.

Examples:

__Statues are erected in cities to honour important military, social or political leaders. (The statue doesn't exist yet).

__Confederate statues are being torn down or defaced as they are regarded by some as racist. (Statues with a particular theme but which are not specified in any other way).

Notes and examples

STRUCTURES

The is used to specify particular structures that are different in relation to other structures. This could be because of things like the size, function, material they are made from or an event that is associated with them. A structure can also refer to non-physical things such as the form or organization of something more abstract. Structures in this context is not referring directly to buildings.

Examples:

The[1] scaffolding on **the**[2] Burj Khalifa building was built in stages to conceal the height of **the**[3] building ([1]Specific structure. [2] Specific building. [3] The previously mentioned building – the reason for using the specific noun phrase 'the building' instead of the pronoun, '**it**', was to avoid confusion as **it** could refer to either the building or the scaffolding around the building).
The scaffolding for Hangar One was 345m long, 94m wide and 60m high (size).
The A frame is used to lift engines out of cars (function).
The scaffolding in Asia is usually made from bamboo rather than steel (material).
The Hyatt Regency walkway collapse was caused by a substandard design change (associated event).
The structure of a sentence can be studied using colour (abstract form).

Exception: When talking about structures in general, even when referring to ones of a special type, then a or an would be used.

Example: You'll need **an** A frame to lift that engine (the capitalised A refers to the shape of the structure and is not a determiner).

Notes and examples

PUBLIC ARTWORKS

Art installations in public places are generally named using a proper noun, so you'd expect that they wouldn't be prefaced with **the**, however they usually are. Note, the first two examples below use general terms to apply to a statue (*angel* and *motherland*, respectively).

Examples:

The *Angel of the North* is in the north of England. (General term)

The *Rodina Mat* in Volgograd is the largest statue in the world.

The *Mission District murals* are in San Francisco (Multiple artworks treated as one).

Exception: When referring to artworks in general, even if they are created by the same artist, are generally prefaced with **a** or **an** (for singular artworks) or a <u>null determiner</u> (for multiple artworks). Note, if the artwork is named then *the name* would be prefaced with **the** but the artist wouldn't be, when referring to plural artworks by that artist (see the second example).

Examples:

A Richard Serra artwork installed in Federal Plaza in Manhattan – called **the** *Titled Arc* - was dismantled after a number of complaints.

__ Henry Moore statues are renowned for being monumental, rounded reclining figures.

Notes and examples

　　　　　　　

MONUMENTS

Monuments are generally erected to send patriotic triumphant messages after great victories. As they are generally unique or internationally well-known they would normally be prefaced with **the.**

Examples:

Some people say that **the** Siegessäule (victory) column in Berlin, inaugurated in 1875, was modelled on **the** Alexander Column in Saint Petersburg. (Column - tall cylindrical structure supporting something).

The Arc de Triomphe de l'Étoile in Paris was erected by Emperor Napoleon after the battle of Austerlitz and, at 50 metres tall, is slightly smaller than **the** similar Arch of Triumph in Pyongyang, which is 60 metres tall. (Arch).

Exception: If the monument is associated with a name, using a possessive noun, or has given its name to a geographical area around it, then it would normally be prefaced with a <u>null determiner</u>.

Examples:

__Nelson's column stand in the middle of Trafalgar Square. (Column named after a person).

__Marble Arch is situated at the junction of Oxford Street, Park Lane and Edgware Road in London. (Arch giving its name to the surrounding area and underground railway station).

__Mount Rushmore features the faces of four former US presidents (geographical feature).

Notes and examples

SACRED OBJECTS

Sacred objects, whether they are used during religious observances or not, are regarded as specific and therefore they would be referred to using **the**,

Examples:

Over 200 million people have visited **the** shrine at Lourdes.

The altar in the church is estimated to be almost 1200 years old.

Exception: When the objects are very common they are preceded by a null determiner (no word). If a single one of the type is being specifically referred to then **a** or **an** would be used, while plural ones of the type are generally preceded by a *numerical determiner* (if the number is known) or **many** (if the number is not known).

Examples:

__Prayer wheels are a common part of Tibetan Buddhist practise (generic reference – <u>null determiner</u>).

There are over *1,000* statues of the Lord Buddha in the Dhammakaya Temple complex in Thailand (approximate *numerical value*).

Many sacred relics existed and were used as part of Islamic devotions during the classical and medieval periods (*unknown number*).

Notes and examples

BUSINESS

FINANCE NOUNS

Words and phrases related to financial matters tend to be very specific and so many of the terms are prefaced with **the**.

Examples:

I went to **the** bank. (The specific bank where my money is).

I filled in **the** form to withdraw some money (The specific form).

The cashier gave me **the** cash in ten pound notes (specific person and specific cash – as it was my cash as opposed to all the other cash: note you could use **my** cash instead of **the** cash in order to personalise it).

Exception: You can use **a** or **an** to refer to a place where a generic transaction will take place or a form that is generic.

Examples:

I had to go to **a** bank to cash **a** cheque (any bank – one of many cheques). Cheque is spelt **check** in US English.

I had to fill in **a** withdrawal form (one of many such forms).

Notes and examples

GENERAL BUSINESS FUNCTIONS

The functions that a business performs are usually not specified using **the** as they tend to be generic. Therefore they'd either use no word (null determiner) for a generic description or **a/an** to show that they are one of many companies performing that service. Note in the latter instance the function may be described in an adjective form (as a descriptor used to clarify the function) or as a noun phrase.

Examples:

The Company is involved in __ engineering (generic description of function performed by a known company).

My firm is **an** electronics manufacturer (noun phrase – adjective [to clarify the type within a category] & noun [general category]).

It is **a** design company (adjective form – design is the adjective).

Exception: The is used when the company is either known already, referred to previously, or it has been specified (usually with a prepositional phrase).

Examples:

We just got a quote from **the** design company (previously known).

The guy from **the** marketing company we spoke to, called me (referred to previously).

He works at **the** engineering firm <u>on the industrial estate</u> (specified with a <u>prepositional phrase</u>).

Notes and examples

OFFICE EQUIPMENT

The is generally used when referring to a piece of office equipment even if there are more than one of them in a particular office. If you need to be more specific (say there are a lot of printers) then use an adjective (**the** colour printer) or a prepositional phrase (**the** printer on Jane's desk) to specify it.

Examples:

I made a copy in **the** photocopier (only one available)

I printed it out on **the** nearest printer (one of many specified with comparative adjective).

Exception: If the equipment is connected to a specific person then use either a possessive noun or a possessive determiner.

Examples:

I printed it out on **Jane's** printer (possessive noun)

I scanned it in with **my** scanner (possessive determiner)

Notes and examples

OFFICE FURNITURE

The doesn't generally get used to describe pieces of office furniture as they tend to be considered to be individual (and generally indistinguishable) items in a collection, so they are normally prefaced with **a** or **an**, or a numerical determiner.

Examples:

In my office there is **a** desk, **an** armchair and **three** office chairs.

Exception: If an individual piece of furniture is considered to be different, distinguishable or outstanding it would be prefaced with **the**, a possessive pronoun or a possessive noun.

Examples:

That is **her** desk over there (possessive pronoun).

Put it on **John's** table (possessive noun).

The desk in the boss's office is made of rosewood (specific using **the** and a prepositional phrase to specify it).

Notes and examples

OFFICE SUPPLIES

Whether or not **the** is used when referring to office supplies depends on whether or not the supplies are being highlighted or of special interest. This would apply whether the supplies are countable or uncountable.

Examples: Highlighted supplies

The copier paper is in that drawer (uncountable – specific reference).

The toner cartridge arrived today (countable – the one we ordered)

Exception: If the supplies are being referred to in general terms then they can be prefaced with **a** or **an**, or a numerical determiner for countable nouns or **any** [negative or questioning amounts], **some** [for positive amounts] or no determiner [generally for unspecified amounts including 0] for uncountable nouns.

Examples:

Have you got **a** pen I can borrow? (countable - any pen)

We bought **three** toner cartridges (countable – specific number).

Have we got **any** paperclips? (uncountable – questioning amount).

I have **some** paperclips here (uncountable- unspecified amount)

We have run out of __ printer paper (uncountable – general)

Notes and examples

QUOTATIONS AND ESTIMATES

The is generally not used when asking for or offering a quotation or estimate, use **a** or **an** instead. The difference between an estimate and a quotation is that an estimate is generally not legally binding but quotations are generally fixed and can form part of legally binding contracts. If the estimated cost is to within the nearest round figure (100s or 1,000s say) then use the adjective <u>rough</u> before the word estimate (I need a <u>rough</u> estimate). In general business terms quotations are usually offered for physical goods and estimates are offered for services (as costs may increase due to unforeseen problems or changes in circumstances).

Examples:

I'd like **a** quotation for 1,000 units FOB, by return if possible.

Is it possible to get **an** estimate of the cost of the refurbishment?

Exception: The would be used to refer to a quotation once it has been offered.

Examples:

What is the validity of **the** quotation as I need it to be valid for 60 days so the order can be placed in our next financial year?

The estimate was a little high, can we negotiate a reduction if I arrange my own workmen?

Notes and examples

ORDER REFERENCES

The is generally not used to preface the word <u>order</u> when ordering goods or services, use **an** instead.

Examples:

I'd like to place **an** <u>order</u> for twenty units for delivery next week.

Exception: The is used by the customer to refer to an order that has already been placed. The vendor (the person or organisation that is fulfilling the order) would use **your** to refer to the order.

Examples:

With reference to **the** <u>order</u> I placed last week, which arrived today, I ordered green units and you delivered blue ones (customer).

Your order has been shipped and should arrive at your factory on Friday the 21st of May (vendor).

Notes and examples

PRODUCT REFERENCES

The is generally used to preface the name of what the company supplies or produces. It can be used to refer to either single items, multiple items or a complete range.

Examples:

I can let you have **a** free sample of **the** book (singular).

Free copies of **the** book can be supplied to libraries on request (indirect plural reference).

All of **the** books are shipped from our distribution centre in Bangkok (direct plurals).

The books we supply range from workbooks through to detailed references (A range of products).

Exception: When you want to place an emphasis on the source of the products, in order to show that you are the sole supplier say, you would use **our** (for a company) or **my** (for a person).

Examples:

Our books are offered under standard industry terms (company).

My books are really good! (Single person).

Notes and examples

COMPANY NAMES

The is generally not used with names of businesses.

Examples:

He designs electronic systems at __British Aerospace

Chevrolet is a brand name of __General Motors

Exception 1: If the business wants to be known for its specific specialisation then **the** can be used.

Example:

The British Welding Corporation

Exception 2: When you are talking about the products from the named company you would use **the.**

Example:

The Boeing 747 is a very popular aircraft.

Notes and examples

TRADE SHOWS

Trade shows, which are generally based on a theme or for an industry and are used to showcase existing products or announce new products, are generally named and that means that they would not be prefaced with **the**. Instead they would be prefaced with a <u>null determiner</u>. Many are so well known they do not need specifying with a prepositional phrase (to say where they are or what they are about, for example).

Examples: Did you go to __Comic con this year? (The only one).

Exception 1: If there are a number of trade shows with the same name in different cities/.countries then the name would be prefaced with **the**.

Example: Did you go to **the** embedded system show <u>in San Jose</u>? (Show that takes place in a number of places; so, it has been further specified with a <u>prepositional phrase</u>).

Exception 2: If the show is not named and is either known, for example if it is the only one of its type that is relevant to a business sector, or is specified with an adjective or a prepositional phrase, then it would be prefaced with **the**.

Examples:

Are we taking a stand at **the** show this year? (The only show the company exhibits at).

Is **the** *food additives* show this month? (Specified with an *adjective*).

Are you going to **the** show <u>in Berlin</u>? (Specified with a <u>prepositional phrase</u>).

Notes and examples

CONFERENCES

A Conference is a meeting that has been prearranged and involves consultation and discussion on a number of topics by the delegates for instance a sales conference or a trade conference. Conferences differ from symposia in that they are often non-academic and can, and often do, take place over a period of a number of days. They are often prefaced with **the**, particularly while they are taking place.

Examples:

The *teaching* conference starts on Tuesday. (Future conference using an *adjective* to specify it).

The conference <u>on food additives</u> is taking place in the Queen Sirikit Conference Centre in Bangkok. (Current conference using <u>prepositional phrase</u> to specify it).

The conference took place in the Taiwan Conference centre in Taipei. (Past conference that is known about – so there is no need to specify it with either an adjective or a preposition).

Exception 1: When referring to conferences in questions then **a** or **an** are used.

Example: Is there **a** sales conference taking place this year?

Exception 2: When referring to conferences in general, particularly plural conferences, then a <u>null determiner</u> would be used.

Example: __Conferences are an important way for the company to bring together its external sales staff and distributors.

Notes and examples

SALES AND MARKETING

When we refer to a company's sales and marketing we are talking about a concept and so the reference would generally not be prefaced with **the**; instead, they would normally be prefaced with a <u>null determiner</u>.

Examples:

____ Sales are up across the whole sector this year.

We decided to invest more in ____ marketing this year.

Exception: When discussing sales or marketing that are specific to a particular company then either **the** or a **possessive determiner** are used.

Examples:

The company's sales increased this year. (Sales specific to the company being discussed and therefore known).

Our marketing is not very effective in the teen market. (**Possessive determiner** used when discussing a company where the speaker and, commonly, the listener work).

Their sales increased when they released their new product. (3rd person possessive determiner used to discuss a company that is being studied by people who do not work in the company).

Notes and examples

ADVERTISING

Advertising is generally an uncountable concept and so it wouldn't be prefaced with **the**. In general, conceptual terms it would be prefaced with a <u>null determiner</u> and in questions and in negative terms it would be prefaced with **any**.

Examples:

___Advertising tells people about the availability of a product (In conceptual terms).

Is there **any** advertising on the BBC? (Question about advertising availability).

We are not doing **any** advertising this quarter. (Negative reference).

Exception: When advertising is specified - in order to associate it with a product or a company or an emotion (with an adjective or a prepositional phrase) then it would be prefaced with **the**.

Examples:

The *clothing* advertising focused on denim products. (Specified with an adjective to associate it with a product).

The advertising <u>that the company undertook</u> paid for itself. (Specified with an <u>adjective clause</u> to associate it with a company).

The advertising <u>during the program</u> drove me crazy. (Specified with a <u>prepositional phrase</u> to associate it with an emotion).

Notes and examples

PRODUCTION

Production is generally regarded as an abstract concept and so it wouldn't normally be prefaced with **the**; instead, it would generally be prefaced with a <u>null determiner</u>.

Example: I will contact __ production and see if we can move your order forward.

Exception 1: If the word is used as an *adjective*, or part of a <u>compound noun</u>, then it would be prefaced with **the**.

Examples:

I spoke to **the** *production* manager and he will see what he can do. (Using the word as an *adjective*).

The <u>production line</u> is working at full capacity. (<u>Compound noun</u> referring to the only one in the company).

Exception 2: When referring to the action of making (producing) something, instead of where it is undertaken, then **the** would be used.

Example: **The** production of the machine was undertaken in Thailand.

Notes and examples

SHIPPING

The word 'shipping, can be used as part of a verb. It is also used as an adjective and as a noun. As a verb part it wouldn't be prefaced with **the**, instead it would be prefaced with an auxiliary verb. As a noun it is used to refer to the (generic) area where products are sent from.

Examples:

I <u>am shipping</u> it next week. (As part of a compound <u>verb</u>).

It was sent to __ shipping yesterday (Place where products are dispatched. It is prefaced with a null determiner because it is being referred to in a generic way).

__ Shipping is by air (the method by which products were shipped).

Exceptions: If it used as an adjective it is prefaced with **the**, if it refers to the specific noun it prefaces, or it could be prefaced with **a** or **an** if it is prefacing a non-specific noun.

Examples:

Your product is currently in **the** shipping <u>department</u>. (Prefacing a <u>specific</u> <u>noun</u>).

He is **a** <u>shipping</u> *clerk* in the factory. (***Non-specific noun***, i.e. one of many).

Notes and examples

IN THE HOME

HOUSEHOLD FURNITURE

Household furniture is a collective and so is regarded on the whole as uncountable. However individual pieces within a house or a home are generally preceded with **the**, even when referring to plural items, particularly whilst talking about it/them whilst inside the home itself. When referring to them whilst outside the home a possessive determiner is generally used. When referring to one of a group then an indicative determiner can be used.

Examples:

I put it on **the** sideboard (singular item).

The dining room chairs need replacing (plural items).

I am thinking of changing **my** bed (outside reference & possessive determiner - note, changing the bed has two meanings in English, most commonly, it is taken to mean changing the bedclothes for clean ones. In this sentence, however, it means buying a whole new bed including the mattress, frame etc.).

Please sit in **that** chair over there (indicative determiner).

Exception: When talking about the acquisition or disposal of furniture use **a** or **an**.

Examples:

I bought **a** new sofa (acquisition).

We donated **an** armchair to the homeless shelter (disposal).

Notes and examples

HOUSEHOLD ITEMS

The is used when there is only one item or a specific group is being referred to in the house.

Examples:

Have you used **the** washing machine today? (Only one in the house).

The cups are in the cupboard over the sink (specific group).

Exception: If there are many items available, or if it being used to quantify some uncountable thing; or if it not known whether there is an item of that type in the house; then use **a** or **an**.

Examples:

Can I have **a** clean plate? (One of many items in the house).

Do you want **a** cup of tea? (Quantify an uncountable noun).

Do we have **an** iron? (Unknown availability)

Notes and examples

HOUSE FIXTURE AND FITTINGS

Fittings or fixtures are parts that are fixed in place and usually perform a particular task. **The** is generally used to preface a single fixed item in the house, it can also be used to preface multiple items of the same type, which are generally specified using a <u>prepositional phrase</u>.

Examples:

The boiler is not working so we have no hot water. (Single item).

The patio doors are warped so we need to replace them. (Plural items).

Exception 1: When referring to single or multiple items from a certain household in terms of specific attributes then they are usually prefaced with **possessive determiners.**

Examples:

Their window was broken by a stray baseball. (Single specified item belonging to known owners).

Our doors are made from plastic. (Plural items with specific attributes).

Exception 2: When using a general reference to certain fixtures they are prefaced with a null determiner.

Example: __ Taps are used to control the flow of water and are called faucets in the USA.

Notes and examples

HOUSE STRUCTURAL FEATURES

The would generally be used to talk about single structural features in a building, it would also be used when talking about collective structural features, providing they are specified (usually using a prepositional phrase, an adjective or an adjective chain).

Examples:

The roof is leaking. (A specific feature on a known building).

The doors _in my house_ are made from pine. (With a _prepositional phrase_).

The _bay_ windows need painting. (Specified using a single _adjective_).

The _stained white plastic_ guttering needs cleaning. (_Adjective chain_ – note guttering is uncountable; so, even though it consists of many parts it is regarded as a singular uncountable entity – hence no plural 's').

Exception 1: When referring to structural features whilst in the vicinity of it then an indicative determiner would be used. If the feature(s) is/are specified using an adjective or a prepositional phrase then **the** would be used, even if the speaker is in the vicinity.

Examples:

Those windows need replacing. (The indicated ones - in the vicinity).

The _rotten_ windows need replacing (The _adjective_ specified ones).

The windows _over the front door_ need replacing (_Prepositional phrase_).

Exception 2: When specifying the features by possession then a possessive determiner would be used.

Example: My windows need replacing.

Notes and examples

ADDITIONAL FEATURES

Additional features in this context are features or structures that have been added to a building after it was built. **The** would normally be used as the features are generally singular and specific. If they are not specified by virtue of them not being the only feature of that type, then they would be specified using an adjective or a prepositional phrase.

Examples:
The conservatory roof is leaking. (Specific additional feature – note it is a compound noun).

The *new* porch looks good. (*Adjective*).

The double glazing *that we had installed* is falling apart. (Specified using an *adjective clause*).

The path *at the side of the house* has weeds growing through it. (*Prepositional phrase*).

Exception: When discussing a feature belonging to the speaker or someone else specified by them then a possessive determiner would be used.

Example: Their loft extension makes the house look ugly.

Notes and examples

DECORATIVE FEATURES

The would normally be used to preface decorative features in a home as they are specific to that home. Decorative features are generally functional as well as being good to look at. A prepositional phrase or an adjective would be commonly used in order to differentiate them from others of their type.

Examples:

She has recovered <u>all of the</u> cushions with red velvet. (Using a <u>determiner</u> containing **the** to encompass every example of that item).

The curtains *in the living room* need replacing. (Specified with a *prepositional phrase* – note curtains are known as drapes in US English).

The wallpaper *that we bought in England* has been used in the dining room. (Specified using an *adjective clause*).

Exception: When discussing the function of the decorations then a null determiner is often used.

Example: __ Rugs are used to cover the floor and deaden sound. (<u>Null</u> <u>determiner</u>).

Notes and examples

ORNAMENTS

Ornaments are items that are placed on display in a home to provide decoration, provide talking points and as reminders of past events. They are generally not used to provide a useful function except, possibly, on special occasions. They are generally prefaced with **the**, even if they are part of a set. They are generally further specified with a prepositional phrase or an adjective.

Examples:

We use **the** *bone china* tea-set when visitors come. (Using an *adjective*).

My wife bought **the** gold ornament *in the cabinet,* at an auction. (*Prepositional phrase* used to specify the ornament).

Exception: People often like to show off their ornaments, usually by saying where or how they were acquired, in this instance a **indicative determiner** is used to refer to them.

Example: That Meissen porcelain figurine was bought in Germany.

Notes and examples

UNCOUNTABLE MATERIALS AND CONCEPTS

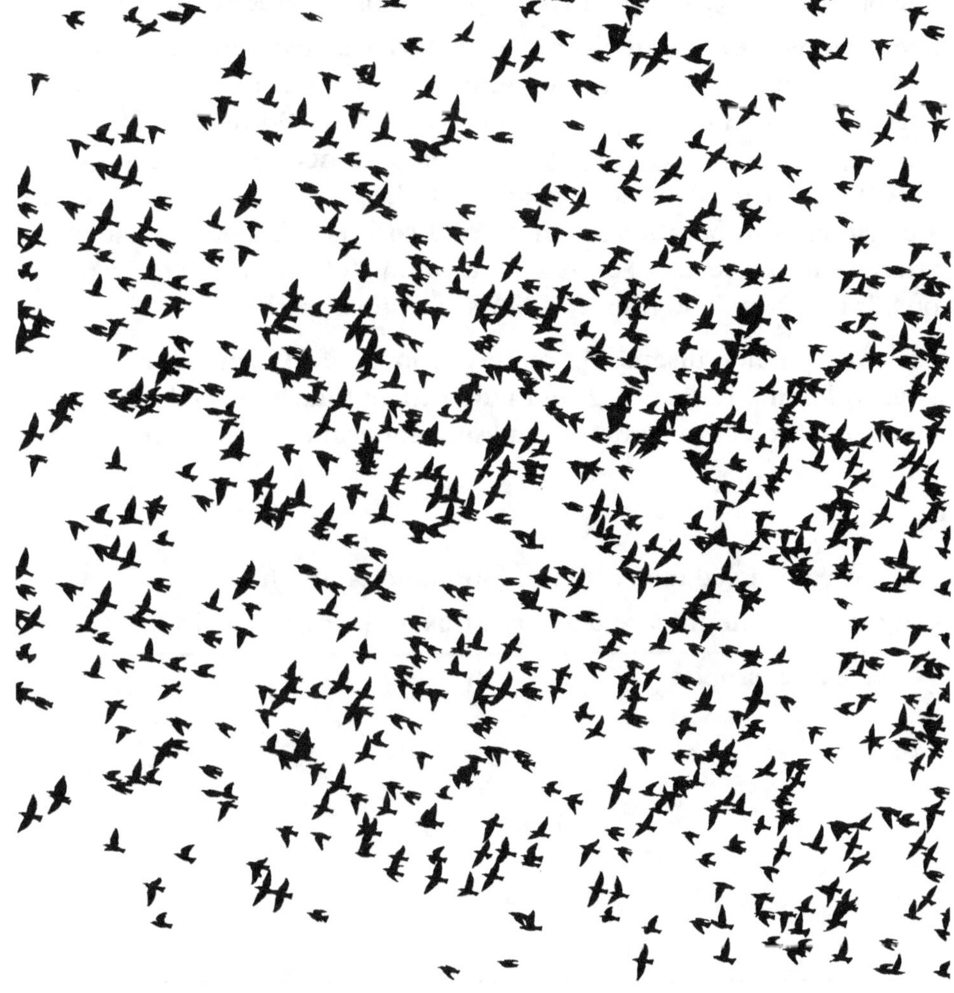

CONSTRUCTION MATERIALS

The would generally be used to describe construction materials that are included in a specific building project, such as the one being worked on or viewed, or when a specific feature is being indicated or highlighted. It is also used to talk about quantities of materials that are specific or different in some way. Building materials are generally uncountable nouns.

Examples:

The concrete beams hold the ceiling up. (The beams being indicated)

The cement is taking ages to dry. (The cement used in this project).

The bricks are very decorative. (Specific highlighted feature.)

The ten tons of cement delivered today has been used already. (Specific as it has been used already and is therefore considered to be extraordinary - normally a null determiner would be used prefaced with a <u>numerical determiner</u>: **ten** tons of concrete have been used. Note the tense used in each instance - in the first sentence the concrete is considered to be a single entity and so it is third person singular; whereas, in the second sentence the volume of the concrete, in plural tons, is the focus and therefore it uses a plural verb).

Exception: When discussing materials in general terms, for example when referring to building methods rather than materials used in a particular project, or when discussing general quantities, then **the** is not used.

Example:

__Concrete is used to create the foundations (method).

Ten tons of cement were delivered this morning (quantity).

Notes and examples

PRODUCTION MATERIALS

The is generally used to preface the materials used in manufacturing as they are specific items that are needed to produce the product.

Examples:

The soy extract is added to the processed heme at this point.

The steel used in the product has been pre-coated.

Exception: When discussing the materials in general terms, for example when the emphasis is on the process rather than the product, **the** is not used.

Examples:

We use __steel in the product instead of __ plastic because it is more robust.

Notes and examples

AGGREGATIONS

Aggregations are intangible but recognisable things that are grouped together and referred to in abstract terms; therefore, they are usually regarded as uncountable. **The** is generally used to preface aggregations, such as news and sports.

Examples:

The instructions contained a lot of diagrams.

The news about the tsunami shocked the world.

Exception 1: When the aggregation includes details of its constituent parts or is coming from, or is owned by, a specific source then it tends to be prefaced with a possessive or an uncountable determiner (i.e. many).

Examples:

His advice was sound (owned by a specific person).

He likes **many** sports (specific determiner used to indicate a lot of different sports: i.e. the constituent parts).

Exception 2: When the aggregation is referred to in a generalised way then no determiner is used.

Examples:

He likes __ sport.

Notes and examples

COLLECTIVES

Collectives are similar to aggregations in that they refer to groups of things but they differ in that collectives refer to tangible (touchable) items rather than concepts. They are also regarded as being uncountable, even though in most cases their constituent parts are divisible and countable. **The** is generally used to preface the name of the <u>collective</u> when it is being referred to in general terms, even if a possessive noun is used to denote ownership, and when it is grouped together, usually in one place.

Examples:

The <u>furniture</u> is being delivered tomorrow.

The <u>cutlery</u> is in the drawer.

The *prisoners'* <u>clothing</u> is washed by the prison laundry (*possessive noun*).

Exception 1: When the collective is owned by someone who is already known then it tends to be prefaced with a possessive determiner.

Example: Their <u>clothing</u> is washed by the prison laundry (The prisoners are already known).

Exception 2: When the collective is not owned or is distributed widely it is referred to using other determiners.

Examples:

Some bric-a-brac was left over after the jumble sale.
Most garbage is sent to the city dump.

Notes and examples

PROBLEMS

Problems are usually specific therefore they would normally be prefaced with **the,** irrespective of whether it refers to a specific problem or an abstract problem, as long as it is known about.

Examples:

I need to talk to you about **the** problem <u>with my order</u> (unnamed problem specified with a <u>prepositional phrase</u>).

I want a refund for **the** <u>low quality of the product</u>. (<u>Named problem</u>).

Did you manage to fix **the** problem? (Abstract reference to an unnamed but known problem).

Exception: If a problem is unspecified or suspected then **a** or **an** would be used.

Examples:

There is **a** problem with my order. (Unspecified).

I think there is **a** bug in the code. (Suspected problem).

Notes and examples

EXERTIONS

References to exertions are normally expressed in a personal context therefore they are generally prefaced with a possessive determiner or a possessive noun.

Examples:

My work requires a lot of thinking. (First person)

His exertions finally produced tangible results. (Third person)

The **slave's** servitude generally lasted a lifetime. (Possessive noun – note the noun is prefaced with **the** as it refers to a specific class of people).

Exception: When the emphasis is on the work itself with the person doing it being of secondary importance, if mentioned at all, then **the** would be used.

Examples:

The struggle produced a range of benefits. (Unknown persons).

The task required him to work long hours (Emphasis on the work).

Notes and examples

FIBRES

In general <u>fibres</u> are both uncountable and generic and so they tend not to be preceded by an article or determiner.

Examples:

__ <u>Cotton</u> is the main fibre used in my shirt.

The robe was made of __ <u>silk</u>.

Exception 1: When the fibre is referred to as an adjective instead of a noun then it will usually be prefaced with an article; however, the article refers to the following noun and not the adjective – see below.

Examples:

He is wearing **a** <u>silk</u> shirt. (The '**a**' refers to the noun, <u>shirt</u>).

The <u>cotton</u> skirt *she is wearing* is very colourful. (Specified with the *adjective clause*)

Exception 2:   When the fibres are referred to in a generic sense, particularly when they are referenced in terms of the raw material they are made from, then they would be prefaced with **the**.

Example:

The cotton is harvested between July and October in the USA.

Notes and examples

GELS

Gels are generally uncountable and are usually referred to in terms of the container they are in. The container would be prefaced with **the** but the gel itself wouldn't be. This is true whether they are used as two nouns (with the infix 'of') or where the gel is used in its adjective form.

Examples:

Someone left the top off **the** *tube* of <u>toothpaste</u>. (*Tube* is the container and <u>toothpaste</u> is the gel).

The <u>honey *jar*</u> is on the shelf. (Honey is the gel in adjective form and jar is the noun).

Exception: When referring to the gel in a generic sense, for example when describing all available amounts, then it is generally prefaced with **the**.

Examples:

The whipped cream is in the refrigerator.

The toothpaste is in the bathroom.

Notes and examples

LIQUIDS

Liquids are uncountable as you can only measure them in terms of the container they are in (carton of milk, glass of water, etc.) or using a measurement (litre of oil, gallon of petrol, etc.); therefore, the liquid itself isn't generally prefaced with **the**, but the container/measurement can be. If you are referring to one container/measurement use **the** to preface it, else preface it with **a** or **an**.

Examples:

The bottle of milk is in the fridge. (One specific bottle).
Can you buy **a** bottle of milk? (Any bottle – not specific).

Exception: When referring to the only container of the liquid that is available or is specified in some way, then it is common to not mention the container itself but to just refer to the contents, in which case the liquid is prefaced with **the**.

Examples:

The milk is in the fridge. (Specific liquid).
The fuel <u>in the tank</u> was contaminated with water. (The liquid has been specified using a <u>prepositional phrase</u>).

Notes and examples

INDIVISIBLE LIVING THINGS

The would generally be used to preface indivisible living things when they are the subject of a sentence, in order to highlight the effect or influence for example, or they are being directly referred to as a specific sentence object.

Examples:

The algae covered the pond (Sentence subject).

I need to cut **the** grass. (The specific grass that I am responsible for).

Exception: When the things are referred to in a generic form, for example as a type, then they wouldn't be prefaced with **the**. As they are uncountable they wouldn't be prefaced with **a** or **an** either; however, they could be referred to using **some** or **any** to refer to an unspecified amount.

Examples:

Whales eat __ plankton. (Plankton is referred to as a type of food).

The farmer planted __ corn. (Corn is the type of crop).

Would you like **some** yogurt? (Unspecified amount on offer).

Is there **any** yeast in this juice? (Questioning existence of unspecific amount).

Notes and examples

RAW MATERIALS

Raw materials are generally referred to in generic terms so they don't tend to be specific - you use some of whatever it is in your process or product - but it isn't likely to be the only ingredient and the amount or percentage is not likely to be specified unless it is by someone involved needing to know the quantities. Therefore the materials are unlikely to be preceded by **the**.

Examples:

The biggest component in a car is __ <u>steel</u> (Subject complement).

Bread is made with __ <u>flour</u> (Object).

Exception: When discussing a specific context for the material then **the** would be used to indicate the specificity.

Examples:

The <u>sugar</u> has run out so we can't make the cake. (Specific as it is the specific ingredient I need to use of which there isn't any).

When will they deliver **the** aluminium? (Specific because it is the aluminium we need for production and is expected to be delivered).

Notes and examples

POWDERS

The is used when referring to powders used in a specific way, in a previously specified amount or for a specific purpose.

Examples:

The flour is mixed with yeast to produce bread. (Specific way).

The salt is added at this point. (Previously specified amount in a recipe).

The skimmed milk powder is added to the Fortified Blended Food to improve the protein quality. (Specific purpose in a specific product).

Exception: Powders are uncountable and are commonly referred to in terms of amounts (often using '**of**' to link the amount and the noun describing the powder), in which case they would not be prefaced with **the.** The nouns are <u>underlined</u>.

Examples:

Add two ounces **of** __ <u>flour</u>. (Specific amount using 'of').

My vacuum cleaner bag is full **of** __ <u>dust</u>. (Abstract amount using 'of').

__ Bricklaying mortar is comprised of 1 part <u>cement</u> to 3 parts <u>sand</u>.

Notes and examples

FATTY SOLIDS

The is not usually used to describe fatty solids. These substances are referred to using concrete nouns but in abstract terms, primarily because the amount in use is generally not specified. See the examples below to study this in action (the nouns are <u>underlined</u>).

Examples:

I like __ <u>butter</u> on my toast.
Do you like __ <u>cheese</u>?

Exception 1: When referring to these substances in questions then **some** or **any** can be used.

Examples:

Would you like **some** <u>chocolate</u>?
Do we have **any** <u>butter</u>?

Exception 2: When the substance has been mentioned previously then it would be preceded by **the** as it is now known. So if you see the substance prefaced with **the** then look back through the document to see where it was first mentioned to find the context (and, often, the amount).

Example: Add **the** <u>margarine</u> to the flour and mix it thoroughly. (Previously mentioned in the list of ingredients in a recipe).

Notes and examples

HARDENED SOLIDS

The is often used with hardened (or hardening) solids as they tend to be specific, either because they have a very specific role to play or they are an intrinsic and important part of something.

Examples:

The <u>putty</u> around my windows is starting to flake off. (Important role)

The <u>concrete</u> will take at least a day to set. (Intrinsic structural part).

There is a problem with **the** cement in the wall. (Object noun).

Exception: When discussing these substances in an abstract fashion, for example their general use, they would not be prefaced with **the**.

Example: The wall was built using bricks and ___ <u>mortar</u>.

Notes and examples

WATER

Water is uncountable in its natural, liquid, state. If it used for some specific purpose, usually by containing, producing or dealing with it, then it would be prefaced with **the**.

Examples:

The water in the radiator is used to cool the engine. (Water in liquid form being contained in order to be used).

The steam in those pipes drives the turbines. (In its vapour form after being specifically produced for a particular purpose).

The ship has a strengthened prow to deal with **the** ice. (In its solid form being dealt with using a particular technique).

Exception: If the water is in its natural state(s) then it would generally be prefaced with a null determiner.

__ Water is leaking from the pipe. (The water is unspecified despite being previously contained).

__ Steam was the power source for the industrial revolution. (Being referred to as a generic concept).

Anti-freeze is needed to protect the engine against __ ice. (It is generic as it does not actually exist; indeed, it can't exist if the anti-freeze is used).

Notes and examples

PEOPLE

HEADS OF STATE

The is used when referring to a head of state as they have a very specific role and they occupy a unique position.

Example: I'd like to present **the** president of the United States, Donald Trump.

Exception 1: When referring to a monarch then they will be addressed with their title, prefaced with a *gender specific determiner* and <u>the role</u> and/or ***the order*** in which that name has occurred would be prefaced with **the**. Any further specific titles (such as the defender of the faith) would follow the name and role and would be prefaced with **the**.

Example: *Her* Majesty Queen Elizabeth **the** ***second***, **the** <u>Queen of England</u>.

Exception 2: When discussing heads of state in general terms then an indefinite article is generally used.

Example: A president is the head of state in a republic; whereas, in a monarchy the head of state is **a** King or Queen. (Note only one 'a' needed to be used even though two alternatives were provided).

Exception 3: When referring to the role rather than the person then a null determiner would be used.

Example: The USA holds elections for __ president every four years (general reference to the role).

Notes and examples

TITLED DIGNITARIES

The would be used to preface a dignitary's rank, if that person was deemed to be specific in some way (usually clarified using the suffix 'of'), or they are attached to or associated with the particular place where the conversation is taking place, or it is part of the title bestowed on them.

Examples:

The bishop of York (specified as being of a particular place).

The Prince of Wales (full title instead of a name).

He is **the** Lord of the Manor (the local manor).

The Right Honourable Jim Hacker (As part of the title of privy counsellor).

Exception 1: If the dignitary is one of many then **a** or **an** would be used.

Example: He is **a** Knight (knights have '<u>Sir</u>' prefaced to their name – e.g. Let me introduce <u>Sir</u> Humphrey Appleby – to denote their rank).

Exception 2: If the rank is from the nobility then **the** wouldn't be used even if they are associated with a place - and most are. Moreover, their first name would not be included in the name, only the surname or their surname would be replaced with the place they nominally represent. Note, in very formal settings a Lord may be announced as "**the** Lord …".

Examples:

__ Lord Maltby of Warmington on Sea. (Surname with place as a prepositional phrase)

__Lord Belvoir lives in a castle. (With the place taking the place of the surname).

Notes and examples

RELIGIOUS LEADERS

The is usually used when the religious leader is either pre-eminent (very senior) or is specific in some way, such as being associated with a local house of worship (who is likely to be regarded as a dignitary in his/her own community).

Examples:

The Archbishop of Canterbury (Anglican Church leader).

The Chief Rabbi (Jewish faith leader in Israel),

The Dalai Lama (Tibetan Buddhist leader).

The Grand Ayatollah (Shia Islamic leader).

The Grand Mufti (Sunni Islamic leader).

The Pope (Catholic Church leader).

The Reverend Timothy Farthing (Anglican vicar of the local church)

Exception: When referring to a religious leader by name **the** is not used. Instead the honorific title is given followed by either their honorific names (as part of their rank) or their given name.

Examples:

__ Pope Francis (Francis is the honorific name – his real name is Jorge Mario Bergoglio) – his function may be appended to the official name using **the** (Pope Francis **the** bishop of Rome).

__ Archbishop Justin Welby (Title followed by full [real] name).

Notes and examples

SENIOR DIPLOMATS

Internationally recognised diplomatic ranks were agreed at the Congress of Vienna in 1815. The most senior diplomat, the ambassador (or the High Commissioner in a British Commonwealth country), is referred to as Her Excellency or His Excellency when talking to them or about them. Other senior ranks within the embassy or mission would have their title, but not their name, prefaced by their rank, in which case it would be prefaced with **the**.

Examples:

Her Excellency Nongnuth Phetcharatana.

He is **the** First Minister at the Embassy.

Exception 1: When referring to them indirectly, for example in the Embassy, then **the** would be used. In addition, if their full title is used, for example when they are being introduced, then the country they represent is prefaced with **the**.

Examples:

What time is **the** ambassador returning from seeing the foreign minister? (The ambassador for this embassy).

Her Excellency Nongnuth Phetcharatana, **the** ambassador for the Kingdom of Thailand. (Introduction).

That lady over there is **the** Thai ambassador (pointing someone out).

Exception 2: Junior ranks would not have their rank prefaced with **the**, primarily because there are more of them. The rule of thumb is that if there is only one of that rank then use **the**, else use **a** or **an** (when using a linking verb) or a null determiner (no word) when using their rank as an appositive.

Example:

Ms. Orndaporn Pewngern is **an** attaché at the embassy in Chile.

Mr. Supachai Teeramungcalanon, third attaché at the Thai embassy.

Notes and examples

LEGISLATORS

The is generally used to refer to an elected member of the legislator when addressing or referring to them in writing. International etiquette suggests that a sitting member or the member elect (elected but not yet sworn in) as '**the** honourable'. It could be used to preface their name or the place they represent (for example in the British parliament the MPs name is not mentioned but they are referred to or addressed, in speech, by the constituency they represent). Privy counsellors, or retired or serving cabinet ministers would be referred to as '**the** right honourable'. Finally, the chair of a committee would be referred to as **the** honourable. Note: Honourable is the UK English spelling and honorable is the US English spelling.

Examples:

The honorable Rand Paul (US Senator).

The member for Witney (UK MP being addressed in the house).

The Right Honourable Gordon Brown (Previous Cabinet minister).

The honorable Trey Gowdy, Chair of the House Benghazi Committee (Committee chairman).

Exception: When introducing the representative you do not need to use **the** if they are in their own constituency (although you could when pointing them out: **The** MP is over there); whereas, outside, or in the presence of other MPs, you would use **the** to introduce the constituency/district they represent. When addressing them in conversations you would use their name.

Examples:

I'd like to introduce you to our local MP, Ben Lake.

I'd like to introduce **the** MP for Ceredigion, Ben Lake.

I'm pleased to meet you Mr. Lake.

Notes and examples

SENIOR OFFICIALS

High ranking government officers are generally known, introduced or addressed by their title. If they are the head, or deputy head, of a department or the secretariat (an office or department of a government ministry), then their title would be prefaced with **the**, in many cases instead of using their name.

Examples:
I have the pleasure of introducing **the** cabinet secretary, Jeremy Heywood (Introduction prior to a speech).

The current US department of defence secretary is General James Mattis. (Giving information).

The current permanent Secretary of the Thai Ministry of Foreign Affairs is Mrs. Busaya Mathelin. (The most senior civil servant in the ministry).

I spoke to **the** European Commissioner for Competition (used instead of their name).

Exception: When talking about previous high ranking officials then **the** is usually not used as they don't occupy that post any more. In which case you'd use **a** or **an**. The exception is that if they are the immediate predecessor to the current incumbent then **the** could be used (The previous foreign secretary was Mohammed Mijarul Quayes).

Example: Today we are paying tribute to Mrs. Elizabeth Abiodun Ashiru, a permanent secretary in Nigeria's Ministry of the Environment.

Notes and examples

PUBLIC SECTOR EMPLOYEES

The is not used to preface the title of a public sector employee because they are regarded as one of many, in fact governments generally take great pains to keep them anonymous (listen for the phrases 'privacy issue', 'protecting our members of staff' or 'we do not divulge personal information'), so **a** or **an** would be used instead.

Examples:

I saw **a** civil servant in the ministry of labour. (Unnamed person).

Fred Bloggs, **a** junior administrator in the ministry, has just been offered a job in the private sector. (Job title as an appositive).

Exception: If the person takes some specific action, or is the person who provides the link to the government (such as the person who instructs an applicant, hands over or processes a permit, for example), then their job would be prefaced with **the**.

Examples:

The clerk took my application to his department head. (The person performing a specific action).

The receptionist told me I had to complete a security form before I would be given a visitor's pass. (Instructing an applicant).

The deputy head signed the permit as her boss was away (Processing a permit).

Notes and examples

EDUCATORS

The would be used to preface the title of an educator if they are a head of department (e.g. professor), they teach a specific class (e.g. art teacher), they are the only one teaching that subject (The home economics teacher...) or are currently teaching, or have just taught, the speaker or listener.

Examples:

The professor gave a lecture (Head of University Faculty – aka the 'Chair').

The head of Science took the class today (Head of school department).

The geography teacher was ill today (the only teacher of a specific subject).

The teacher was unhappy about the noise in the class today (the one that just taught the speaker).

Exception 1: When referring to a teacher that has special responsibilities towards the speaker then the possessive determiners **my** or **our** can be used.

Example: My teacher said that my art project was really creative.

Exception 2: When referring to a teacher or lecturer who is part of a department then **a** or **an** are generally used.

Examples:

He is **an** assistant professor in the Education faculty.

She is **a** lecturer in biological science.

Mr Smith is **a** chemistry teacher.

Notes and examples

SENIOR PRIVATE EXECUTIVES

The is used to preface the rank/role of senior private sector executives, people who work for privately owned named companies or corporations. **The** would also be used if the company was not named but is specified in some way.

Examples:

The current chairman of Xerox is Robert J. (Bob) Keegan and **the** CEO is Jeff Jacobson. (Association of job titles with named people).

The Managing Director gave all the staff an inspirational speech. (Unnamed executive).

The CEO of the country's leading environmental company has endorsed the measure. (The company is special as it is a leader in its field).

Exception: If the corporation itself is not named then **the** wouldn't be used, **a** or **an** would be used instead.

Examples: The congressman was approached by a prominent CEO who expressed concerns about the new law. (Note that the congressman, although unnamed, was specified as he was the person that was approached and is being reported upon and therefore known).

Notes and examples

SENIOR COMMERCIAL OFFICERS

This table contains a list of the most common Chief Officers (also known as the 'C suite'). Each of the acronyms (Acr.) would be prefaced with **the** when referring to them (He is **the** [company] CLO).

Acr.	Responsibility	Acr.	Responsibility
CA	Architect	CAIO	Artificial Intelligence
CAE	Audit Executive	CBO	Brand
CAO	Academic	CAO	Accounting
CAO	Administrative	CAO	Analytics
CBDO	Business Development	CBO	Business
CCO	Commercial	CCO	Communications
CCO	Compliance	CCO	Content
CCO	Creative	CCO	Customer
CDO	Data	CDO	Design
CDO	Development	CDO	Digital
CDO	Diversity	CEngO	Engineering
CEO	Executive (aka M.D)	CeXO	Experience
CFO	Financial	CGO	Gaming
CHRO	Human Resources	CIO	Information
CIO	Investment	CITO	IT
CISO	Information Security	CIO	Innovation
CKO	Knowledge	CLO	Learning
CLO	Legal	CMO	Marketing
CMO	Medical	CNO	Networking
CNO	Nursing	COO	Operating
CPO	Privacy	CPO	Process
CPO	Procurement	CPO	Product
CQO	Quality	CRDO	R&D
CRO	Research	CRO	Revenue
CRO	Risk	CSO	Sales
CSO	Science	CSO	Security
CSO	Strategy	CSO	Sustainability
CTO	Technology	CVO	Value
CVO	Visionary	CWO	Web

PRIVATE SECTOR EMPLOYEES

The is only used with the <u>job title</u> of a private sector (privately owned) company company if they are special in some way, they have a position of responsibility, a specialist in their field or if they have special attributes.

Examples:

She is **the** company software engineer (she is the only software engineer).

He is **the** senior design engineer. (Position of responsibility).

She is **the** only female sales person in the company. (Special attribute).

Exception: If the person is one of many people in that position in the company, or they hold a particular position in the industry, then **a** or **an** would be used.

Examples:

He is **a** maintenance man for the shopping mall. (One of many in that company).

She is **a** marketing executive. (One of many in the industry – note no company was mentioned).

Notes and examples

PROFESSIONALS

The would only be used to preface a professional person's job title if they are either a specialist (particularly if they are the only or most senior) or they are undertaking a specific task Note, a professional is someone who uses their intellectual prowess and knowledge to serve a client. **The** would also be used if a specific known group is involved in a specific action.

Examples:

The company accountant found some problems in the accounts. (They are specific to the company).

The lawyer drew up the sales contract. (The legal expert that undertook that action).

The scientists made a surprising discovery. (A group working together on a particular action).

Exception 1: If the professional is not known, possibly because they haven't been chosen yet, or they are one of many involved in something then **a** or **an** would be used. Unknown groups involved in an action would also be prefaced with **a** or **an**.

Examples:

If you have legal problems then you should consult **a** lawyer. (Unknown as they haven't been chosen yet).

He is **a** diplomatic chauffeur for the embassy. (One of many).

A research group is being formed to study it. (Unknown group).

Exception 2:   If the professional would be the only one, or the first, in the profession that would be consulted by the client in case of problems or issues, then a <u>possessive determiner</u> would be used.

Examples:

<u>My</u> solicitor drew up my new will.

Their financial advisor told them about the new tax laws.

Notes and examples

TRADESMEN

The word tradesman is generally regarded a non gender specific title; it can refer to a male or a female who is very skilled and often qualified in one area.

The would be used to preface a tradesman's title if they are working on a specific problem or task, or they are doing it for a specific person, such as the speaker. **The** would also be used if the tradesman is named, usually in response to a question about who they are.

Examples:

The car mechanic found the problem straight away. (The tradesman who did a specific task).

The plumber called today. (The tradesman who is working for the speaker).

The electrician is called Bert Briggs. (In response 'What was the name of the electrician").

Exception 1: If the tradesman's name is additional information then **a** or **an** would be used.

Example: An electrician, called Bert Briggs, fixed the problem.

Exception 2: If the tradesman is not known or hasn't been chosen yet then **a** or **an** would be used.

Examples:

A technician came and fixed the washing machine today. (Unknown tradesman performing a generic task).

A heating engineer is needed to fix the boiler. (Not chosen yet).

Notes and examples

MANUAL WORKERS

Manual workers are so named because they tend to work with their muscle or hands; indeed, the word 'manual' was derived from the Latin word 'manus' meaning hand or strength. These workers tend to be regarded as unskilled or semiskilled.

Most manual workers tend to be anonymous and unspecified; therefore, they wouldn't be prefaced with **the**. Their positions are usually regarded as one of many, even though there may be the only person employed in that role, and so they'd be prefaced with **a** or **an**.

Example: He is **a** council gardener.

Exception: When the worker has done something specific, specified using a prepositional phrase or an adjective clause, then their position (job title) would be prefaced with **the**.

Examples:

The road sweeper <u>outside my house</u> is singing loudly. (<u>Prepositional phrase</u>).

The furniture removal man *who injured his back* is now back at work. (*Adjective clause*).

Notes and examples

STUDENTS

Whether **the** is used to preface the noun phrase, including the plural noun 'students', depends on the context and whether the students have been specified in some way. For example, they may be specified using a prepositional phrase or adjective clause, or by their action(s) if they have performed some specific task(s). Whether **the** prefaces the noun clause containing the singular noun 'student' depends on whether they are identifiable in some way either through a prepositional phrase or an adjective or adjective clause or through their deeds.

Examples:

The students in my class... (Specified using a prepositional phrase).

The students who failed the exam can retake it in... (*Adjective clause*).

The students presented flowers to the retiring lecturer. (Unknown students performing a specific action).

I am going to talk to **the** students. (Unknown number of unidentified students with the implication being that all eligible or present students would be involved).

The student *who won the prize* is from Laos. (Individual specified using an *adjective clause*).

Exception: When a teacher refers to their own students (or an individual student in their class) they would often use the possessive determiner **my**. If the student is unknown, or their identity is not important, then **a** or **an** is used for single students or **some** or **any** for unknown groups of students.

Examples:

My students all passed their exam. (Students of the speaker).

A student set the Dean's car on fire. (Unknown student).

Some students demonstrated outside the President's office. (Unknown students).

Notes and examples

CLUB MEMBERS

Clubs, also known as associations or societies, usually with membership rules and fees, are organisations that are dedicated to a particular interest or activity. **The** is used when referring to members of a club even though they may be unidentified. Note, they can be referred to as clubs, associations or societies. Clubs tend to be smaller, associations tend to be formed to bring together people with similar interests in a particular area and societies are much larger groups.

Examples:

The members of the apathy society couldn't be bothered to attend the general meeting.

The association chairman said that **the** members need to be consulted before the proposal is put forward.

Exception 1: When referring to the overall membership in abstract terms then a null determiner would be used.

Example: __ Members need to pay their subscriptions by Friday.

Exception 2: If an individual member is being referred to but not specified then **a** or **an** would be used. Note, if all members raised objections then **the** would be used (**The** members of the club raised objections to the committee's decision); whereas, if a few members objected then **some** would be used instead (**Some** members of the...).

Example: A member of the club raised an objection to the committee's decision.

Notes and examples

ENTHUSIASTS AND FANS

The would generally be used when describing fans of particular teams or performance artists.

Examples:

The fans were good natured. (Note. The fans belonged to unnamed, but known, club or clubs – possibly the rival clubs in a match – and it is used in this case to create an overall impression of the atmosphere).

The fans queued all night to get tickets for the concert. (The assumption is that the people queuing are fans of the artist(s) taking part).

Exception 1: When referring to an unknown fan or group of fans, usually in the context of something they did or said, then **a, an** or **some** would be used.

Examples:

A Liverpool fan said the club had a good chance of winning the FA cup this year. (Singular fan).

Some Millwall fans went on a rampage after the shock defeat. (Plural fans).

Exception 2: If the fan or fans are being discussed in a generic sense then a <u>null determiner</u> would be used.

Examples: There are __ Manchester United fans all over the world.

Notes and examples

CREATIVE PEOPLE

People who practise the creative arts are generally known as artists /'ɑː.tɪst/, as are people who are skilled at particular aspects of their profession. If they are particularly skilled or talented they are often called 'artist*es*' /ɑː'tiːsts/. They are generally referred to in a non-specific way using **a** or **an**, even if they are better described using adjectives.

Examples:

He in **an** artist. (General reference - we don't know what he creates).

She is **a** *famous* <u>sculptor</u>. (With a further description using an adjective and a <u>noun</u> that better describes the type of art she creates).

Exception: If the artist is not directly mentioned by name but his/her artwork is being referred to, then the would be used.

Example: The artist who painted the 'girl with the pearl earring' belonged to the group of artists known as the Dutch Golden Age painters. (If the painter is named, such as with an appositive, then their name would not be prefaced with the: The artist, Johannes Vermeer, who painted the 'girl with the pearl earring').

Notes and examples

FAMILY MEMBERS

Family members are almost always personal and would therefore be preceded by a possessive determiner.

Examples:

<u>My</u> sister has two children; **<u>her</u>** son, **<u>my</u>** nephew, and **<u>her</u>** daughter, **<u>my niece.</u>**

<u>My</u> grandfather's father is **<u>my</u>** great-grandfather.

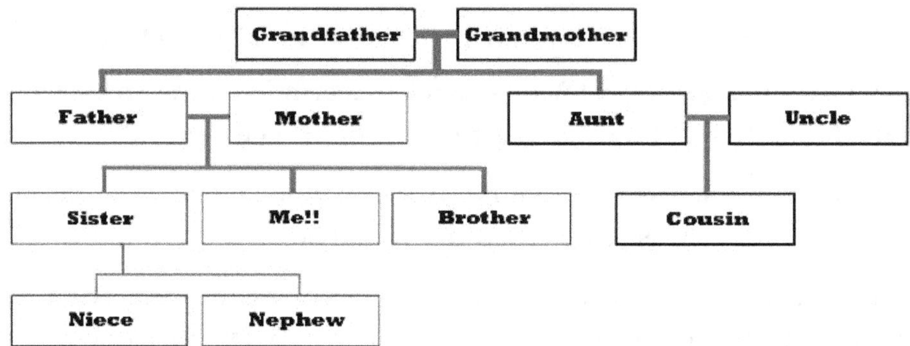

The diagram above shows a typical family relationship tree.

Exception 1: When referring to other people's family members in an uninterested way, for example by the police when referring to the victim or perpetrator of a crime, **the** could be used.

Example: The grandfather was also injured during the break in. (Referring to the grandfather of the family that were the victims of the crime).

Exception 2: When referring to a change in familiar status **a** or **an** would normally be used.

Examples:

I am **a** father now my wife has given birth. (The speaker referring to himself and describing his new status).

What is it like being **a** grandfather? (Enquiring about a newly acquired status).

What exactly is a second cousin? (asking about a family relationship).

    Website: www.englishbook.shop

FRIENDS

Friends are generally personal and therefore they would be prefaced with a possessive determiner.

Examples:

<u>My</u> friend lives in Lincoln (Possessive determiner prefacing a simple noun).

<u>Her</u> best friend has got a new job (Prefaced with an adjective).

Exception 1: If the friend is referred to in a generic, non specific, way then a or an would be used.

Example: Everyone needs **a** friend.

Exception 2: When referring to them in a disinterested way, such as during official discussions, then **the** may be used.

Example: The friend said there was no motive for the attack (From a police report describing the relationship between the victim and the person providing the testimony).

Notes and examples

PEOPLE IN GENERAL

The is not usually used to describe people in general as they are not specified or different in any way. If a single person is being referred to **a** or **an** would be used, a <u>null determiner</u> would usually be used to describe multiple people.

Examples:

A person is being sought in connection with the crime. (Note the use of the passive voice when describing an unknown person).

__ People are coming forward to give blood after the disaster. (Plural people).

Exception: When looking for an unknown person, for example in connection to a crime or with a particular talent or skill, or someone who has been mentioned earlier then **the** would be used.

Examples:

The person we are looking for, in connection with this crime, is described as six foot tall, with red hair and a limp. (In connection with a crime).

The person we need must have good software skills. (Particular talent or skill).

A woman left the baby on the steps of the orphanage. According to witnesses **the** woman was crying. (Previously mentioned).

Notes and examples

OFFICIAL GROUPINGS

POLITICAL PARTIES

The is generally used when the party name is used as part of a compound noun or when it describes all members of the party as a plural group noun.

Examples:

The Labour party used to represent the working man. (Compound noun.)

The Christian Democrats are again the largest party in the German Bundestag (all members as a group.)

Exception 1: When the focus of the sentence is not on the party itself, but more on the general membership, then **the** wouldn't be used; however, other determiners are usually used (See below).

Example: <u>Few</u> Republicans are conservative.

Exception 2: When the party name is used as an <u>adjective</u> prefacing the *type* then it is not prefaced with **the** unless it refers to a specific person.

Examples:

Many <u>Republican</u> *politicians* vote in favour of <u>Democrat</u> *policies*. (Adjective forms used to qualify the party that the *nouns* are allied to).

The un-named <u>Tory</u> minister was caught taking a bribe. (The is used to specify this individual with the <u>party name</u> in adjective form providing the context).

Notes and examples

GOVERNMENT DEPARTMENTS

The is always used when discussing or writing about government ministries. This is because they are unique and specific. Department and sections within the ministries would also be prefaced with **the**, as they each have a unique role. They also tend to be capitalised.

Examples:

The US Department of State (US foreign ministry).

The Foreign Office (UK foreign ministry).

The Ministry of Foreign Affairs (Foreign ministry in many countries around the world).

Notes and examples

COMMISSIONS AND ENQUIRIES

Commissions and special inquiries are entities that are set up, usually by the legal branch of government, to look at specific wrongdoing by members of the government, governmental employees or government agencies (such as the police, armed forces, departments etc.). They are usually headed up by a senior figure in the legal system, either active or (commonly) retired who could be a judge, a high ranking member of the legal investigative apparatus (such as the FBI in the USA), a senior civil servant, a professor or (less commonly) a specialist in the field being investigated. They usually take the name of the senior investigator or chairperson, or if it was an inquiry about a particular event or person then it would be named after the event or person, and would be prefaced with **the** while they are active or after they have delivered their findings. If the findings result in a report then the report name would also be prefaced with **the**.

Examples:

The Hutton inquiry (undertaken by Lord Hutton of Bresagh into the suicide of government scientist David Kelly).

The Aberfan disaster inquiry (Inquiry into a coal waste slip that killed 144 people, mainly children, in 1966).

The Shipman inquiry (inquiry into the issues surrounding the case of mass murderer Harold Shipman).

The Macpherson report (report containing the findings from an inquiry into racism in the UK police force).

Exception: If the inquiry has been announced and the team hasn't been assembled yet, then it would be prefaced with **a** or **an**.

Examples:

A Royal Commission is being assembled to look at the facts.

An inquiry has been launched into Russian collusion in the US 2016 election.

Notes and examples

　　　　　　　　　Website: www.englishbook.shop

GOVERNMENT AGENCIES

The is generally used to preface government agencies, particularly when the word 'agency' is used, as they are unique and for a very specific purpose. Agencies are defined as being semi-autonomous in that they are not directly controlled by a cabinet government minister or secretary, but are funded by the government. Many of these agencies are represented by acronyms instead of their full name.

Examples:

The FBI (US - Federal Bureau of Investigation).
The CIA (US - Central Intelligence Agency).
The NCA (UK - National Crime Agency).

Exception: Places run as agencies, but using proper nouns, will not be prefaced with the. Note, the second example uses a numerical determiner (10).

Examples:

_ Camp David (US Presidential Retreat).
10 Downing Street (UK Prime Minister's office and residence).

Notes and examples

ORGANISATIONS

The is generally used to preface the name of an organisation, such as an association, a confederation (representing a group such as a trade body), a union or a transnational body.

Examples:

The Royal Air Force Association (association)

The CBI (<u>C</u>onfederation of <u>B</u>ritish <u>I</u>ndustry - confederation)

The Teamsters (Union – organised labour)

The United Nations (transnational body)

Exception 1: The is not generally used when referring to an entertainment club unless that club is aimed at a specific clientele.

Examples:

__ Ministry of Sound (nightclub)

__ Eight club (exclusive membership club)

The art club (aimed specifically at London's art elite)

Exception 2: The is not generally used when referring to organisations named after a founder or using a proper noun.

Examples:

__ Boodle's (using a proper noun)

__ Annabelle's (named after the founder's wife)

Notes and examples

INSTITUTES

The is generally used to preface the names of institutes, even if they are named after a founder, as they are generally targeted at specific sectors.

Examples:

The women's institute (targeted at women)

The Howard Hughes Medical Institute (aimed at medical research)

Exception: The generally wouldn't be used if the institute is not specifically targeted at a sector or discipline, or is not specifically named, unless it is describing where an event is taking place and the name is part of a <u>prepositional phrase</u>.

Examples:

I work in **a** government research institute (generic).

I work <u>in **the** Devawongse Varopakarn Institute of Foreign Affairs</u> (the specific place where I work).

The course took place <u>at **the** Devawongse Varopakarn Institute of Foreign Affairs</u> (activity taking place there).

Notes and examples

COUNCILS

A council is a formally constituted (elected or appointed) body of people who meet regularly for advisory (for example *the advisory council on historic preservation*), deliberative (for example *The Council of Princes and Ministers*), or legislative (such as a parish [village], town, city, municipal or county council) purposes. If the title states the purpose of the council then it would generally be preceded by **the**.

Examples:

The privy council (A formal body of advisors to a monarch or Governor General with few formal powers - the adjective 'privy' was derived from the Latin word 'privatus' meaning personal and it used to mean they are private advisors and their advise is not made public).

The Nursing and Midwifery council (A formal group for nurses and midwives that set the standards of education, training, conduct and performance).

Exception: Legislative councils generally have the name of the place they administer and the word 'council' grouped together in a (proper) compound noun and so they generally wouldn't be preceded by **the**.

Examples:

__ Ceredigion county council.
__ Birmingham metropolitan council
__ Arvada city council
__ St. Neots town council
__ Abbots Ripton parish council.

Exception 2: When referring to the action(s) or responsibilities of the council then the simple word 'council' would be used (without the name of the area they represent) as it is assumed that the local council is being referred to and so it would be preceded by the.

Examples:

If you call **the** council they will come and take it away.
The council has just passed a new law regulating the amount of air you can breath before having to pay tax on it.
Elections for **the** council will be held next week.
He has a seat on **the** council (He is an elected member.)

BOARDS

Boards are a group of people who have the decision making responsibility for an organisation. In general terms they differ from councils in that councils tend to be in the public (government) sector; whereas, boards are generally in the private sector (but not always - for example boards are often temporarily convened for matters such as disciplinary proceedings or recruitment in the public sector). In formal terms the differences between boards, councils and committees are:

- Board - a Board is a group of people who have all the powers to decide and control the working of an organisation and generally act on behalf of the owners of the organisation. Board members are generally appointed.
- Council - A Council also controls an organisation but works on behalf of the people it represents. Council members are generally elected.
- Committee - A Committee is a subgroup of the original organisation, normally formed to deliberate over specific issues. Members can include both appointed and elected representatives.

When the whole board is being referred to by name or by virtue of it having immediate responsibility or being previously named then it would be preceded by **the**.

Examples:

The Federal Reserve Board is an organisation that is tasked with helping to implement the monetary policy of the United States (named board).

There was a meeting of **the** board of directors today (the board of the company the speaker works in).

Exception 1: Individual board members are normally preceded by **a** or **an** as they are regarded as one of many. The activities of the board are also preceded by **a** or **an** as they represent one of many such activities.

Examples:

He is **a** main board member. (Individual member).

There was **a** board meeting today. (Board activity).

Exception 2: If a person fulfils a particular role on the board their role would be preceded by the.

Example: He is **the** Chairman of the board.

FAMILIES

The is generally used to preface the names of famous or well-known families.

Examples:

The Kardashians (famous TV personalities).

The Clintons (well-known political family).

Exception 1: The generally wouldn't be used when referring to one member of the family as their name (a proper noun) would be used instead or **a, an** or **one** would be used if the name of the person that is being referred to is not known.

Examples:

__ Bill Clinton (named individual in the family).

A Kardashian was robbed in Paris (unknown individual).

Exception 2: The generally wouldn't be used when referring to a family that is not well-known; unless the family is being specified in some way – such as for their location or their notoriety.

Examples:

Do you know **the** Smiths on our street? (Specified by location).

The Kirks are causing trouble again (notorious).

Notes and examples

WORKING GROUPS

A working group or a working party is a group of people that are brought together to fulfil a particular task. Examples of their work are: to build on previous work, to bring together parts of an organisation, to clarify ideas, create strategies, directives, specifications or standards and/or to develop plans of action. When discussing any working group using its name or the particular work/function it is involved in then it would be prefaced with **the**.

Examples:

The *Bioethics Council* advises the US President on the ethics involved in biotechnological advances (n*ame*).

The *Moving Picture Experts Group* (MPEG) is a working group of authorities that sets the specifications for audio and video compression and transmission.

The *Bluetooth Special Interest* group (The function of the group is to set the standards for all aspects of Bluetooth development).

Exception: When referring to the results of the deliberations of a group then a null determiner would be used.

Example: The company complies with __ISO 9000 (Refers to standard 9000 from the International Organisation for Standardisation [ISO]).

Notes and examples

COMMITTEES

Committees are generally set up for a special purpose. They are generally preceded by **the** as they are usually the only body dealing with a particular issue.

Examples:

The committee will discuss the issue at the next meeting (the speaker is assuming that the listener will know which committee is being referred to).

He is a member of **the** ways and means committee.

He was elected to be **the** committee chairman (using the committee as an adjective and using **the** to specify the singular role he will undertake).

Exception 1: If the committee does not exist yet it would be prefaced with **a** or **an.**

Example: The department is setting up **a** committee to study the issue.

Exception 2: When referring to multiple committees they are prefaced with a null determiner.

Example: __Committees are the bane of local government.

Exception 3: If an individual member of a committee is being discussed they are generally prefaced with a unless they are fulfilling a special role on the committee.

Examples:

He is **a** committee member (ordinary member).
He is **the** committee secretary (specific role).

Notes and examples

NGOS

NGOs (<u>N</u>on <u>G</u>overnment <u>O</u>rganisations) or QUANGOs (UK <u>Q</u>uasi <u>A</u>utonomous <u>N</u>on <u>G</u>overnment <u>O</u>rganisations - they are called 'quasi' because they are generally funded, but not controlled, by the government) are entities that are set up to fulfil specific roles in society. Their roles are officially designated as providing "a variety of service and humanitarian functions, bring citizen concerns to Governments, advocate and monitor policies and encourage political participation through provision of information". In general they are usually referred to using their name preceded by a null determiner.

Examples:

__ Médecins Sans Frontières is a French medical NGO that provides doctors and medical staff for disadvantaged people around the world.

__ CARE International was set up to help fight poverty around the world.

Exception 1: If the name is preceded by the country of origin or their purpose then they would be preceded by the. If the controlling interest is appended to the name then the would also be used.

Examples:

The *Danish* Refugee council (*country of origin*).

The Clinton *Health Access* Initiative (*purpose*).

The Wikipedia *foundation* (*controlling interest*).

Exception 2: When the focus of the sentence is towards the subject and the name of the NGO is not important then **a** or **an** would be used.

Example: She works for **an** NGO in Africa. (Note, it is preceded with **an** rather than **a**).

Notes and examples

CHARITIES

A charity is a local, national or international organisation that was set up to provide specific goods or services to people in need. They are generally private, non profit making organisations that operate outside government control and usually enjoy some form of tax exempt status in return for which they submit to government oversight. They would normally have a specific purpose or the geographical area they cover is expressed in their name and therefore they would usually be preceded by **the**. If the organisation that set it up is included in the name or they enjoy royal patronage then **the** would also be used.

Examples:

The *Samaritans* (*purpose* - based on a biblical tale of someone from another culture helping a person in need)

The *National* Autistic Society (*geographical area* expressed in the name).

The *Rotary* foundation (o*rganisation that set it up*).

The *Royal* National Lifeboat Institute (*under royal patronage*).

Exception: If the charity has a name that doesn't directly specify what they do or there is no indication that they are a charity then then they would be preceded by a null determiner.

Examples:

__ Christian Aid (no indication what they do).

__ MENCAP is a leading mental health charity (no indication of them being a charity).

Notes and examples

STAKEHOLDERS

Stakeholders are a group of people without whom an entity would cease to exist or would not be needed. These can range from people supplying goods and services through to the consumers of those goods or services, plus any others like the government who would have an oversight of or a regulatory interest in the entity. For example, the stakeholders in a hospital would include the medical, clerical, building services and support staff, the patients, creditors, debtors, suppliers, management, the regulatory authorities, drug and consumables suppliers, equipment suppliers and the owners. Taken together they are uncountable and, in most cases, are not completely identifiable and shouldn't, therefore, be prefaced with **the**. However, in general they are referred to as a single group and would be prefaced with **the**. In addition, if the stakeholders who replied or take an interest, in say a proposal, are overwhelmingly in favour of something they would, as a group, be referred to using **the**.

Examples:

The government consultation was sent to **the** stakeholders for their feedback (it was sent to those who could be identified).

The stakeholders largely agreed with the proposal (the majority are in favour and are therefore assumed to be speaking for all).

Exception 1: If a sizable percentage disagree then the determiners such as **'most'**, **'the majority of the'**, **' a few of the'** or **'some of the'** would be used.

Examples:

Most stakeholders agreed with the proposal (a small minority disagreed).

The majority of the stakeholders agreed with the proposal (a sizable minority disagreed).

A few of the stakeholders disagreed with the proposal (the government is playing down the uncomfortable number that disagreed).

Some of the stakeholders disagreed with the proposal (a larger than expected number disagreed).

Exception 2: When defining who are considered to be stakeholders a null determiner would be used.

Example: __ Stakeholders in our company include the staff, owners and customers.

MILITARY FORMATIONS

Military units are generally anonymous formations of personnel and, as such, they are generally prefaced with **a** or **an**. If they are led by a particular named person, or they are subdivided into a fraction of a larger formation (usually using a cardinal number) or if a strategic group is covering a particular section of the battlefield then a <u>null designator</u> would be used. Formations are organised into commands and given a designation based on the number of troops as shown below.

Formation Name	No. of troops
Region or Theatre (US: Theater)	1,000,000–10,000,000
Army Group or Front	400,000–1,000,000
Army	100,000–200,000
Corps	20,000–50,000
Division or Legion	6,000–20,000
Brigade	3,000–5,000
Regiment or Group	1,000–3,000
Infantry Battalion, Cavalry Squadron, Armoured or Combat Regiment	300–1,000
Infantry Company, Armoured or Engineering Squadron, Artillery Battery or Cavalry Troop	80–250
Platoon	26–55
Section or Patrol	12–24
Squad or Crew	8–12
Fireteam or Cell	3-4
Fire And Maneuver Team	2-3

Notes and examples

MILITARY FORMATIONS

Examples continued…:

___ Captain Mainwaring's platoon is designated for special duties. (Named leader's formation prefaced with a null determiner).

"___ Number one platoon, Warmington on Sea Company, *Attention*!" (Platoon designated with a cardinal number to address a particular part of the overall formation and prefaced with a null determiner. Note a *military order* given to the troops is often capitalized even in part of sentence).

__ Army group *South* was tasked with covering the retreat. (Strategic formation designated with an area *adjective* following the noun).

Exception 1: When discussing a particular formation it would normally be given a designation, usually in the form of a *preceding adjective* (commonly in the form of a ordinal number) or a compound noun. In this case **the** would preface the name.

Examples:

The *101st* Airborne division led the assault. (Prefaced with a numeric designator).

The Argyll and Sutherland Highlanders became famous during the Aden crisis (Designated with a compound noun).

Exception 2: When addressing the commander of a formation then a *possessive determiner* would be used.

Example: You will lead *your* company on the main assault on the ridge. (Formation designated with a *possessive determiner*).

Exception 3: When discussing a formation named after a person (for example the commander) then a possessive noun would be used. This terminology would generally be used by commanding officers instead of using the numbered designator in order to personalise the actions.

Example: ___*Colonel Dawson's* regiment will execute a flanking manoeuvre. (Third person designation using a possessive noun prefaced with a null determiner).

SUPPORT GROUPS

Support groups provide members with help and/or emotional support to help them to cope with withdrawing from addictive substances or habits. These things include things like drugs, alcohol abuse or gambling. In general they are not prefaced with **the.**

Examples:

__Alcoholics Anonymous is a support group for people addicted to alcohol.

__Gambler's anonymous is a support group for people addicted to gambling.

Exception: When referring to events linked to the group or materials produced by the group then **the** would be used.

Examples:

The Heroin anonymous meeting will be held at 8 p.m. this evening (Event).

The ASH smoking cessation literature is available in the foyer (Materials).

Notes and examples

ANIMALS AND OTHER LIVING CREATURES

PETS

Pets are generally associated with specific people and so they are usually prefaced with a possessive determiner.

Examples:

Our dog likes to lie on the sofa.

Their cat died of old age.

Exception 1: If the pet's, or pets', ownership is not known **the** would be used to refer to animals specified by the action they undertook or their appearance.

Examples:

The dog was running around the park biting people. (Pet's actions).

The dog that won Crufts was beautifully groomed. (Pet's Appearance).

The dogs were barking all night. (Plural pets).

Exception 2: If plural pets, or animals assumed to be pets, are involved then a null determiner would be used.

Examples: __ Horses need a lot of looking after.

Notes and examples

FARM ANIMALS

The would be used with farmyard animals as they tend to be specific to a specific farmer, farm, group of people – such as a farming family or a collective - or place. Note, it would apply to both single animals (**the** bull) or groups of animals (**the** cows).

Examples:

The lambs on their farm are being fattened for market. (The specific lambs belonging to a farm belonging to a group of people).

The cows in Switzerland wear bells around their necks. (The ones belonging to a place).

Exception 1: Because they are owned by a farm or farmer they can be prefaced with a possessive determiner, like **my** or **our**.

Example: His cows are milked at 6 am every day.

Exception 2: <u>**Indicative determiners**</u> are used when the speaker is in close proximity to the animals in question or they have been indicated previously.

Examples:

<u>**These**</u> sheep will be sheared on Saturday. (In close proximity to the animals).

The pigs used in the research were specially bred. <u>**These**</u> pigs have a particular genetic make-up that makes them ideal for this type of research. (Previously described and made specific using *the*, with the indicative determiner being used to describe why they are specific).

Notes and examples

WILD ANIMALS

Wild animals are generally referred to in generic, non-specific, terms; therefore, they would not be prefaced with **the**.

Examples:

__ Elephants in Asia are different from __ African elephants because their ears are smaller. (Generic reference to all animals in those places).

__ Goats have been known for killing trees by chewing the bark from around the circumference. (All animals of this type irrespective of the place).

Exception: When a specific animal (or group of animals) is being discussed, particularly in terms of appearance, action or relationship with something else, then **the** would be used.

Examples: The leopard was lying in the grass watching **the** gazelles grazing. (Singular animal being specified in terms of its action and the plural animals are specific in terms of their relationship to the first animal).

Notes and examples

ANIMALS IN GENERAL

Animals in general refers to all animals within a group or species. They don't tend to be specific and therefore they wouldn't be prefaced with **the**. When discussing individual animals then **a** or **an** are used; whereas, plural animals would be prefaced with a <u>null determiner</u>.

Examples:

A bear was seen in the company car park (Single animal of a particular type).

An anteater eats __ ants. (Showing difference between the treatment of non-specific singular animals and plural animals)

__ Bears hibernate during the winter (Plural animals within a generic reference – i.e. all animals of that type).

Exception: When drawing attention to a specific type of animal, in terms of some specific feature, then **the** would be used. Note that the reference is in the singular but refers to all animals of that type.

Examples: The duck billed platypus is the most unusual animal on earth.

Notes and examples

AQUATIC ANIMALS

Aquatic animals live in water, the term can refer to mammals, such as whales, that have live births or fish that lay eggs. Most aquatic animals can't be specified, or individually recognised, so they aren't generally specified using **the**. Singular examples are prefaced with **a** or **an** but plural specimens are prefaced with a <u>null determiner</u>.

Examples:

A dead whale was washed up on a beach in Wales. (Singular example).

__ Siamese fighting fish are ferocious towards each other. (Plural referring to all of that type).

Exception: When referring to a specific species or group of aquatic animals, particularly when referring to their relationship to other creatures, then **the** would be used. Note, the group is singular.

Examples:

The fish we eat need to be carefully managed to avoid over-fishing.

Note: the word fish is derived from old Anglo-Saxon (*fisc*) and is an irregular noun, so the plural of fish is fish (and not fishes), like the other Anglo Saxon derived irregular noun sheep. The word 'fishes' evolved in the 14th century to talk about fish that are used as food. In modern use either fish or fishes could be used to talk about plural fish in general.

Notes and examples

INSECTS

Insects are generally difficult to differentiate from each other; therefore, they don't tend to be specified with **the**. In addition, they are generally referred to as an overall generic group and would commonly be prefaced with a <u>null determiner</u>. Single examples are generally prefaced with **a** or **an** if they cannot be recognised individually but are specific in some way.

Examples:

__ Cockroaches are a sign of a dirty kitchen. (Note that they are described using the plural, thereby referring to a group of individuals rather than a generic group).

A stick insect (phasmid) is difficult to see in its natural habitat. (Single insect type with a specific ability).

Exception: When an insect or group of insects has done something, has a known characteristic or is outstanding in some way then **the** would be used.

Examples:

The moth flying around the lamp in my room was driving me crazy. (An insect specified by its actions).

The mayfly will only live as an adult for one day. (An insect known for a particular characteristic – note it applies to all insects of that type even though it only describes a single example).

The average locust contains 13–28 g/100g of protein against 19–26 g/100g for prime beef. (Outstanding in a particular way).

Notes and examples

REPTILES

Many reptiles are usually referred to in terms of their actions because these actions are of most concern for people. The action would normally be prefaced with **the**; however, the reptile itself may not be unless it is named or it needs to be named.

Examples:

The snakebite from **the** asp *had* to be treated quickly. (The reptile, asp, was named as the reptile that undertook the action – note: this sentence could be written "**A** snakebite from **an** asp *has* to be treated quickly". The difference being that the first sentence refers to an event that actually happened; whereas, the second example is giving advice about a possible event. You should also note the *tenses* in each sentence).

When suffering from a snakebite you should try and identify **the** snake so you can be treated with the correct anti-venom.

Exception: When describing a specific characteristic of a type of reptile it can be prefaced with **the** or not. If it is prefaced with **the**, it describes a specific group and refers to the type in the singular (even though it applies to all of that type); alternatively, if **the** is not used then the same meaning would use plural nouns and verbs. Study the following examples.

Examples:

The Boa Constrictor kills its prey by squeezing it to death. (Singular reference to the whole type using **the**).

__ Boa Constrictors kill their prey by squeezing them to death. (Plural reference to the whole type using plural nouns and verbs with a <u>null determiner</u>).

Notes and examples

MICROSCOPIC ANIMALS

Microscopic animals, or life forms, are generally referred to as bacteria or viruses. They are never referred to as individuals, because it is almost impossible to isolate them; so, they are always referred to as a group. They could be referred to using the singular, prefaced with **a**, or the plural, with both the type in the plural as well as any associated type(s), in order to refer to the actions of the type. For example consider the following:

Examples:

A bacteriophage is a virus that infects and replicates within a bacterium.

__ Bacteriophages are viruses that infect and replicate within bacteria.

Exception: When using an appositive to name a particular bacteria then **the** would be used.

Examples: The bacterium, Yersinia pestis, was responsible for the Black Death, which is estimated to have killed 30–60% of Europe's population in the mid 1300s.

Notes and examples

ENDANGERED ANIMALS

Endangered animals are generally prefaced with **the** as the context of the reference is usually very specific, i.e. it will most likely be about their endangerment. Note, they are generally referred to in the singular, and the reference uses a singular verb, even when referring to the whole group or species.

Examples:

The tiger is facing extinction in all of its Asian habitats. (No reason was mentioned for the endangerment).

The critically endangered black Rhinoceros is facing extinction due to poaching. (Reference giving a specific reason for the endangerment).

Exception: When talking about the animal in general terms, such as when discussing its attributes such as habitats, food source, etc. then a <u>null determiner</u> would be used.

Example: ___ Tigers live in Asia and feed on live prey.

Notes and examples

PLANTS

CROPS

Crops are generally regarded as uncountable, even if, like apples, individual items can be counted; however, they are generally prefaced with **the**, even when they are referred to in plural terms. **The** would also be used to refer to specific examples of this type of crop, usually followed by an adjective clause or prepositional phrase to clarify which subset is being referred to.

Examples:

The wheat is nearly ready for harvesting. (The uncountable crop that is specified by being of one type and being the produce of a known person or group of people).

The plums are early this year. (Even though this refers to a plural designation it references the whole crop of individual items).

I loved **the** pears <u>you brought me</u>. (Specified using an <u>adjective clause</u>).

The tomatoes <u>in my garden</u> are nearly ripe. (Specified using a <u>prepositional phrase</u>).

Exception: If the crop is being referred to in generic terms, in other words it refers to all crops of that type from anywhere and produced by unknown people then a <u>null determiner</u> would be used.

Examples:

___ Rice is a staple food for most of Asia. (Generic reference to all rice of all types. Note, Asia is a generic reference to all people who live or originate in Asia, ***the people of Asia*** could have been used instead in order to make the reference more explicit).

I like ___ pineapple. (Note the use of a singular reference to pineapple, which indicates that the speaker likes the taste. If they were referring to all aspects of the fruit they'd say '**I like pineapples**).

Notes and examples

FLOWERS

Flowers are generally regarded as generic and so they would be prefaced with either a <u>null determiner</u> for all variations of that type or **a** or **an** when referring to a single specimen.

Examples:

___ Flowers brighten up the house (All flowers indicated by a null determiner).

He gave his love **a** rose. (Referring to a single one of the type).

Exception: When referring to specific flowers, either a single flower or an uncountable number of them then **the** would be used. If the flowers can be seen or have a defining characteristic, such as they all bloom together, they do not need to be further specified; however, if they are unseen or otherwise unknown to the listener then they would be accompanied by an adjective, an adjective clause or a prepositional phrase to specify them.

Examples:

The flowers look lovely. (The ones that can be seen).

The daffodils bloomed early this year. (All of that type acting together).

The *red* roses give the impression of being in an English garden. (Specified with an *adjective*).

The snowdrops *<u>that I planted</u>* haven't bloomed yet. (Specified with an <u>*adjective clause*</u>).

The bluebells <u>in the woods</u> are particularly beautiful this year. (Specified with a <u>prepositional phrase</u>).

Notes and examples

WEEDS

Weeds are generally not specified as they are regarded as a generic nuisance. Therefore, they wouldn't normally be prefaced with **the**, instead they'd be prefaced with a <u>null determiner</u>. When making enquiries about this indicative indicators such as **this** and **those** are commonly used to identify them to the listener.

Examples:

___ Weeds were growing out of the driveway of the abandoned house. (Generic reference used as an observation).

___ Japanese knotweed is regarded as a nuisance as it helps to destroy structures and is difficult to get rid of. (Named weed referred to in a general way in order to highlight its proven features that are common to its type).

What are **those** weeds called? (**Indicative reference**, usually accompanied by a pointed finger).

Exception 1: When weeds are referred to in a specific context, such as being in a certain place, are usually prefaced with **the** and specified using an adjective clause or a prepositional phrase.

Examples: The weeds *growing among the crops* were a nightmare for the farmer. (Specified using an *adjective clause*).

The weeds <u>in my garden</u> outnumber the flowers. (Specified using a <u>prepositional phrase</u>).

Exception 2: When referring to abstract attributes of a weed, for example how the speaker feels about weeds of a certain type, then the weed's name is generally prefaced with **the**. If plural weeds are being referred to then a <u>null determiner</u> would be normally be used unless they are further specified using a *<u>prepositional phrase</u>*.

Examples:

I think **the** dandelion is a beautiful flower. (Abstract reference to a weed of a certain type).

____ Clover is considered to be lucky even though it ruins the perfection of the lawn. (Plural generic reference).

In my opinion, **the** daisies *<u>is my lawn</u>* brighten it up. (Plural reference specified with a *<u>prepositional phrase</u>*).

TREES

Trees are often viewed in terms of groups and thus described with group nouns such as forest, wood, spinney, copse, stand, group, weald, plantation or clump. They may or may not be used with the plural noun 'trees' forming part of a prepositional phrase together with 'of' to clarify the description. With either usage they tend to be prefaced with **the**. Individual trees that are notable, usually being classified using an adjective, an adjective clause or a prepositional phrase, would also be prefaced with **the**.

Examples:

Most of **the** trees <u>in the wood</u> are Lombardy Poplars. (The <u>prepositional phrase</u> clarifies which trees are being discussed).

Something frightening is lurking in **the** forest. (Without the word 'trees' as the forest is assumed to mainly consist of trees).

The stand <u>of beech trees</u> was planted fifty years ago. (With the word 'trees' in a <u>prepositional phrase</u> – note this sentence would have been prefaced with an *indicative determiner* if it is being directly indicated, by pointing for example: '*That* stand <u>of beech trees</u> was planted fifty years ago.').

The *tall* tree is blocking the light. (Specified with an *adjective*).

The tree <u>that we carved our initials into</u> *when we were young* has been chopped down. (Specific tree specified with an <u>adjective clause</u> – note the *adverb clause* specifying the time).

The tree <u>in my garden</u> provides shade on hot summer evenings. (A particular tree specified with a <u>prepositional phrase</u>).

Exception 1: If the group of trees is unspecified then it would be prefaced with **a** or **an**.

Examples:

They live in the middle of **a** forest. (The focus of the sentence is the type of lifestyle, in that it gives the impression that they like their privacy).

I parked under **a** tree (the tree is one of many and is not specific).

Exception 2: When discussing plural trees in general terms a null determiner will be used.

Example: Trees help to make the landscape look beautiful.

GARDEN PLANTS

Garden plants are specifically grown by someone and are therefore regarded as personal and are generally prefaced with a **possessive determiner**.

Examples:

I need to put some manure around **my** roses.

Her tomatoes are nearly ripe.

Exception: When describing their state, for example how they are growing, thriving or wilting, they would be prefaced with **the** - even when using the proper noun (their name) to describe them. They are specified with a prepositional phrase that states where they are and/or how they are related to the speaker if there is any doubt.

Examples:

The Gardenias <u>in my garden</u> are doing very well even though it can get quite cold and dry here. (Specified with a <u>prepositional phrase</u> as it is possible to grow gardenias in both the garden and indoors).

The raspberry bushes seem to be dying. (Not specified with a prepositional phrase as it is assumed by the speaker that the listener knows exactly which bushes are being discussed).

Notes and examples

VEGETABLES

Vegetables are generally prefaced with **the** when discussing their preparation, in cooking for example, and when referring to vegetables growing in a particular place. Note, they are usually referred to as plurals.

Examples:

Are **the** Brussels sprouts cooked yet? (They are specific as they are the only vegetables currently being cooked).

The peas are ready to pick now. (The peas that both the speaker and listener know about).

Exception: If vegetables are referred to singular items then they'd be prefaced with **a** or **an.**

Example: The schoolboy was crunching on **a** carrot when he entered the room.

Exception 2: If questions are being asked about a quantity greater than zero then the name would be prefaced with **any.**

Examples:

Have you grown **any** potatoes this year? (Note, the 'any' could be removed - 'Have you grown potatoes this year?' - and the sentence would now ask whether you are growing potatoes instead of something else).

Did **any of the** cauliflowers survive the frost? (Using the compound determiner '**Any of the**' to ask whether one or more of the vegetables survive the conditions that all of the vegetables suffered).

Notes and examples

ENDANGERED PLANTS

When an endangered plant is being discussed in terms of the particular type of plant, such as a flower or a vine, then the name would be used as an adjective and the type would be used as the noun and the resultant uncountable noun phrase would be prefaced with **the**.

Examples: The Rafflesia Flower (*Rafflesia arnoldii*), also known as **the** corpse flower, is thought to be at risk of extinction. (Note, it is common to leave the type off in conversation – leaving it to be assumed – so you can say '**The** Rafflesia is at risk of extinction').

Exception: If the plant is being discussed without mentioning the type then a <u>null determiner</u> would be used.

Example: __ Endangered plants are listed in a federal register.

Exception 2: If the number of endangered plants is known it would be used as a *numerical determiner* to emphasize the danger the plant is in - note the use of 'only' to add further emphasis.

Example: Only *140* Texas Wild Rice clumps are thought to exist. (In this instance the word 'Rice' is part of the compound noun and does not refer to the type. To refer to the type, use the word '<u>plant</u>' – **The** Texas Wild Rice <u>plant</u> is at risk of extinction).

Notes and examples

PHARMACEUTICAL PLANTS

When plants are used to make therapeutic drugs the name of the plant is generally not prefaced with **the**; a null determiner would be used instead. They can be referred to as a singular or a plural noun form.

Examples:

__ Foxglove, also known by its scientific name Digitalis Lanata, is a critical ingredient in drugs used to correct cardiac arrhythmias. (The name of the plant is referred to as a singular, uncountable noun together with a singular verb).

__ Opium Poppies are a natural analgesic (painkiller) but are currently banned worldwide; mainly due to pressure from drug companies. (Plural [group] reference discussing all plants of this type).

Exception: When discussing the preparation of a previously known drug based on a plant ingredient **the** would be used.

Example: The quinine is extracted from the bark of the Cinchona tree and can be mixed into food or drink before being given to the malaria patient. (Extract from a plant - if we are talking about where a drug is derived from then **the** would not be used: __ Quinine is derived from the Cinchona tree).

Notes and examples

MICROSCOPIC PLANTS

The most common microscopic plants are algae. They are never referred to as individual plants, because it is almost impossible to isolate them; so, they are almost always referred to as an uncountable group. As they are indivisible they would generally be prefaced with a null determiner - note, the singular verb.

Examples:

The pond was covered in __ Algae.

__Phytoplankton is an extremely important part of the ocean's food chain.

__Yeast is not regarded as a plant but instead it is regarded as a fungus.

Exception 1: When the plant has been previously referred to, it should be prefaced with **the** when mentioning it again in order to confirm that the same thing is being referred to. If it is referred to in the immediately adjacent (next) sentence then **this** could be used instead.

Examples:

What is the difference between pondweed and algae? Answer: **the** algae is actually a group of separate plants; whereas, **the** pondweed is a single plant.

Phytoplankton is eaten by larger animals from Krill to Whales. **This** phytoplankton is not the only microscopic life form in the ocean's food chain; the protozoa is also eaten by larger animals.

Exception 2: When categorising the plant with an adjective or a prepositional phrase it would be prefaced with **the**.

Examples:

The *microscopic* plankton was examined under a microscope (categorised with an *adjective*).

The algae *in the pond* was choking the life out of it (categorised with a prepositional phrase).

Notes and examples

TEXTS AND LEGAL DOCUMENTS

CONTRACTS

Contracts are generally prefaced with **a** or **an** because they are generally not named, even though the parties to the contract may be named. When discussing contracts in general terms a <u>null determiner</u> would be used. If a contract covers a specific set of circumstances and would apply to both current and future people it would be named using an *adjective* and prefaced with **a** or **an**.

Examples:

The two companies signed **a** contract agreeing to share their technology. (Two previously named or known companies are entering into legally binding cooperation).

____ Contracts are legal documents that state and explain the terms of a formal agreement between two different people or groups. (General reference/definition prefaced with a <u>null determiner</u>).

I had to sign **an** *employment* contract stating my rights and responsibilities when I joined the ministry. (Specifically named contract using an *adjective* thus forming a compound noun).

Exception 1: When quoting from the contract it would be prefaced with **the**, even if it not named, as it assumes that both parties to the conversation know about which contract is being referred to.

Example: **The** contract states that the inventor is entitled to royalties of 1% of each product based on the sale price when the invention is sold.

Exception 2: When referring to a violation of a contract or towards particular benefits or responsibilities **the** is generally used to preface the contract and is generally specified with an adjective or a prepositional phrase.

Examples:

He broke **the** *employment* contract by not turning up to work for three months. (Specified with an *adjective* – note, when one party violates the terms of the contract then they are referred to as having '**broken**' it.).

The contract *I signed* states that I am entitled to royalties. (Contract specified with an *adjective clause*).

The *unfair* contract was terminated <u>by the court</u>. (Specified with a <u>prepositional phrase</u> that clarifies who/what nullified the contract. Note the *adjective* that clarifies which contract is being discussed and, in this case, why).

Exception 3: When a person is referring to a contract that is specific to them then they would normally use a ***possessive determiner***.

Examples: ***My*** contract states I am entitled to 20 Days holiday per year.

AGREEMENTS AND POLICIES

Contracts and agreements share similarities and can be confused. To clarify: an agreement is any understanding or arrangement reached between two or more parties and is usually informal; whereas, a contract is a specific type of agreement that is legally binding and enforceable in a court of law. Agreements are generally unspecified, the fact that the agreement exists is normally the important message and not the applicable parts of it, and they would normally be prefaced with **a** or **an**.

Examples:

We have **a** *verbal* agreement that stipulates how we will react under certain circumstances. (Note the *adjective* that clarifies what type of agreement it is but it is still prefaced with **a**).

We have ***an unwritten agreement*** to help each other. (*An unwritten agreement* is one that has never been written down nor were the rules specified. It is usually between friends or family members and would often be societal mores).

Exception: When the terms of an agreement are either being explained or where the terms have been broken then **the** would be used.

Examples:

Under the terms of **the** agreement we are both jointly liable for the costs. (Referring to a previously discussed agreement).

The *tenancy* agreement states that we are responsible for maintaining the property. (An *Adjective* is being used to specify the agreement).

A policy is a written agreement to act in a certain way. It originally meant **'the cunning acts that politicians indulged in'** but has since come to mean a government's behaviour. It can also refer to a legally binding agreement with an insurance company that states how they will react when presented with a claim. When referring to government actions or for future insurance policies it is prefaced with **a** or **an**:

Examples:

Hitler's government had **a** policy of extermination based on certain ethnic and religious characteristics.

I need to buy **a** life insurance policy. (It doesn't exist yet).

Exception: If the policy is in force then **the** would be used.

Example: The policy states that I am entitled to free dental care.

TREATIES

Treaties are legal agreements between two or more sovereign states and/or international organisations (for example the UN). They are also known as international agreements, protocols, covenants, conventions, pacts, or exchange of letters. Whether a treaty is prefaced with **the** or not depends on where in the negotiations the announcement that refers to it is being made. For example before the treaty is being first announced then **a** or **an** are used. If the treaty negotiations are progressing then the first mention is prefaced with **a** or **an**, the next mention will be prefaced with the, usually with the treaty name, with subsequent mentions using the pronoun 'it'.

Examples:

A security treaty has been proposed between ASEAN countries and Israel. (Initial proposal prefaced with **a**).

A trade treaty is being negotiated between the UK and South Korea. **The** treaty is expected to cover both manufactured goods and intangibles such as banking and insurance. **It** is expected to be announced in the next 12 months. (Currently under negotiation – first mention prefaced with **a**, the next mention is prefaced with **the** and thereafter it is referred to using the pronoun **it**.)

Exception: Once a treaty has been signed and announced it would be subsequently be prefaced with **the**.

Examples: The Bowring treaty was signed on 18 April 1855 between the United Kingdom and the Kingdom of Siam that liberalized foreign trade in Siam, modern day Thailand. (Long standing treaty being discussed in terms of its main attributes).

Notes and examples

MEMORANDA

A memorandum can be one of three things: In its most common form it is a short note that acts as a reminder and is normally shortened to 'memo', it can also be a formal written communication in business and finally it can be a brief diplomatic communication. They would generally be prefaced with **a** or **an** as the fact that they exist is usually the important point.

Examples:

I sent you **a** memo to remind you about our meeting. (A short note acting as a reminder).

A memorandum of association is the document that governs the relationship between a company and the outside world. (Often called the 'memorandum and articles' of the company – the articles refers to the 'articles of association' that governs how the relationships <u>within</u> the company are governed).

A memorandum of understanding is a document that outlines the legal facts that both parties believe have been agreed to and is often used in diplomatic exchanges and agreements. These would normally be signed by all the involved parties.

Exception: When referring to the terms of a memorandum,**the** would be used.

Examples:

I'd like to draw your attention to section two of **the** memorandum. (Referring to one part of the memoranda covering this topic).

We need to liberalise our trade policies as per **the** memorandum. (Referring to the overall memorandum).

Notes and examples

FORMAL LETTERS

Formal letters form the basis of professional communications in legal, commercial or diplomatic contexts. They would often accompany other documents to explain their context. Even though they are generally regarded as vital and are often specified they are generally prefaced with **a** or **an**.

Examples:

I sent you **an** *application* letter for the job I saw advertised. (Letter specified with an adjective and sent by the speaker).

A letter was sent to your last known address on the 16th of last month. (A formal communication in the 3rd person to state that an official letter had been sent).

Exception 1: When referring to something that is contained within a specific letter or to formally confirm having received it then **the** would be used. The letter would be specified with an adjective or a prepositional phrase.

Examples:

It was mentioned in **the** *covering* letter. (Specified with an *adjective* - a covering letter is sent with and explains other enclosed documents).

We confirm receipt of **the** letter <u>of the 10th inst</u>. (Specified with a <u>prepositional phrase</u>. Note, *inst.* Is a formal way of saying 'in the current month' and is short for 'instant'. Further note the use of 'we' to denote that the correspondent is not acting alone but is part of a larger group or company).

Exception 2: When a series of letters are being exchanged between parties then the **possessive determiners** could be used. Note, this is regarded as being a slightly less formal way of referring to the letter(s) than using **the**.

Examples:

I think **our** *last* letter made our position plain. (Specified with an *adjective*).

With reference to **your** letter <u>of the 13th of March</u> I can confirm that the price includes the shipping charges. (Specified with a <u>prepositional phrase</u>).

WILLS

A will, or more formally last will and testament, is a document that states the intent of how a deceased person's effects are to be handled. They are legal documents and are usually enforceable in a court of law. Because they are generally very specific to a particular person they would generally be prefaced with a possessive determiner or a possessive noun.

Examples:

She left all her money to the cat's home <u>in **her** will</u>. (Note that the will appears in a <u>prepositional phrase</u> as it is not considered to be as important as the [scandalous to some people] fact that the money had gone to a cat's home instead of, possibly, her family).

Fred dictated **his** *latest* will to his lawyer just before he died. (A *comparative adjective* has been used to specify the will).

Martha's will is being read today. (Specified using a ***possessive noun***).

Exception: In formal communications regarding the will, say from the solicitor's office that is handling the probate, or when the will is well known or previously discussed, then **the** would be used.

Examples:

The reading of **the** will is taking place at the legal offices of Sue, Grabbit and Runne. (Formal declaration regarding the will without naming whose will it refers to, with the implication being that the interested parties would themselves know. Further clarification could have been added using a <u>prepositional phrase</u> 'The reading of **the** will <u>of the late George Ward</u> is…')

The final will ended up being regarded as very controversial (Previously discussed will).

Notes and examples

DEEDS

Deeds are legal instruments, usually in the form of documents, which confirm the title, or ownership, of something. They are usually prefaced with **a** or **an** because they are generally not specified.

Example: We will need to draw up **a** new deed to cover this new property.

Exception 1: When discussing a specific deed that refers to a specific piece of property then it would generally be specified with an *adjective* or a <u>prepositional phrase</u> and prefaced with **the**.

Examples:

The *house* deeds are <u>on the table</u>. (Specified with an *adjective* – note the <u>prepositional phrase</u> in this sentence is used to confirm their position and is not specifying the deeds themselves).

Our corporate counsel retained **the** deeds <u>to the property</u>.

Exception 2: A **possessive determiner** is commonly used to refer to personal property and would normally be specified with an *adjective* or a prepositional phrase.

Examples:

Our *sale* deed outlines the terms of the sale. (Specified using an adjective).

My deeds <u>for the property</u> show the boundaries of the land. (Specified using a prepositional phrase).

Notes and examples

CONVEYANCES

A conveyance is a document that is used to transfer the title or ownership of something – note the noun 'conveyance' is generally used to describe something that is used to carry or transfer something from one place to another. They are generally specific because they are used in the transfer of specific pieces of property so the would be used.

Example: We have to agree to the payment details before **the** conveyance can be concluded.

Exception 1: When discussing the need for a conveyance **a** or **an** would be used (**a** or **an** are generally used for things that don't exist yet).

Examples: We will need to draw up **a** *conveyance deed* to define the terms of the transfer. (Note the *compound noun* that defines a particular type of conveyance).

Exception: When providing an explanation or definition of conveyances a <u>null determiner</u> would be used.

Examples: ___ Conveyances are used to transfer property between parties.

Notes and examples

COVENANTS

A covenant is essentially a legally binding promise to either do, or not do, something. It is generally not used instead of an agreement but could form part of agreement or deed or as an addition to an agreement or deed. It would usually be prefaced with **a** or **an** when it is being referred to in terms of it being present or when it is an addition to an agreement.

Examples:

There is **a** covenant in the agreement that covers one of the parties being unable to comply. (Stating the covenant is present).

An additional covenant in **the** agreement states that the goods cannot be resold before payment has been made in full. (A notable addition to the main agreement covering things that each party will NOT do – agreements generally cover things that each party should do. Note, the agreement is specific, as it is known about, and so it is prefaced with **the**).

Exception 1: When asking questions about a covenant, or covenants, being present, then **any** is generally used. When referring to an unknown number of covenants on answering a question then **some** would be used.

Examples:

Are there **any** specific covenants in the agreement? (Asking a question about the presence of at least one covenant).

I was told by the lawyer that there may be **some** special covenants in the will. (Indicating the presence of at least one covenant).

Exception 2: A <u>null determiner</u> would be used when discussing plural covenants in general terms, for example what they are.

Examples: __ Covenants add special terms to legal agreements. (Using a <u>null determiner</u> when defining covenants).

Exception 3: When discussing the terms or effects of a covenant **the** is generally used.

Example: The covenant states that the funds from the will to the youngest daughter be held in trust and become available when she reaches the age of 18.

DRAFTS

A draft is a preliminary document that is used to incite comments and feedback that will be used when creating the final agreement. Although it may not be directly specified it would generally be prefaced with **the** as it is associated with a particular result. Note, it could be used as either a *noun* (I will write the *draft*) or an *adjective* (I wrote the *draft* agreement). It can also be used as a verb that describes the action of creating a document (I will **draft** an example).

Examples:

I will have **the** *draft* on your desk by noon. (Previously discussed draft – used as a *noun*).

We have a lot of queries about **the** *draft* contract. (Previously discussed pre-contract – used as an *adjective*).

Exception: When discussing the necessity of a draft or when explaining it then **a** or **an** would be used.

Examples:

Will we need to have **a** draft or can we start to draw up the contract itself? (Asking about the necessity).

We will need to create **a** draft so we have a discussion document to assist in our negotiations. (Explaining the necessity).

Notes and examples

PROPOSALS

Proposals refer to actions or agreements that don't exist yet; therefore, they are generally prefaced with **a** or **an**. Note, a proposal refers to a proposed series or actions; whereas, a draft is the first stage in a final document.

Examples:

Can you send me **a** proposal giving me a ballpark figure of the likely cost? (Asking for a proposal to be created – note 'ballpark figure' [US English] or 'rough idea' [UK English] indicated a request for an indicative number that is not legally or contractually enforceable).

Thank you for taking the time to discuss your ideas with me today. I will send you **a** proposal tomorrow that will outline how we can move forward on this matter. (A proposal will be created to state what further actions will be undertaken if both parties are in agreement with its terms and move to a contract stage).

Exception: When a known proposal has been received or being directly referred to then it would be prefaced with **the**.

Examples:

Have you received **the** proposal yet? (The proposal that you were expecting and, hence, you knew about).

Has **the** proposal been sent to the customer yet? (Referring to a particular proposal. Note, the proposal is known about, possibly from having been previously discussed).

Whether the word 'proposal' is prefaced with **the** or not, depends on at what stage the proposal is at. For example consider the following two sentences:

A proposal needs to be sent to the customer that includes the non-disclosure agreement and the outline specifications. (Discussing a proposal that doesn't exist yet except as a concept).

The proposal you are sending to the customer needs to include a non-disclosure agreement and the outline specifications. (Discussing a proposal that is being prepared and therefore exists).

LAWS

Laws are usually prefaced with **the**, because they are generally specific, even when referring to them in the abstract (i.e. they are not named) or if they don't exist yet but are being debated. Moreover, they are generally referred to as 'act' when quoting their terms – such as in relation to wrongdoing.

Examples:

The law is very clear on this matter. (Abstract reference).

The law currently being debated in congress will increase taxes to 99%. (A specific law that is currently under discussion).

Members of the government are exempt from the provisions of **the** new law. (The law that has been previously mentioned – note it is being clarified with the adjective 'new').

They have been charged under **the** misuse of drugs act. (Referring to a specific law).

Exception: If there isn't a specific law in effect or the idea of a particular future law currently is being considered then it would be prefaced with **a** or **an**.

Examples:

There ought to be **a** law against it. (There is no law prohibiting a particular act – although the speaker is indicating that they would like one).

The UK government is considering **a** law to ban all forms of fun and entertainment. (A prohibitive law is being considered).

Notes and examples

ESTIMATES

The dictionary definition of an estimate is a 'guess', in business the word refers to the potential – non-legally binding - cost of something that is being proposed, such as a series of actions or the delivery of certain items. If the estimate doesn't exist yet or is being asked for then it would be prefaced with **a** or **an**.

Examples:

We need to send **an** estimate to the customer. (It doesn't exist yet).

Can you send me **an** estimate that includes all of the possible costs? (An estimate is being asked for).

Exception: When referring to an estimate that has exists – it has been written or given to the customer – then it would be prefaced with **the** when referring to it.

Examples:

I will send you **the** estimate by email. (The estimate has been created and will be forwarded to the customer).

The estimate you sent doesn't mention cleaning up after the job has been done. (The estimate is in the hands of the customer; therefore, it exists).

Notes and examples

SPECIFICATIONS

A specification is a detailed and/or technical description of how something will or should be done or made. As they are specific (it is the root of the word) they would generally be prefaced with **the**. Note, they are commonly referred to in the plural form (specification**s**) and would always be prefaced with **the** in this form.

Examples:

The specification is for a 10mV input amplified to provide a 100 watt output. (A specific singular existing specification).

The specifications say that the transmitter's output should be 10dB (Plural specifications - a group of individual specifications to produce the whole).

Exceptions: If a singular specification is being discussed, whether it exists or not, would normally be prefaced with **a** or **an**.

Examples:

Is there **a** specification that covers the input voltage? (Enquiring whether a particular specification exists).

A specification needs to be added to state the effects of moisture on the circuit. (The specification doesn't exist yet).

Notes and examples

BILLS

Bills have two forms: the first is a notice or statement referring to a proposed new law or an event, the second refers to a request for payment. If they exist already they would be prefaced with **the**. They can also refer to a statement of content or value.

Examples:

The new bill, that the MPs in the UK house of commons will be voting on tonight, outlaws all forms of speech that hasn't been specifically approved. (A specific bill that was specified using an adjective 'new').

Can you ask the waiter for **the** bill? (Refers to the itemized cost of something, such as a meal).

The bills are coming in faster than we are able to pay. (Multiple requests for payments – note, plural bills would always be prefaced with **the**).

The *bill of lading* states that there are five tons of ammonium nitrate in this truck. (*Statement of content*).

Exception: If the bill doesn't exist yet then it would be prefaced with **a** or **an**.

Examples:

A bill is going through the UK parliament to ban non-approved sites on the Internet. (Refers to a proposed law that hasn't previously been mentioned).

We need to send them **a** bill for our services (a future request for payment).

Notes and examples

CERTIFICATES

When referred to in legal terms a certificate is primarily an official document which states that the information on it is true. They are commonly used in business supply chains as part of quality control systems. They can also be used as a legal document to attest to the fact that a named person has successfully completed a course of study or training and have achieved the desired competencies in the subject, skill or craft. They are often required to prove competency before the person is allowed to work in a field where poor workmanship may cause injury to others. They are generally prefaced with **a** or **an**.

Examples:

A certificate of conformance (C of C) is signed by a competent authority to say that the product meets the agreed standards.

A certificate of analysis differs from **a** certificate of conformance in that the former would normally contain the test results that confirm compliance with the standards.

She has **a** BTEC certificate in Electronics Engineering. (Attestation that the person has reached the required standard in an academic subject).

Exception: When referring to a specific instance of a certificate it would be prefaced with **the**.

Example: The certificate of compliance was missing from the last shipment.

Notes and examples

SWORN STATEMENTS

Sworn statements are written statements that are offered by a party in a lawsuit. The statement is generally followed by a paragraph wherein the person attests that the information is true. They will usually sign and date the paragraph, which is known as an endorsement paragraph. Sworn statements are generally referred to using **a** or **an** as they are not specific.

Example: He gave **a** sworn statement regarding the circumstances regarding the contract.

Exception: If a sworn statement has just been referred to previously, during a court case for instance or it specified using by a clause, then it would be prefaced by **the**.

Examples:

The sworn statement has been proved to be wrong. (Previously known.)

The sworn statement *given by the defendant* states that... (specified using an *adjective clause.*)

Notes and examples

AFFIDAVITS

Another class of court documents are called affidavits. Affidavits contain similar statements and claims to sworn statements, but have been signed, witnessed, and certified by a public official such as a notary public, a justice of the peace or a court official, such as a magistrate or a judge. This certification allows an affidavit to be perceived as a more credible form of evidence than a simple sworn statement. Lying on an affidavit can, in most jurisdictions, lead to a criminal charge of perjury or obstruction of justice. Affidavits are generally prefaced with **a** or **an**.

Examples:

He presented **an** affidavit to the court.

She made **a** sworn affidavit that the facts were true (sworn means she attested to the veracity before a court approved official - strictly speaking the word 'sworn' does not need to be used as it is assumed that it was sworn or it wouldn't be regarded as valid; but, the word is often used by legal representatives appearing before a jury to add gravitas i.e. to cause feelings of respect and trust).

Exception: If they are specific, for example if they are specified with a clause, they would be prefaced with **the**.

Examples: **The** affidavit *you presented to the court* clearly states... (Specified using a *clause*).

Notes and examples

SUMMONS

A **summons** is an order to appear in person at a given place and time. It is most commonly used in the context of a writ issued by authority of law; usually compelling someone's attendance in a civil suit, or in certain low level criminal cases. A failure to appear results in a default judgment against the defendant or, in a more serious criminal case, a warrant being issued for an arrest of the individual.

They would generally be prefaced with **a** or **an** as individually they are one of many such documents issued by the court.

Example: He was given **a** summons to appear for the magistrate.

Exception: If the summons is specified, such as where the contents are being described, then it would be prefaced with **the**.

Example: The summons states the time and venue of when and where you should appear.

Notes and examples

SUBPOENAS

A **subpoena** is a demand for evidence. It goes to a person, to make them testify or produce evidence. The main difference between a summons and a subpoena is that with a summons the court controls the person; whereas, with a subpoena the court controls the evidence. They are generally regarded as being one of many such documents issued and therefore they would be prefaced with the **a** or **an**.

Example: A subpoena has been issued by the grand jury to order him to present evidence.

Exception: When describing the contents of a subpoena or when it has previously been discussed it would be prefaced with **the.**

Examples:

The subpoena contained a statement regarding the matter under investigation. (Discussing the contents).

The issuing of **the** subpoena came as a shock to all concerned (Previously discussed).

Notes and examples

WARRANTS

A warrant is a writ from a court commanding police to perform specified acts, for example to arrest someone or to search a particular place. It can also mean formal and explicit approval for an action. They are generally regarded as undefined; therefore, they would be prefaced **a** or **an**.

Examples:

The policemen say they have **a** warrant to search our house. (Unspecified as the householder hasn't see it yet).

The company had **a** warrant to buy the shares when they reached $1.20. (Only a single right has been mentioned; otherwise, it is unspecified).

Exception: When discussing the purpose, contents or the specific terms of a warrant **the** would be used.

Examples:

The arrest warrant was granted by a magistrate. (Purpose).

The warrant discussed the terms in great detail. (Contents).

Paragraph two on **the** warrant discuss the terms of sale (Specific terms).

Notes and examples

WRITS

A writ is a legal document from a court of law which informs someone that they will be involved in a legal process and instructs them what they must do. Writs are normally prefaced with **a** or **an** (singular) or a <u>null determiner </u>(multiple writs).

Examples:

The high court issued **a** writ to overturn the decision by the lower court. (Singular writ).

There are 5 types of writ that can be issued by a court:

- **Habeas Corpus** (literally 'give me the body': created by the Magna Carta) - orders authorities to bring someone before a court to confirm whether they should continue to be held.
- **Mandamus** - a high court issued command to do something.
- **Prohibition** - forbids a stay order in an ongoing court case.
- **Certiorari** - overturns a previous court's decision.
- **Quo-Warranto** - stops a person from holding a public office to which he is not entitled.

Exception: When the contents of the writ or the purpose of a previously specified writ is being discussed then **the** would be used.

Examples:

The writ normally contains the date of execution in it. (Content).

The writ overturned the circuit court decision issued last year. (Purpose).

Notes and examples

COMMISSIONS

A commission is a formal choice of someone to undertake a task or range of tasks. It may also apply to someone who has the authority to be an officer in a country's armed forces. It would generally be prefaced with **a** or **an**.

Examples: She was given **a** commission to be an officer in the Air Force.

Exception 1: Commissions are bestowed on individuals so they are commonly prefaced with a possessive determiner.

Example: Her commission was signed by the Queen.

Exception 2: When discussing the specific purpose of a commission then it may be prefaced with **the**.

Example: The commission he was given was for him to paint an official portrait of the President.

Notes and examples

LETTERS PATENT

Letters patent (always plural) are publicly published written orders issued by a head of state, generally granting an office, right, monopoly, title, or status to a person or corporation. They are also used for the creation of corporations or government offices, granting of city status or a coat of arms, or appointing representatives of the head of state. They are essentially public proclamations by the head of state and in many countries a person cannot assume office until they are the subject of letters patent. Note, the opposite of openly available are '**letters close**', which are sealed (or completely private). The most common form of letters patent are **patents** used to protect intellectual property. The word 'patent' comes from the Latin **patere**, which means "to lay open". They are generally prefaced with a <u>null determiner</u> for a plural or **a** or **an** for a singular patent.

Examples:

__Letters patent were issued confirming the appointment of the ambassador.

I had **a** patent issued for a welding system.

Exception: When the purpose is specified or the contents are being discussed then **the** will be used.

Examples:

The letters patent were issued in 1882. (Specified with a date).

The patent is about electronic power control. (The contents are being discussed).

Notes and examples

PRESS RELEASES

A press release is a public statement given to the press to publish but there is no obligation to do so, unlike a formal government announcement. They are generally not specified when first issued so they'd be prefaced with **a** or **an**.

Examples: The Company issued **a** press release to explain the privacy issues on their website.

Exception 1: If the press release is being specified, for example with a clause, then it would prefaced with **the**.

Examples:
The press release *they issued* was full of mistakes. (Specified with a *clause*).

Exception 2: If the press release is being referred back to its source then a **possessive determiner** (my, your, his, her, its, our or their) would normally be used.

Example: **Their** press release didn't mention how they are going to correct the problem.

Notes and examples

TECHNOLOGY

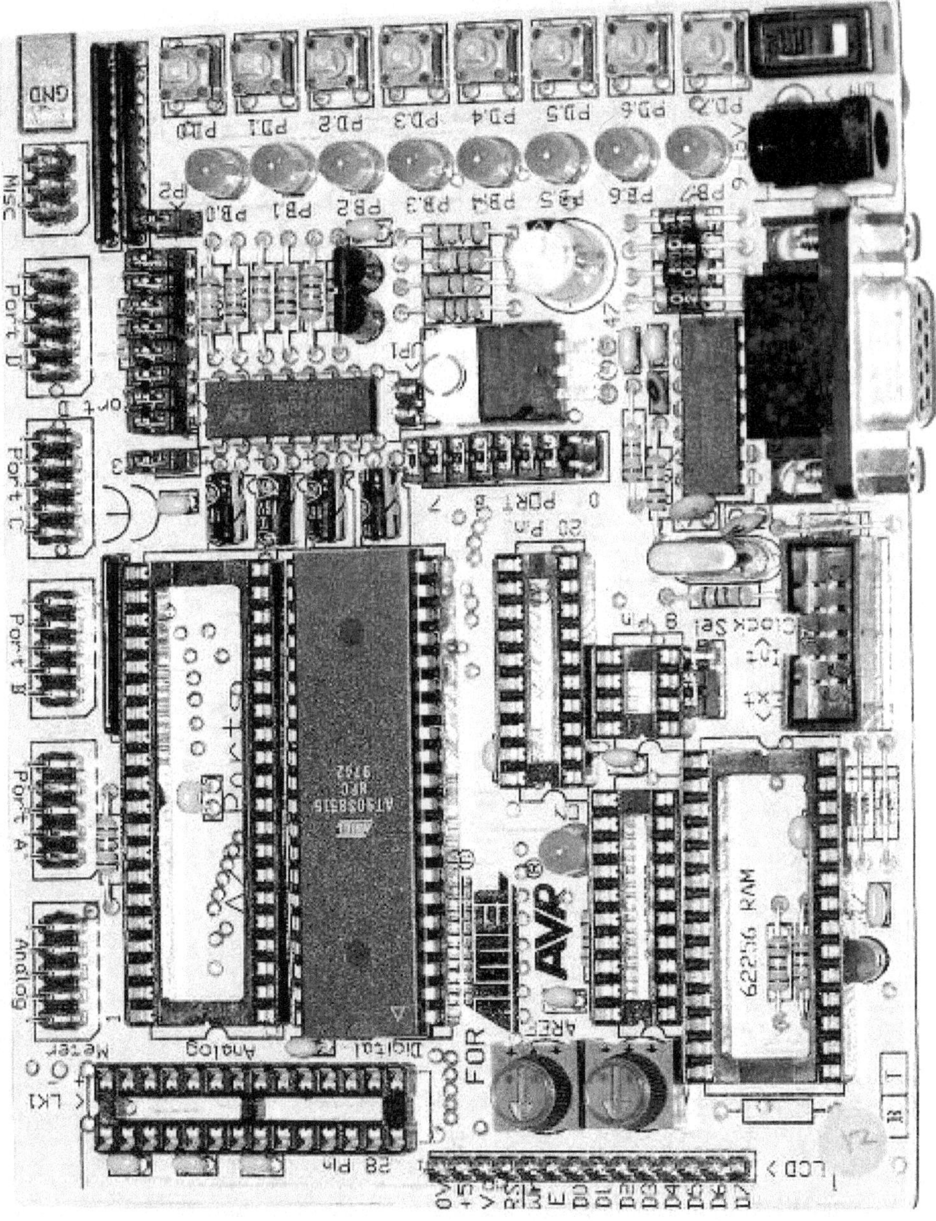

TECHNOLOGICAL EQUIPMENT

Even though technological equipment (such as mobile phones, computers, tablets, etc.) tend to be singular and specific, they aren't commonly used with **the**. Instead they are generally personalised using possessive nouns or determiners.

Examples:

I borrowed **Bert's** laptop (possessive noun)
I lost **my** mobile phone (possessive determiner)

Exceptions: When referring to technology that is not owned by the person speaking then **a** or **an** are generally used. When we refer to the equipment in a specific way, such as talking about a certain aspect of the equipment, then **the** is used.

Examples:

I want to buy **a** mobile phone (I don't yet own it).

She bought **an** iPad (One of many on sale).

The mobile phone *I bought* has stopped working (the specific aspect is that I bought it – note how it is specified with a *clause*).

Notes and examples

PARTS OF A COMPUTER

The is generally used when referring to parts of a computer because they have a specific function. In general we ignore the parts until they are failing or we upgrade them.

Examples:

The hard drive in my computer is failing (specific: the computer is not functioning correctly because the specific device is failing).

I need to upgrade **the** RAM in my computer (The specific part that is inadequate).

Where is **the** Ethernet port? (Specifying what cannot be found).

Exception 1: When we refer to parts that we do not have in the system then we generally use **a** or **an**, because it has no specific function in our system (yet) but is merely one of many available.

Examples:

I bought **a** new router for my computer (It wasn't part of my current system)

Have you got **an** Ethernet cable you can lend me? (Do you have any of the thing I need but don't have).

Exception 2: When we refer to a part without talking about what it is part of (assuming that the listener knows), or it is regarded as a separate piece of equipment (although it is a part of the whole), then we'd generally use a personal determiner or possessive noun.

Examples:

My hard drive is 3 Terabytes (possessive determiner).

Julie's monitor is curved (possessive noun).

Notes and examples

COMPUTER SOFTWARE

Software is not usually referred to using **the** even though it is specific, mainly because the software (which is uncountable) is referred to by its name, which is generally a proper noun and wouldn't normally be prefaced with a determiner at all.

Examples:

I have uninstalled __ Microsoft Office from my computer.

At one time __ Lotus 1-2-3 was a hugely popular piece of software.

Exception: The functions the software performs, or the result of the functions, would usually be prefaced with **the** as they are specific and usually the reason the software was purchased.

Examples:

The table function in __ Word has some strange quirks.

The graph was made using __ Excel.

Notes and examples

COMPUTER GAMES

The is not generally used when talking about named computer games, a <u>null determiner</u> would be used.

Examples:

__World of Warcraft is a very popular game.

I bought a new copy of __ Sim City.

Exception: Specific levels within a game and certain characters, functions or difficulties in the game are commonly prefaced with **the**. Occasionally game names are prefaced with **the** when the name refers to the characters in it.

Examples:

The final level in a computer game is usually the most difficult (level).

The Sims is a game where you control simulated humans (named after characters in the game).

Notes and examples

COMMUNICATION DEVICES

The is commonly used to refer to a communication device even if the device itself is not specific or it is being referred to by an abstract reference to its function.

Examples:

They heard a distress call on **the** radio (it could be one of many but is regarded as specific as the call was heard on it).

I spoke to her on **the** phone (Abstract reference to the concept of speaking via a telephone).

The *office* intercom is not used much any more (Specified with an *adjective*).

Exception: If you refer to the device itself, in isolation from the function it performs, then use **a** or **an**, or a possessive determiner or possessive noun.

Examples:

I bought **a** new house phone (one of many).

I am happy with **my** walkie-talkies (possessive pronoun).

Jane's fax is not working (possessive noun).

Notes and examples

SPECIALIST EQUIPMENT

Specialist equipment is generally specific and so it would be prefaced with **the** when describing its function, where only one of its type exists in that place or that its type is unique in some way.

Examples:

The environmental test chamber is used to test how equipment will function under different environmental conditions. (Describing the function).

The bathroom sling over the bath is used to provide access to disabled people. (The only one in that place).

The Belaz 75710 dump truck is the largest in the world (The type is unique).

Exception: When making a general reference to all specialist equipment of that type then a <u>null determiner</u> would generally be used. If advice is being given to use a particular piece of equipment then use **a** or **an**.

Examples:

__ Dive computers are used by scuba divers to take depth and time information and apply it to a decompression model to track the dissolved nitrogen in their bodies during a dive.(General reference).

A wheelchair ramp will be needed to provide access to the facility. (Advising on a piece of specialist equipment).

Notes and examples

ELECTRONICS

Electronics (Always plural – the singular is an adjective) are generally referred to as a generic thing, commonly as an adjective, and would be prefaced with a <u>null determiner</u>.

Examples:

__Electronics are in use all around us. (Generic reference).
I am **an** electronics design engineer. (Used as an adjective – note the determiner.)

Exception 1: When referring to the specific use for electronics installed or used in a certain installation then **the** is used.

Example: **The** electronics control the way the reactor works.

Exception 2: If a particular installation or major piece of equipment is controlled by electronics then the noun 'electronics' would be prefaced with a **possessive determiner**.

Examples: A modern aircraft is controlled by **its** electronics with the pilot mainly having a supervisory function except in an emergency.

Notes and examples

ELECTRONIC EQUIPMENT

A particular piece of electronic equipment would normally be prefaced with **a** or **an**, as it is one of many such pieces of equipment.

Example: He bought **a** new amplifier as his old one wasn't powerful enough.

Exception: If the piece of equipment is specialised, in limited supply or unique to a location then it would be prefaced with **the.**

Examples:

The cutting laser has a broken plasma tube. (Specialised –the adjective 'cutting' explains the specialisation).

The main electronic control system has a fault. (Limited supply – the adjective 'main' indicates that it is the primary system with possibly a single back up).

The CRT scanner in the hospital's east wing is now fully functional (Unique to that location).

Notes and examples

MECHANICAL EQUIPMENT

Mechanical equipment is generally specific to a particular task therefore it/they would normally be prefaced with **the** and further specified using a possessive noun, an adjective and/or a prepositional phrase.

Examples:

The *boat's* engine developed a fault last night. (Specified using a possessive noun. Note, if the mechanism is the only one, such as when discussing it whilst in or on the vessel or structure, then the possessive noun can be omitted; therefore, the example would now be '**The** engine developed a fault last night'. Alternatively, if the speaker wants to convey a sense of urgency, for example to alert others, who are directly involved, to the possible consequences, then a *possessive determiner* would be used. In which case the example would be '*Our* engine developed a fault last night', implying that, unless it is fixed, there could be serious consequences).

The *main* bearing needs replacing. (Specified using an *adjective* - note it is common to further specify it with a prepositional phrase so the phrase 'in my engine' could be used after the noun 'bearing').

The tyre *on my motorcycle* burst yesterday. (Specified using a *prepositional phrase* - note the noun 'tyre' is spelt 'tire' in the US).

Exception 1: When discussing mechanical systems or component's uses in a general or abstract sense then **a** or **an** would be used.

Example: A tractor was used to plough the field.

Exception 2: If ownership of the mechanical device is important then a possessive determiner or a possessive noun would be used.

Examples:

<u>Your</u> water pump needs priming for it to work properly. (Using a <u>possessive determiner</u>).

My <u>neighbour's</u> car is on fire. (Using a <u>possessive noun</u>. Note, the possessive determiner, **my**, used to link the following noun phrase, neighbour's car, to the speaker. Further note, the noun 'neighbour' is spelt 'neighbor' in US English).

ELECTRICAL EQUIPMENT

If the electrical equipment is specific, such as being unique or large for example, then it would be prefaced with *the* and specified with an adjective, a possessive noun and/or a prepositional phrase. Prepositional phrases are very commonly used when discussing large pieces of equipment.

Examples:

The *high voltage* electrics need to be replaced. (Specified using an *adjective phrase* - note the sentence assumes that the reader/listener knows which electrics are being discussed, if not a <u>prepositional phrase</u> - such as 'in the factory' - would be added after the noun 'electrics').

The *ship's* generator needs to be repaired. (Specified with a <u>*possessive noun*</u> in order to state that the electrical component is an integral part of that particular machine, system or, in this case, vessel/mode of transport).

The transformer <u>outside my apartment</u> blew up last night. (Electrical component, 'transformer', specified with a <u>prepositional phrase</u>).

Exception 1: When discussing electrics in an abstract sense, in other words when no particular piece of equipment is being discussed, then a <u>null determiner</u> would be used. The noun 'electrics', referring to electrical components or systems, is always plural, the words 'electric' and 'electrical' are adjectives.

Example: __ Faulty electrics are the most common problem in modern cars and the cause of most fires.

Exception: When discussing the need for one particular component out of many available or the function of component, then **a** or **an** would be used.

Examples:

I need **a** charger to charge my mobile phone. (One of many available). **An** alternator is used to charge the car battery. (Discussing the function of the component).

EQUIPMENT MANUALS

Manuals for equipment of all types fall into two main categories: User manuals are designed so that the purchaser can learn how to operate the equipment; whereas, service manuals are for those people who need to fix the equipment if it is malfunctioning. In general, user manuals are prefaced with **a** or **an**; whereas, service manuals are prefaced with **the**. The exception to this is when the equipment in question has already been referred to in which case **the** would always be used.

Examples:

A user manual is normally included with all types of household appliances.

The service manual for the washing machine is available as a download.

Have you tried reading **the** manual? (Previously specified equipment, possibly prefaced with" "I can't get the video recorder to work' and referring to the user manual that is specific to that piece of equipment).

Exception: When a manufacturer or supplier is referring to either type of manual then they would generally use   a <u>possessive determiner</u>; whereas, a third person, such as reviewer, would generally use a *possessive noun.*

Examples:

<u>Our</u> manuals are available online in many different languages. (<u>Possessive determiner</u> used by a manufacturer).

The *company's* manuals are well written. (Using a *possessive noun* prefaced with **'the'** to show that only that one company's manuals are being referred to. If the company name is being introduced into the discussion for the first time, it would take the form of a *possessive noun* prefaced with a **null determiner**, such as '__*Audio Technics'* manuals are well written'. Note, if the example sentence is part of a longer discussion of a company then a <u>possessive determiner</u> could be used instead, in this instance either possessive nouns, prefaced with the, or possessive determiners are acceptable. So the example sentence would now be: '**Their** manuals are well written').

VEHICLES AND TRANSPORT

PUBLIC TRANSPORT

Generally public transport vehicles or systems are not individualised and so they would generally be prefaced with **a** or **an**.

Note: If you have to go **up** in order to use a form of transport you would use the preposition _on_ to describe it. You would go '_on_' aircraft, buses, motorcycles, ships, ferries, trains, bicycles and when walking [_on_ foot]. For example: I flew here _on_ a helicopter.

If you go **down** or **straight** in order to use a form of transport you'd use _in_ (You go '_in_' a car, a taxi, a motorcycle rickshaw [tuk-tuk] or a boat). For example: I went there _in_ a taxi.

Examples:

I came here on **a** number 57 bus (describe named type of vehicle). You should you take **a** taxi (describe the type of transport).

Exception 1: If you are describing being in/on a public transport vehicle then you would refer to it using **the.**

Example: I am on **the** train, I will be home at 9.

Exception 2: When talking about problems with a public transport system, or vehicle, or when offering, suggesting or asking to share a vehicle then it is common to use a **possessive determiner** to refer to it.

Example:

My train was late today; so, I was late for work. (Refers to the personal consequences caused by the problem with the transport I used).

Our ferry hit the pier when it tried to dock. (Makes a general observation without naming any consequences suffered by the speaker; therefore, a third person plural determiner was used).

Can I share **your** taxi as my car won't start? (Asking to share a temporarily possessed vehicle).

Notes and examples

AIR TRAVEL

Flights are normally not specific as any given flight is regarded as one of many and are not sufficiently of interest to be specified, so they'd be prefaced with **a** or **an**.

Example:

I need to book **a** flight to Rome. (Any flight on any airline as long as it goes to Rome).

I have to go as I have **a** flight to catch (unspecified flight).

Exception 1: When referring to a specific flight, such as one that has been sought, booked or taken, then it would be prefaced with **the**. Note they are commonly specified with a *prepositional phrase* or an *adjective clause*.

Examples:

I want to get a seat on **the** flight *at 2 p.m. tomorrow.* (Flight being sought).

I managed to reserve a seat on **the** flight *that I was hoping to take*. (Booked flight – specified with an adjective clause).

I got an upgrade on **the** flight. (The flight that I took – note the details of the flight are assumed, for example in this instance the speaker must be talking about the flight they have just experienced so it doesn't need to be specified further).

Exception 2: When naming the operator of the airline a <u>null determiner</u> would commonly be used.

Example: I flew here on __ Thai Airways.

Exception 3: If you are referring to how a journey by aircraft went, such as to comment on the experience or question it then a *possessive determiner* would be used. Note, you could use **the** or a *third person pronoun* to answer the question, because the question has specified it.

Examples:

My flight is delayed so I will miss my connection. (Commenting on a current personal experience).

Did she catch *her* flight? (Asking about a third person's flight – it is assumed that the listener would know which flight and which person is being talked about).

Question: How was *your* flight? (Question the experience).

Answer: The flight was a bit turbulent. (Alternatively, a *third person singular pronoun* could have been used: '*It* was a bit turbulent', or even a single adjective: 'Turbulent').

SHIPS

Ships are generally specified with a name (proper noun) and so they would be prefaced with a <u>null determiner</u>.

Example: I went on __ MS Harmony of the Seas and it was great. (<u>M</u>otor <u>S</u>hip Harmony of the Seas is the name of the ship).

Exception 1: If the method of transport was by sea then it would use the verb 'ship' to describe the method and the vessel would be referenced with **a** or **an**. Note, in the example below the goods being carried are referred to using the noun 'shipment' that would be prefaced with **the** as it the thing that is under discussion. For example:

The <u>shipment</u>	was <u>shipped</u>	on **a** <u>ship</u>.
Goods [cargo]	**Action**	**Method**

Exception 2: When referring to any actions taken by a specific, but unnamed, ship then **the** would be used. Note it would normally be specified using a *prepositional phrase* or an *<u>adjective clause</u>* to state why it is of interest or has importance.

Examples:

The ship *in the harbour* has developed a list. (Specified with a *Prepositional Phrase*).

The ship *<u>that polluted the bay</u>* has been seized by the coastguard. (Specified with an *<u>adjective clause</u>*).

Notes and examples

BOATS AND FERRIES

Boats and ferries are commonly not specified as the service they provide is generally more important than the name of the vessel. The service would be prefaced with **the** as it is specific. It can be prefaced using **the** if it is the only one of its type or it is specified with a *prepositional phrase*.

Examples:

I took **the** ferry as the bridge was closed. (Only service of its type).
I went on **the** boat *to the mainland.* (Specified using a *prepositional phrase*).

Exception 1: When asking about the availability of a ferry service, or whether it is a potential travel option, then **a** or **an** would be used. Note the service would normally be specified with an *adjective clause* or *a prepositional phrase.*

Examples:

Is there **a** ferry *that goes out to the island*? (Specified with an *adjective clause*).

Have you used **a** water taxi *in Bangkok*? (Specified with a *prepositional phrase* - note, it refers to a service in a specific place)

Exception 2: When asking about the definition of a boat then it normally be prefaced with **a** or **an** because it cannot be specified yet.

Example: Is **a** submarine, **a** ship or **a** boat? (None of the nouns are specified and so they are all prefaced with the indefinite article **a**).

Notes and examples

TRAINS

Trains are generally not specified and are usually referred to by the service they offer rather than the train itself; therefore, they are generally prefaced with **a** or **an**.

Examples: He caught **a** train in order to visit his mother.

Exception 1: When talking about a particular train journey then **the** would be used. Note, the journey is discussed in the abstract as '**the train**'. If a particular train is being discussed then it would be prefaced with **the** and specified with a *preposition phrase* or an *adjective clause*. Note, it refers to the physical train rather than abstract 'experience' of the journey.

Examples:

The train was dirty, slow and uncomfortable. (The train refers to the journey by train. It could be rewritten as '**The** train was slow and uncomfortable.' Note, it uses 'dirty' to describe the condition of the carriage the traveller was in and not to how the overall conditions of the train were for everyone or the physical appearance of the train).

The train *on platform 7* is the 16:50 express to Exeter. (Specified with a *prepositional phrase* – interestingly, the preposition '**on**' is used to state that the train is '**next to**' or '**at**' a particular platform and it isn't actually '**on**' the platform but the passenger would need to be on that platform in order to board [get on] it).

The train *that was involved in the accident* was involved in another collision 5 years ago (specified with an *adjective clause*).

Exception 2: When referring to the experience of a personal train journey then a **possessive determiner** may be used. Note, it refers to the journey (experience) rather than the train itself.

Example: **My** train was smooth and luxurious.

Notes and examples

BUSES

Busses are usually known by a number, specifying the route, or by the destination and are commonly prefaced with **the** as they are specific to reaching a certain place. This rule would apply even if any one of a number of different busses could be used. Note: If you stop a bus on the street you are '*catching*' it; whereas, if you get on the bus at the terminus you are '*boarding*' it. (I *caught* a bus on the street – I *boarded* the bus at the station).

Examples:

You need to catch **the** number 37 bus and get off at Silom. (Identified using a number).

I think **the** Sliema bus goes there. (Identified using the name of the final destination).

You need to catch either **the** 93 bus, which goes every half hour, or **the** number 7, which goes every ten minutes but takes longer to get there. (When referring to a choice on offer – even though a number of buses with the same number are being discussed - they are all treated as one as the number refers to the route the bus takes [the service] rather than the bus itself).

Exception: When referring to the act of travelling using a bus then **a** or **an** would generally be used.

Example: If you catch **a** bus it will cost less than a euro to get there;

Notes and examples

TAXIS

Taxis are generally not specified and so they'd be prefaced with **a** or **an**. Note, you '**grab**', '**hail**' or '**flag**' a taxi on the street or '**call**' a minicab to arrange a pick up by phone. If you obtain it via the Internet you would '**book**' it. **Taxis**, that offer metered journeys, are also known as **cabs** in the US. If they can only be hired via the phone or Internet, can't be hailed on the street and only offer do the journey for a fixed price they are known as '**minicabs**' or '**private hires**'.

Examples:

I will grab **a** taxi and I'll be there in half an hour.

Do you know where I can get **a** taxi?

Exception 1: When referring to a taxi that is or had been under hire then **the** would be used.

Examples:

Hurry up, **the** taxi is here. (Currently under hire).

I'm sorry I'm late, **the** cab got stuck in **traffic**. (Previously hired)

Exception 2: The places where taxis stand waiting for customers are known as taxi **ranks** (UK) or **stands** (US) and are prefaced with the and specified with a prepositional phrase.

Examples: You can get a taxi at **the** taxi rank on Mitchell Street.

Exception 3: If you are enquiring as to the existence or the whereabouts of a taxi rank then use **a**.

Example: Is there **a** taxi rank near here?

Notes and examples

PRIVATE TRANSPORT

Being privately owned, private transport is often specified with a **possessive determiner** rather than **the**.

Examples: <u>My</u> personal vehicles include a Ferrari and a Harley.

Exception 1: If a communally owned vehicle is being discussed, or if the vehicle is specified with a *prepositional phrase* or an *adjective clause*, then it would often be prefaced with **the**. With transportation where the person is in control from inside the machine, that person is known as the **driver** [for example; cars, pickups and trucks); whereas, transportation where the person is in control from outside the machine (for example: bicycles and motorcycles) then that person is known as the **rider**.

Example:

Do you mind if I borrow **the** car, dad? (Communally owned).

Who owns **the** truck *in my drive*? (Specified using a *prepositional phrase*).

Was **the** pickup *involved in the accident* totally destroyed? (Specified with an *adjective clause*).

Was **the** rider of **the** motorcycle hurt? (Previously known: where either the rider or the machine had been previously discussed. Even though only one of the two were mentioned they would both be prefaced with **the**. An example of a previous sentence would be: 'I saw a motorcycle collide with a car today', which directly specified the motorcycle for use in the following sentence and indirectly specified the rider as there needed to be one in order for the motorcycle to operate).

Exception 2: When asking questions about an item of personal transport then **a** or **an** would normally be used.

Example: Have you got **a** bike?

Notes and examples

OTHER TYPES OF TRANSPORT

Other types of transport include hovercraft, skateboards, hydrofoils, horses, buggies, carts, go-carts, Segways, ski-lifts, funicular railways and underground railways etc. They are generally prefaced with **a** or **an** when they are singular or with a <u>null determiner</u> when they are plural. This would apply in both statements and questions.

Examples:

A horse can take a drunk rider home in its own. (Singular | statement)

__ Hovercraft used to be used to cross the channel. (Plural | statement)

Did you ever drive **a** go-cart? (Singular | question)

How many German cities have __ underground railways? (Plural | question)

Exceptions: When discussing the type of transport in an abstract sense, for example when referring to all examples of that type, then **the** would normally be used to specify the type.

Example: The horse drawn buggy largely died out when the internal combustion engine became popular.

Notes and examples

TIMES AND DATES

ASKING FOR THE TIME

The is used to ask for the current time. Note that the word **time** is preceded by **the**, and so would the answer if the word **time** is used, as it is referring to the specific time being asked about. However, if the answer is a simple noun phrase or a simple sentence, then **the** is not used.

Examples:

What is **the** time? (Impolite way of asking for the current time)
or
May I ask you what **the** time is please? (An alternative and polite way of asking for the current time)

The time is now 3 o clock (Giving an answer about the current time using the word time – this is a formal answer).

3 o clock (informal noun phrase answer).

It's about 3 p.m. (Simple sentence answer – this is approximate and informal)

Exception: If the time refers to when a future event is going to take place, then **the** is not used (the question determiners, what or when, would be used instead). However, the name of the event would use **the**, to show that it is specific.

Example: What time does **the** concert start?

Notes and examples

TIME PERIODS

The is used when referring to a period of time because it is specific in that it has a beginning and end. It could refer to an exact (concrete) period as measured (in minutes, hours, days etc.) or an abstract time (as measured against how long a task took relative to how long something else took to do or measured against the current time).

Examples:

The time allowed to complete the exam is three hours (<u>concrete</u> time)

The time I took to do the crossword was slightly less than **the** time it took you to read that book (<u>abstract</u> reference to another time period – note: the second time period is also specific).

Exception: If the word time is purely used as an abstract concept (with no reference to another time or event) then **the** is not used.

Examples:

__ Time is the fourth dimension.

I'll do it when I have __ time. (note: In UK English it is common to preface the time with **the** in this sentence - I'll do it when I have **the** time - as it refers to the specific time that would be allotted to that task. In other words, either use is generally acceptable).

Note: It is common in Asia to use the words '**the time**' in a sentence starting '**It took**' to describe the duration: This is incorrect – do not use ~~the time~~!

Example: It took ~~the time~~ three hours to get here.

Notes and examples

DAYS OF THE WEEK

The is not generally used when referring to a day of the week, particularly when it is used to indicate when an event will take place. The day is either prefaced with **a**, to indicate one of many, or nothing when talking about a particular day that is within the same week as the current day. Note that days of the week are always capitalised.

Examples:

Christmas falls on **a** Monday this year (one of many Mondays).

I will see you <u>on Monday</u> (null determiner as it is a direct reference, using a <u>prepositional phrase</u>, to a particular day this week - in this case it means next Monday).

Exception 1: If the day referred to is not in the same week, then **the** is used to clarify which day is being referred to.

Example:

I will see you on **the** Monday after next (not next Monday but the one after that).

Exception 2: If the day is being used to create a reference or give a name to a particular event, particularly those taking place at regular intervals then use **the.**

Example:

The Sunday before Easter is Palm Sunday.

Notes and examples

MONTHS

The is not generally used when referring to the name of a month, particularly when it is used to indicate when a single or repetitive event will take place. The day is either prefaced with the preposition **in**, to indicate that it is the month that the event is happening in, or **by** when talking about a deadline for some event. When referring to specific dates within the month preface it with **of**, note the use of _on_ to specify the actual numerical date which is specific and prefaced with **the**. The names of months are always capitalised.

Examples:

My birthday is **in** __ November (repeated event).

We hope to get the project finished **by** __ May (singular deadline).

He is arriving _on_ the 9th **of** __ June (date within a month)

Exception 1: If the month is being specified, with or without a year specified, then it is generally referred to using **that**, rather than **the**.

Examples:

I know **that** June is very hot here (every year).

That December, in 1997, was when I met your mother (within a specific year).

That January was cold (referring to a previously mentioned year).

Exception 2: If the month is being used as an _adjective_ or as part of a compound noun then use **the**.

Example:

The _April_ showers are really heavy this year.

Notes and examples

YEARS

The is not generally used when referring to the number of a year. The year is either prefaced with the preposition **in**, to indicate that it is the year that the event is happening, or already happened, in, or **by** when talking about a deadline for some long term event. When referring to specific dates within the year it is usually prefaced with a comma, whereas the month will be prefaced with **in**. Years are normally written as numerical values but are often spelt out in words in formal documents (sometimes followed by the year in numerical form in parentheses).

Examples:

She was born **in** 1983 (single past event).

The new BTS line in Bangkok should be finished **by** 2019 (future).

I will retire **in** October, 2020 (future event in a month within a year).

The law will expire **in** two thousand and seventeen (2017) (formal).

Exception: If the year is being specified by the use of a <u>prepositional phrase</u> (usually in literature or legal documents) than use **the** to preface the word year and not the numerical reference to the year.

Example: He was born <u>in **the** year</u> 1773.

Notes and examples

HEALTH AND HEALTHCARE

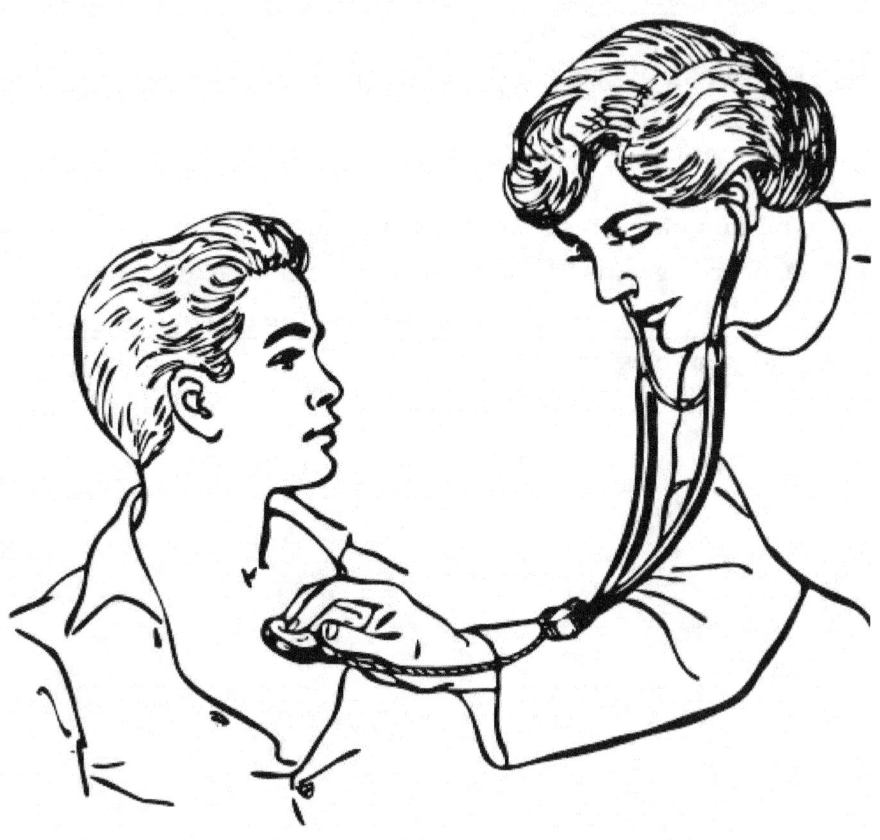

MEDICAL DEVICES

The is generally used only when referring directly to specific items of medical equipment, for example where they are used with a specific patient or are stored in, or available from, a particular place.

Examples:

The measured dosage system in use with <u>Mrs. Jones</u> is working correctly (used with a <u>specific patient</u>).

The defibrillator in <u>the ambulance</u> is faulty (in a <u>particular place</u>).

The endoscope is in *the* 2nd drawer down (available from a specific place - note the use of *the* to indicate that the place is specific).

Exception: When describing the general use of an instrument than **a** or **an** are used.

Examples:

A sphygmomanometer is used to measure blood pressure

An Electrocardiogram (ECG) measures the electrical signals going to the heart.

Notes and examples

MEDICAL SERVICES

Medical services can refer to specific pieces of equipment such as ambulances, specific services such as trauma relief or to specially trained people such as paramedics. They can be available anywhere in the community (front line medical services) or only in hospitals (such as in accident and emergency, A&E, centres). They are primarily for dealing with things like accidents or medical emergencies (such as heart attacks). In common use the service provider would not be specified, except in a general sense, as it is the service that is being provided that is of more importance. Therefore **a** or **an** would be used if it is one of many, or is indistinguishable from others; on the other hand, no word (null determiner) would be used when referring to a place/service in a general way.

Examples:

Have you called **an** ambulance? (One of many available).

He was taken to __ A&E when he crashed his car (general description).

Exception: When referring to a specific piece of equipment (such as the one being used on a specific patient) or a particular person (such as the one that attended to the patient), then **the** would be used.

Examples:

The ambulance, she was in, broke down on the way (equipment).

The paramedic that treated him was very professional (person).

Notes and examples

MEDICAL SPECIALISTS

The is generally used when referring to a medical specialist because there is either only one or they were the one that was consulted on the specific medical matter. You would use **the** either with the special discipline or in a general reference where the specific discipline is not known.

Examples:

His backache was cured by **the** chiropractor in the hospital (Only one of them).

I only visited **the** physiotherapist once (the one consulted).

I went to see **the** specialist today (general reference - the person specialises in my disorder and is specific to me as he/she is the one I saw).

Exception: When referring to a specialist in a generic sense, for example when they are unknown, or where the patient hasn't been seen yet, (use **a** or **an**) or they have been named (usually you'd refer to them by name in this case)

Examples:

He was referred to **a** psychiatrist for assessment (unknown name).

I was told I need to see **an** oncologist (haven't met yet).

I was diagnosed by __Dr. Kelly (named person).

Notes and examples

PARTS OF THE BODY

Parts of the body are usually referred to using a possessive determiner as they belong to a person.

Examples:

The problem is with **your** liver (singular).

My arm is broken (one of two).

His kidneys are not functioning correctly (plural).

Exception: When talking about body parts in an abstract way, for example during medical training or when giving symptoms to other medical specialists, then **the** is used.

Examples:

The heart pumps blood around the body (singular during training).

The lungs take in oxygen to enrich the blood (plural).

The heart is arrhythmic (discussing symptoms).

Notes and examples

MEDICAL COMPLAINTS

Medical complaints are generally referred to using **a** or **an**, primarily because they are referred to in general terms (one of many) even though it is specific to the person suffering from it.

Examples:

I got **a** sprained ankle when I played football.

She said she had **a** head ache and so she couldn't attend the meeting.

He has **a** tumour on his brain (refer to the thing causing the problem).

Exception: When referring to the complaint on subsequent occasions then **the** is used to refer to it, as it is now specific. Note, in the second example a <u>prepositional phrase</u> is used to help to specify it.

Examples:

The tumour is now in remission.

The fracture <u>in his foot</u> has healed sufficiently to take the plaster off.

Notes and examples

DRUGS AND MEDICINE

The is generally used to refer to the specific drugs, or the type or group a drug belongs to, given to or taken by a particular person.

Examples:

The heart drug he was prescribed had some side effects (Type of drug)

The heroin he took killed him. (The specific drug)

Exception 1: When the drug being referred to is not as important as the treatment regime then **a** or **an** are generally used to preface the drug type.

Examples:

He was given **a** beta blocker and sent home (The treatment – the focus of the sentence - was being given a drug).

Have you already taken **an** aspirin? (Asking about prior treatment where a drug was involved – note **any** could have been used if the questioner wanted to know if more than one drug or type of drug was consumed).

Exception 2: When referring to drugs in a general, usually uncountable, sense that is not related to any particular person then a null determiner is generally used.

Examples: __Cannabis has never killed anybody (Cannabis is a general uncountable reference)

Notes and examples

PROSTHETIC DEVICES

A prosthesis is an artificial device that is used to replace a body part, which has been lost because of disease, accidents, congenital conditions or trauma. They are generally referred to in an abstract or generic way; therefore, they would be prefaced with **a** or **an**.

Examples:

He was fitted with **an** <u>artificial leg</u> after losing his to a landmine.

Hegesistratus was the first person to be documented (by Herodotus) to have been fitted with **a** <u>wooden foot</u>, in 450 BC, to replace the one he cut off to escape the Spartans.

Exception: When talking about a specific type of prosthesis or an inherent technology then **the** would be used.

Examples:

The silicon finger felt very realistic.

The Contoured Adducted Trochanteric-controlled Alignment method (CATCAM), invented by John Sabolich, revolutionised lower extremity prosthetic devices. (The method is specified).

Notes and examples

FOOD

COOKING UTENSILS

The is generally used when referring to cooking utensils as they tend to be specific, either to the place they are in (say at home) or the cooking task they are generally or specifically used for. Note the name of the utensil is specified either using an <u>adjective</u>, or a *compound noun*, to describe its use.

Examples:

The <u>frying</u> pan is in the cupboard (place)

The *milk-pan* is used for boiling milk (use).

Exception: If a general task that the utensil as a type (usually as a plural) can perform is being described then use a null determiner (no word). If a specific task that the utensil as a type is/was actually being used for is being described then use **a** or **an**.

Examples:

__ Frying pans are used to fry food (used with plural generic noun).

I used **a** Wok to create the stir-fry (one of a general type).

Notes and examples

MEALS

The is not generally used when referring to meals.

Examples:

Have you eaten ~~the~~ lunch?

We are having ~~the~~ dinner together tonight.

Exception: If the meal is a special event *or* is otherwise specified in some way then **the** would be used.

Examples:

The anniversary dinner took place in a hotel (it was a special event).

I ate **the** packed lunch I made (it is specific as I made it - note, it is specified with the adjective clause 'I made').

Notes and examples

MENU ITEMS

Menu items refer to an aggregation of connected choices; they can apply to selections of food on offer in a restaurant or a group of selectable items on, say, a computer program. They would generally be referred to using **the** as they represent a specific choice of the many of that type on offer.

Examples:

Choose **the** soup of the day as it is delicious (specific recommendation).

I will have **the** soup of the day please (specific choice).

Exception 1:n If there is only one item of that type on offer you can use **the**. With a number of items on offer, using **the** implies that the person is choosing an item from the menu (possibly with a finger pointed to it) and without **the**, it implies that the person may be choosing from a chalkboard or possible even taking a chance that they serve their choice here.

Examples:

I will have **the** special please (Only dish on offer).

I will have **the** duck please (Indicated choice from a menu)

I will have __ duck please (asking for something not overtly on offer)

Exception 2: When making a choice using a computer program the decision of whether or not to use **the** depends on whether the item is represented by a choice from a pull down menu with no specifying noun (do not use **the**) or a button or checkbox, with a specifying noun (use **the**).

Examples:

To save click on __file then __save (pull down menu with no specifying noun note __file is the selection, **the** file is the selected object).

Click on **the** save <u>button</u> on the toolbar (button using a <u>specifying noun</u>).

Exception 3: When referring to an item that can't be pronounced then use an indicative pronoun when pointing to an item or by number if the menu is numbered (note, the word **number** is used in this case).

Examples:

I'll have **this** please (indicative)
I'll have **number 6** please (numerical)

FOOD IN GENERAL

Food is generally regarded as uncountable and generic, so it wouldn't normally use **the**.

Examples:

I love eating __ lamb chops

Do you like __ Thai food?

Exception 1: If you are talking about specific food or the food eaten during a particular meal, then **the** would be used, unless you are not focusing on the specific food but are merely describing your choice (one of many on offer), in which case use **a** or **an**.

Examples:

What was **the** steak like? (The specific type of food that was eaten)

I'll order **the** hot-pot (the one that is specific to this restaurant).

The pasta I had at **the** Italian restaurant last night was awful (The specific food eaten at the specified place).

I would like **a** hamburger (one of many on offer).

Exception 2: When discussing a particular type of food offered by a particular place then **the** is used, even if the noun is plural. Note that, in the 1st example below, the name of the restaurant is not specific, in this case because it is part of a chain, but in the 2nd example it is because an emphasis was placed on the place as being unique.

Examples:

I don't like **the** hamburgers at Chester's Grill (one of a chain).

I like **the** salmon sandwiches they serve at **the** Savoy (unique place)

Notes and examples

FOOD INGREDIENTS

Food ingredients are generally regarded as uncountable and generic when you are choosing, sourcing or buying them, so it wouldn't normally use **the**. As they are uncountable they are usually quantified by using a measure such as; a cup of (250 millilitres ≈ 8.80 fluid ounces – used for liquids or powders) something, a teaspoon of (5 ml or 1/16 fluid ounce) *or* a tablespoon of (0.5 fluid ounce ≈ 14.8 ml).

Examples: Ingredients and/or measures are <u>underlined</u>.

__ <u>Shrimp paste</u> is used a lot in Thai curries (general nonspecific reference).

You need to add <u>a teaspoon of baking soda</u> to the mixture (amount of the ingredient to be added).

Exception 1: When describing how to make something (in a recipe for example) then **the** would be used to refer to an ingredient because both the item and the amount have already been specified in the ingredients list.

Example: …Next you add **the** milk while constantly stirring the mixture.

Exception 2: In US English a specific part of a food may be prefaced with **the**, to draw attention to it, particular if it isn't to be included as an ingredient; however, in UK English **no** tends to be used instead.

Examples:

A hotdog please and hold **the** mustard (don't add mustard - US).
A hotdog please with **no** mustard (UK)

Notes and examples

STAPLE FOODS

Staple foods are the most commonly found foods found around the world and are crucial to human survival as they are used to feed so many people. Despite the fact that they are crucial they are not prefaced with **the** as they are uncountable and would use the compound determiner, <u>a lot of</u>, to talk about them in general terms. Their attributes may be preceded by **a** or **an** if you are referring to one particular attribute or **the** if you are referring to a specific attribute that you would like to highlight (by, for instance, using a *superlative*).

Examples:

Maize (corn) is **the** *most* common staple food in the world (A single specific [and superlative] attribute).

<u>A lot of</u> rice is eaten in Asia as it is **a** staple food there. (One attribute of many that applies to a substantial proportion).

Exception: If the name of the staple food is being used as an *adjective* then use **the**.

Examples:

The <u>*potato*</u> crop failed this year (<u>*adjective*</u>).

Notes and examples

SPICES

Spices are uncountable, although the seeds or plant parts they are derived from (such as peppercorns) could be counted, and so they would normally be prefaced with a **quantifying determiner**, such as **a** or **an** (or **one**) for a single measure or a **number** for multiple measures, and be used as part of a _prepositional phrase_.

Example: Adding **a** pinch _**of salt**_ usually makes the stew taste better. (The spice, _**salt**_, is part of the _prepositional phrase_. Prepositional phrases prefaced with **of** are generally used to quantify uncountable objects; for example, **a** ton **of** potatoes, **a** cup **of** milk or **two** teaspoons **of** sugar).

Exception: When the speaker wants to draw the listener's attention to a particular spice then they would preface it with **the**.

Example: The pepper in this omelette is making me sneeze.

Notes and examples

HERBS

Herbs used in the kitchen are generally regarded as uncountable and so they would normally be prefaced with a <u>null determiner</u>. Note, in the US the word is pronounced with a silent 'h' – as in 'erbs', in the UK it is pronounced with the 'h' – 'herbs'. A <u>null determiner </u>would also be used when discussing the cultivation of **a** herb ('**an** herb' in the US) or the general usage of a particular herb.

Examples:

You need to add __ oregano to this dish.

__ Cress is very easy to grow and is often grown by young children. (Discussing cultivation).

__ Parsley is commonly used to accompany white fish meals. (Discussing the usage of a herb).

Exception: When referring to herbs being grown then it is common to preface them with **the** and specify them with a prepositional phrase or an adjective clause to say where they are being grown.

Examples:

The thyme <u>in my garden</u> seems to have died. (Specified with a prepositional phrase).

The rosemary <u>that she planted</u> is doing very well. (Specified with an <u>adjective clause</u>).

Notes and examples

FAST FOOD

What we term 'Fast Food' refers to two different types: processed food, which is food that is pre-cooked and packaged in such as a way as to easy to prepare, using such things as a microwave oven, and take away food, where a limited number of menu items are pre-processed so they can be prepared and presented quickly in order for the client to eat them on the premises (using the deliberately uncomfortable furniture - so you don't stay too long), outside in the street or at home. Fast food is generally preceded by **a** or **an** and described using either the overall type of food or the vendor, despite the fact that it could be any combination of individual dishes from their menu. Note, in the UK it is called takeaway (Do you fancy a takeaway?) and a take out in the US (I didn't want to cook so I had a take out).

Examples:

Do you fancy **a** pizza? (Any type of pizza).

I won't cook tonight I will grab **a** *McDonalds* on the way home (name of the vendor - note, the dish isn't specified).

Exception: When describing the attributes of a consumed meal **the** is commonly used together with an adverb or a prepositional phrase to say when it was consumed. If a particular dish is being described it would also be preceded by **the**, with or without the adverb/preposition.

Examples:

The Indian I had *yesterday* gave me stomach ache (using an *adverb* - note it is common to say where the food came from if it is ethnic food, rather than what dishes it consisted of, so in this case it was Indian cuisine).

The Chinese *from that new takeaway* was great (using a *prepositional phrase* - note the shop selling takeaway food is also called a takeaway).

I thought **the** Pad Thai tasted a bit stale to be honest (particular dish - in this case a Thai noodle dish - with no time adverb/preposition as the focus was on the food itself with the time being known already).

Exception 2: If the meal was the last one consumed it would normally be preceded by **that** or **this** if it is still being consumed.

Examples:

That KFC tasted greasy (last meal consumed).

This Thai food is really spicy (meal being currently consumed).

EDUCATION AND LEARNING

GENERAL EDUCATIONAL NOUNS

The is commonly used when referring to nouns used in general education, the main reason being that students need to be guided towards the specific thing, out of many similar things, that is being used or referred to.

Examples:

The teacher gave us homework to do. (Refers to person)

She is one of **the** teachers. (Refers to a group of people)

If look at **the** whiteboard you will see an example. (Refers to a thing)

You need to answer all **the** questions in the exam. (Refers to a group of things)

Exception: When referring to general items or people that are not specific, open to all or an unknown one of many then **a** or **an** are used instead.

Examples:

He was given **an** award for outstanding work. (General item).

A class survey is being undertaken. (Open to all)

The class started without **a** teacher. (Unknown person of a type)

Notes and examples

WITH NOUNS USED IN STUDY

Nouns that are used to refer to studying are generally abstract and would not be preceded by the. They can be preceded by a possessive determiner, if it is associated with a specific person, or an indefinite article, if it refers to a general thing that is not being specified, usually because it isn't relevant or noteworthy.

Examples:

His studies included *an* oriental language. (Possessive determiner - note, it is one of many oriental languages so it uses an indefinite article if it was specified then it would use a null determiner, His studies included __ Japanese. If the noun 'language' was used, for instance, to clarify that he wasn't studying something else like Japanese culture, then **the** would be used, His studies included **the** Japanese language).

I can't come with you for coffee as I have **a** class at 1 p.m. (Indefinite article).

Exception: When referring to a specific thing, usually because it is different, special or noteworthy in some way, then **the** would be used.

Examples:

The heating went off during **the** lesson. (the lesson was special as the heating had gone off).

The examination was hard. (The exam I just took - note, if the speaker suspects that the listener doesn't know which exam they were talking about then they'd use an *adjective* [The *maths* examination was hard] or an *adjective clause* [The examination *that I just took* was hard] to specify it).

Have you all completed **the** exercise? (The one I just gave you to do).

Notes and examples

ACADEMIC SUBJECTS

Academic subjects are not prefaced by **the.**

Examples:

I love ~~the~~ mathematics.

~~The~~ Science is my favourite subject.

Exception: Where something specific is being referred to in the context of the subject (in adjective form) or they form part of a compound noun then **the** may be used.

Examples:

The mathematics exam was difficult (subject name used as an adjective).

The science project is due in today (subject name forming part of a compound noun).

Notes and examples

RESEARCH AND STUDIES

The is generally used after the research project has already finished, it has reached a significant milestone or where a discovery was made that was either unrelated to the field being investigated or is contrary to expectations. **The** would also be used when referring to the person that undertook the research.

Example:

The Festinger and Carlsmith (1959) study found that people became more interested in boring tasks if they were paid less. (Named researchers).

The study on the effects of Viagra unexpectedly found it could help with erectile dysfunction. (Unexpected results).

Exception 1: When reporting on the results of a particular piece of research, news outlets use **a** or **an** before the word 'study' or no determiner before the word 'research' in order to place the emphasis on the conclusion. The research or study group would then be named in the following sentence prefaced with **'the'** in order to emphasise that it is the same piece of research.

Examples:

A study has found that viewers are more accepting of advertising on streamed services. **The** study by Telaria found that …

Research has shown that coffee helps your heart. **The** research by…

Exception 2: If the study is unnamed or not cited then it would be prefaced with **a** or **an.**

Example: A study, by an Oxford Scientist, has found that diesel exhaust particles, PM2.5 and PM10, appear to cause lung cancer.

Exception 3: If the author or researcher is referring to their own work they would either used the indicative determiner **'this'** (when referring to it using the passive voice) or the possessive determiner **'my'** (when using the active voice).

Examples:

That positive behavioural reinforcement is not as effective as expected has been proved by **this** research (passive).

My research proves that chewing gum makes you look stupid (active).

BOOKS

The is used to preface the book's name when discussing a particular book. Note that the definite article refers to the book's title and not the subject matter. **The** would also be used when the author's name is linked to the book using 'by', in this case the book title may or may not be mentioned, depending on whether the listener/reader is expected to know which book is being referred to. If the author is not mentioned then **this** or **that** would be used to refer to the book (see the 3ʳᵈ example below).

Examples:

The <u>Verb Types and Tenses</u> book explains how to use modal verbs giving copious examples. (<u>Book title</u>).

The <u>book</u> *by Kevin Kirk* got excellent Amazon reviews [hint-hint!]. (<u>Previously mentioned book</u> using a *prepositional phrase* to specify the author).

That book taught me how to use the passive voice correctly. (No author mentioned with direct reference to previously mentioned book).

Exception 1: When discussing the subject matter, rather than the specific name of a book, or series of books, then use **a** or **an**.

Example: You should read **a** <u>verb tense</u> book if you want to really understand the subject. (<u>Subject matter</u>).

Exception 2: When referring to the book using the author's name then use either a possessive noun, to link the book directly to the author, or a possessive determiner if the author has been referred to already. Note, if the author is known for only one book then the book's subject matter or title wouldn't normally be mentioned.

Examples:

Kevin Kirk's book on determiners allows you to see exactly how articles are used. (**Possessive [compound] Noun.**)

His adverb book groups adverbs in terms of their function. (**Previously mentioned author.**)

Plato's book has shaped politics for a millennia. (**Author** is known mainly for one book).

THEORIES AND THESES

Theses and theories are generally the work of one person or are associated with one person therefore they'd either be prefaced with a possessive determiner or a possessive noun.

Examples:

My thesis was about English language learning methods. (**Possessive determiner**).

Kevin's theory is about alternative ways to learn English (**Possessive noun**).

Exception: When talking about theses in the 3rd person/passive voice **the** is generally used.

Examples:

The dissertation by Kevin needs some changes. (Third person).

The thesis <u>was written</u> by someone other than the candidate. (<u>Passive voice</u>).

Notes and examples

WORKSHEETS AND HANDOUTS

Worksheets and hand outs are generally related to a specific class or lesson and so they would normally be prefaced **the**. This applies even when referring to plural numbers of worksheets/handouts.

Examples:

I can't attend the class today, can you get me a copy **the** handout if there is one? (Single).

The worksheets in the class today were quite complicated. (Plural).

Exception: When referring to worksheets or handouts across a whole course of study then a <u>null determiner</u> would be used.

Example: __Worksheets for each class will be available for downloading on the website after each class.

Notes and examples

DEMONSTRATIONS

Demonstrations are generally very specific as they apply to a particular method or the observable performance of an experiment (with a known outcome) and so they would generally be prefaced with **the**. Note, demonstrations can also refer to street protests against some measure and they would also be prefaced with **the**.

Examples:

The demonstration of Boyle's law went wrong when the tank sprang a leak. (Academic demonstration).

The <u>science demonstration</u> will take place at 4 p.m. (<u>Compound noun</u>)

The demonstration took place outside the White House. (Political demonstration).

Exception: When referring to demonstrations in general, they would normally be prefaced with a <u>null determiner</u> or *any*. *All* may be used to refer to every demonstration associated with a course.

Examples:

Are there *any* political demonstrations planned for this weekend?

___ Dangerous demonstrations must take place under safe conditions.

All demonstrations will be carried out by qualified staff.

Notes and examples

WORKSHOPS

The difference between a workshop and a demonstration is that a workshop will involve both the demonstrator/teacher and the audience/students who will act out pre-prepared actions. Another difference is that workshops tend not to be as specific as a demonstration and so they tend to be prefaced with **a** or **an**.

Example: A dance workshop will follow the class.

Exception: When referring to a particular workshop, particularly one that has already been undertaken, then it is often prefaced with **the**.

Example: The workshop that followed the drama class last week was very interesting.

Notes and examples

ACADEMIC CLASSES

Classes tend to be very specific with an adjective or a prepositional phrase used to specify them, so they'd generally be prefaced with **the**.

Examples:

The *science* class started late as the teacher was stuck in traffic. (Specified with an *adjective*)

The class <u>in the science building</u> was sparsely attended. (Specified with a <u>prepositional phrase</u>).

Exception 1: When discussing classes in general then a <u>null determiner</u> would be used.

Example: __Classes will take place in temporary classrooms while the main classrooms are being refurbished.

Exception 2: When asking questions about classes then **a** or **an** can be used to ask about a specific class or **any** can be used for classes in general.

Examples:

Is there **a** science class this afternoon? (Specific class.)

Are there **any** classes taking place over the weekend? (Classes in general).

Notes and examples

TUTORIALS

Tutorials generally take the form of a specialist teacher/lecturer talking to a small group of students. They are not generally treated as specific so they would be prefaced with **a** or **an** for singular tutorials or **any** with plurals. **Some** can be used when the availability is vague or unknown.

Examples:

I have **a** tutorial sometime this week. (General reference).

I had **an** <u>academic writing</u> tutorial with my English teacher today. (With a specifying <u>adjective chain</u>).

Did you have **a** tutorial today? (Singular question).

Will there be **any** tutorials while Dr. Reid is in hospital? (Question related to multiple tutorials).

I don't have **any** tutorials this semester. (Negative reference).

I think this subject has **some** tutorials but I'm not sure (Vague reference to an unknown number or possibility).

Exception: When talking about past tutorials or when the tutorial has been specified with a prepositional phrase or an adjective - in order to create an association in someone's mind - then **the** would be used.

Examples:

The tutorial <u>on academic ethics</u> was thought provoking (Specified with a <u>prepositional phrase</u> in order to associate it with thinking).

The <u>law</u> tutorial took place in the *dean's* office (Specified with an <u>adjective</u> to describe the type and a *possessive noun* inside a prepositional phrase in order to associate it with a place).

Was **the** tutorial interesting? (Past tutorial).

Notes and examples

LECTURES

Lectures tend to be very specific and so they'd generally be prefaced with **the**. They are usually specified using an *adjective, adverb* or a prepositional phrase, any of which can be used with either singular or plural lecture references.

Examples:

The *biological science* lecture was interesting. (Singular with *adjectives*).

The lecture *today* was cancelled. (Singular with *adverb*).

The lectures on US history only went back 200 years. (Plural with prepositional phrase).

Exception 1: Immediately prior to or following a particular lecture an **indicative determiner** is usually used. Note, it is not specified by using an adjective or a prepositional phrase due to its immediacy.

Examples:

This lecture is about dating fossils. (Prior to).

That lecture was boring. (Following).

Exception 2: When discussing lectures in questions then **a** or **an** (for singulars) or **any** (for plurals) would be used. Note an *adjective* or prepositional phrase could be used to differentiate it from other lectures.

Examples:

Is there **an** *English essay writing* lecture this afternoon? (Compound adjective).

Was there **a** lecture *on organic chemistry* yesterday? (Prepositional phrase)

Are there **any** lectures *in this course*? (Prepositional phrase referring to a known course).

Exception 3: When discussing lectures in general (usually plurals) then a null determiner would generally be used.

Example: Attendance at ___ lectures is compulsory.

Notes and examples

LECTURE NOTES AND RECORDINGS

Materials associated with lectures are generally regarded as specific as they are related to a particular lecture, course or subject.

Examples:

Can you record **the** lecture for me today as I have to go to the dentist?

Can I have copy of **the** lecture notes for my friend?

The lecture notes *for this course* are available online. (Specified using a *prepositional phrase*). [1*] - See note below

Exception: When referring to recordings or lecture notes in general, for example across all courses, then a <u>null determiner</u> would be used. [1*] Note the use of the prepositional phrase in the 2nd example.

Examples:

Permission from the lecturer must be obtained before ___ recordings are made.

___ Lecture notes *for all courses* are available online. ([1*] Note this sentence refers to lecture notes for all courses: whereas, **the** is used when referring to notes that are specific to one particular course).

Notes and examples

POWER POINT PRESENTATIONS

There are two components to a PowerPoint presentation - the individual slides and the overall presentation, consisting of the complete collection of related slides. They are usually specific to a particular presentation or lecture and so they'd generally be prefaced with **the**. Note that the PowerPoint presentation as a whole is generally referred to as **the presentation** and an individual slide would be referred to as **the slide** or **the screen.**

Examples:

The presentation was very professionally made. (Referring to the overall presentation that the listener/reader saw).

If you **refer** to **the** screen you will see how the two methods compare in terms of their measured outcomes. (Referring to a slide by its presentation on the screen).

I changed **the** third slide in **the** presentation as there was a spelling mistake. (Referring to an individual slide in a presentation).

The previous slide showed the test subject scores before the class and **the** following slide will show the outcome. (Referring to relative slides in a presentation).

The next few slides will introduce you to the concepts inherent in the research. (Referring to a relative group of slides).

Exception 1: Whilst giving a presentation the current slide would generally be referred to using an indicative determiner, **this** or **that.**

Example: This slide shows you how the system components connect together. (Refer to currently shown slide - note the noun 'slide' could be omitted and the indicative determiner would then become an indicative pronoun - **This** shows you how…).

Exemption 2: When referring to a presentation in general, such as before it is given, then **a** or **an** would be used.

Examples:

I will be giving **a** presentation this afternoon. (Referring to an unseen and unspecified presentation.)

I removed **a** slide from the presentation as it wasn't needed. (Referring to an unimportant slide that didn't need to be specified).

SPEECHES

Speeches are specific, they generally have a defined theme and are given by specific people or people occupying a specific office. Therefore, they are usually prefaced with **the**.

Examples:

The speech *on string theory* was fascinating. (Singular – made specific using a *prepositional phrase*).

The speech *we attended* was very long (specified with an *adjective clause*).

The speeches will be followed by a Q and A session. (Plural – made specific by being previously known or discussed).

Exceptions: When the focus is not on the speech but instead on the speaker, the event or the type of speech - without naming the presenter - then **a** or **an** would be used. If plural generic speeches are being discussed then a <u>null determiner</u> would be used.

Examples:

After lunch <u>the president</u> will give **a** speech. (With the focus on the <u>presenter</u>).

An <u>*after dinner*</u> speech is customary in state banquets. (Particular event – note the <u>*compound adjective*</u> denoting the type of speech, which tells you when the speech is likely to occur).

The conference will be opened with **a** *keynote* speech. (A particular type of speech represented by an *adjective*).

___Speeches are routinely made in the UN. (Generic plural speeches).

Notes and examples

TALKS

The main difference between a speech and a talk is that a speech would normally be a lot more formal and would generally be about a particular topic. An academic talk* on the other hand tends to be a lot less formal, usually involving a small group and may be interrupted by the listener or the topic may change as the talk progresses. In the context of lectures, a speech is a very formal type of lecture, often involving a lectern and a formal setting; whereas, a talk is informal and may take place in an informal setting like an office or a cafeteria. Given the informality, talks are generally prefaced with **a** or **an** even if they have been specified using a prepositional phrase.

Example: Professor Smith is giving **a** talk <u>on insects</u> this afternoon. (An informal lecture with a topic loosely specified with a <u>prepositional phrase</u> – i.e. the specific aspects of the insects is not known at this time).

Exception: After the talk has happened it is generally referred to in more specific terms, as the topic is now known. Therefore, **the** would be used.

Example: The talk <u>by Professor Smith</u> was fascinating. (Note the <u>prepositional phrase</u> that is used to specify who led the talk).

---

*Political talks are different as they are more formal and would involve key political/diplomatic actors from two or more sides trying to resolve an issue, usually behind closed doors. You can usually tell the difference as an academic talk is singular (talk); whereas, diplomatic talks are plural (talk<u>s</u>) When referring to talks in progress or that have already finished **the** is generally used; however, if they haven't started yet then a null determiner would be used.

Examples:

The talks between North Korea and the USA were very fruitful (already finished).

The talks on the subject of Burmese citizenship for the Rohingya are still continuing (in progress).

__Talks between the two countries are scheduled to take place in September (not yet happened).

CONFERENCES

Conferences describe meetings between people to 'confer' (current meaning: discuss - from the Latin 'conferre' meaning to deliberate, compare or consult). These range from large scale well organised meetings of people involved in a particular industry or with a common interest, through academic conferences, where academics present results and undertake workshops etc. to press conferences which are called to present current progress in a particular matter where reporters can ask questions. Conferences are usually regarded as one of many and would be preceded by **a** or **an**.

Examples:

I'm sorry he is not in the office, he is at **a** conference this week. (Note, if the conference is in the local office and would likely to be available shortly you would say 'he is **in** conference').

I am having **a** conference call with our Beijing office this afternoon (A multi user call is called a conference call).

The police are calling **a** press conference this afternoon to announce the progress in the murder investigation.

Exception 1: When discussing one specific conference, usually specified using an adjective or a prepositional phrase, it would be prefaced with **the**.

Examples:

Are you going to **the** *Electronics* conference? (Specified with an *adjective*)

I would like you to attend **the** conference *in Kabul* next week (specified with a *prepositional phrase*).

Notes and examples

GUIDEBOOKS AND INSTRUCTIONS

Guidebooks and instructions are generally printed (or digital) material that are used to provide information on how to do something (instructions) or to provide general information (guides). The main difference between them is that guides are not intended to be followed in a step by step fashion; whereas, instructions are as they refer to tasks undertaken in chronological order in order to achieve a desired result. Guidebooks are generally preceded by **a** or **an** (as they are regarded as one of many available on that topic) and instructions are generally preceded by **the** as they are specific to a particular procedure. Another difference is that a guidebook/guidebooks can be referred to as a singular (prefaced with a or an) or a plural (prefaced with a null determiner); whereas, instructions are always plural but may be referred to as **a set of** instructions, also known as a programme (program in US English) when referring to instructions that may deviate from chronological order depending on the circumstances. Instructions are generally shorter than guidebooks.

Examples:

Is there **a** guidebook *for this town*? (Specified with a *prepositional phrase*).

I bought **a** guidebook so we don't get lost (Unspecified with the assumption that the listener knows what the guidebook's subject matter is).

I followed **the** instructions but it still didn't work.

A computer program is created from **a set of** instructions that determine how it should work.

Exception: When referring to instructions that may not exist then a null determiner would be used. If they definitely don't exist then it would be prefaced with **no**.

Examples:

Does the machine come with __instructions? (Referring to instructions that may not exist).

There were **no** instructions in the box. (Indicating that the instructions definitely do not exist).

SEMINARS AND WEBINARS

Seminars are a form of academic instruction, by a university or a commercial or professional organization. They generally bring together small groups for either singular or recurring meetings, usually on a particular subject, where the attendees are expected to actively participate. The lead instructor or presenter will present the subject and lead the discussions using a combination of visual materials and demonstrations and may include interactive equipment for more practical subjects. Seminars are delivered in person to other people in the room; whereas, webinars take place over the Internet and require no physical proximity. Although they are on specific topics they are usually prefaced using **a** or **an**, even if they are specified further with a <u>prepositional phrase</u>.

Examples:

There will be **a** webinar <u>on the new AVR microcontroller</u> later today on avrfreaks.com.

A seminar <u>on decoding the human genome</u> will take place in conference room 2 at 7 p.m. today.

Exception 1: If the seminar has already taken place or a webinar is available for viewing (but not participating in) via the Internet then **the** would generally be used.

Examples:

The seminar last night was boring.

The AVR webinar is now available on Youtube.

Exception 2: When referring to seminars or webinars in general they are prefaced with a <u>null determiner</u>.

Example: ___Webinars are an important part of the high tech marketing mix.

Notes and examples

SYMPOSIA

A Symposium (plural: symposia) is a formal gathering usually in an academic setting where all, or the majority, of the participants and the audience are experts in their fields. They differ from conferences in that they cover a single topic or subject and are completed in a single day. A symposium is generally viewed as a small scale conference with discussions on the topic, prefaced by experts presenting speeches on their specialist subject. Although they are on single specific topics they are usually prefaced using **a** or **an**, even if they are specified further with a <u>prepositional phrase</u>.

Example: A symposium <u>on ethics in science</u> will take place in the main hall on Friday at 5 p.m.

Exception: When referring to a symposium that has already taken place or takes place at regular interviews (such as annually) then it is generally prefaced with **the**.

Examples:

Sorry, you missed **the** symposium as it took place last night. (Past).

The symposium will take place in San Jose this year. (Regular event).

Exception 2: When referring to a number of symposia then it would be prefaced with a <u>null determiner</u>.

Example: ____Symposia on various aspects of diversity will take place over the semester. (Plural).

Note: The word 'Symposium' comes from the Greek word 'symposion' meaning "a meeting of the educated" or "a drinking party". They originally came about from cronies meeting in small drinking groups to discuss different political viewpoints in classical Athens.

Notes and examples

EDUCATIONAL EQUIPMENT

Educational equipment generally comes in two forms. The first is equipment that is used to demonstrate a technique or perform an experiment and would be used by the teacher. The other type is equipment that is used by students in order to try out experiments for themselves. As they are generally available pieces of equipment that can be used by any teacher and/or group of students they tend to prefaced with **a** or **an**.

Examples:

The teacher used **a** bicycle to demonstrate centrifugal force. (Solely used by the teacher).

We used **a** Bunsen burner to heat the still. (Type in general use).

Exception: When a piece of equipment has been specified then it would be prefaced with **the**.

Examples:

The microscope <u>that we use in the classroom</u> broke when we dropped it on the floor. (Singular piece of equipment, note the use of the <u>adjective clause</u> to specify it).

The new physics kits haven't arrived yet. (Plural pieces of specific equipment).

Notes and examples

EDUCATIONAL ESTABLISHMENTS

The is generally not used to preface the names of educational establishments such as schools, universities or colleges.

Examples:

Kimbolton School

Mahidol University

Coleg Ceredigion (Ceredigion College)

Exception: The would preface the name if they specialise in a particular subject or discipline.

Examples:

The London School of Economics (Specialist University)

The College of Librarianship (Specialist College)

Notes and examples

CERTIFICATES AND DIPLOMAS

Certificates and diplomas are commonly confused and interchanged. A certificate is primarily an official document which states that the information on it is true. It can also mean a document that confirms a pass in an exam or course. Therefore, the word can be used both outside and within the educational system. A diploma is a document given by a college or university to show that you have passed a particular examination or completed a course, so it is only used in academic context. Education certificates are generally issued for short periods of study and diplomas for longer periods of study. As a general rule both certificates and diplomas are prefaced with **a** or **an**.

Examples:

Once you have completed the course you will be given **a** certificate of participation.

I have **a** *25 yard breaststroke swimming* certificate. (Even when specified with an *adjective chain* the word is still prefaced with **a**).

This two year course leads to **a** national diploma. There is also **a** three year course that leads to **a** higher national diploma.

Exception: When discussing a known or previously discussed certificate or diploma then it would be prefaced with **the.**

Example: The certificate I got from the back street college had a spelling mistake.

Notes and examples

MUSIC

ORCHESTRAS AND BANDS

The is usually used to preface the name of an orchestra, an ensemble (group of musicians with similar instruments) or bands named after the leader. If the band is composed of a type of musician, or is known for a type of music, it may also use **the**. Note that ensembles is the generic term referring to collectives of musicians of any size, they are usually referred to by the number of players: One – soloist. Two – duo. Three – trio. Four – quartet. Five – quintet. Six – sextet.

Examples:

The Royal Philharmonic Orchestra (orchestra).

The Tokyo String Quartet (ensemble).

The Count Basie Band (band named after the leader).

The Beatles (A beat band)

The Fat Boys (hip-hop band of self-described types).

Exception: Most popular music bands or single musicians are not prefaced with **the**. However their most striking feature may be preceded by **the**, usually as part of an appositive.

Examples:

José Plácido Domingo, **the** famous tenor (famed tenor singer).

Abba, **the** chart-topping Swedish band.

Notes and examples

MUSICAL INSTRUMENTS

The is generally used to preface musical instruments when making generic references to all instruments of that type.

Examples:

I am learning to play **the** guitar (generic reference applicable to all guitars).

The lute has always been a popular instrument in English music (specific reference to one particular type of musical instrument)

Exception: If you are talking about doing something other than playing it or describing its uses then don't use **the**, use **a** or **an** instead.

Examples:

I am buying **a** saxophone today (One of many on offer)

French folk music often features **an** accordion (with the focus on the origin and type of music rather than the instrument).

Notes and examples

TYPES OF MUSIC

When describing a type of music then it generally not preceded by **the**, because it is regarded as a generic reference. This applies even if it is specified as a particular type.

Examples:

I like __ classical music.

My wife likes __ traditional Karen folk music.

Do you like __ Czech hip hop music?

Exception: If the type of music is used as an adjective or forms part of a compound noun then use **the**. If the music was heard at a particular venue or time and/or its attributes are being discussed **the** is usually used as it refers to specific music.

Examples:

My great grandfather used to go to **the** <u>music</u> hall (compound noun).

The music was found on an old recording (Specific place)

The loud music hurt my ears (Specific attribute)

Notes and examples

CONCERTS AND LIVE SHOWS

The names of live shows and concerts are usually preceded by **the** as long as they are either named or are at a specific time and at a specific place. This applies even if the concert features a named performer.

Examples:

I went to **the** concert on Tuesday at the Royal Albert Hall (the concert that took part at a particular time and in a particular place, specified using prepositional phrases).

We went to **the** Lady Gaga concert last week.

Exceptions: If the reference is to an unspecified concert, for instance if you are referring to when it happened, some attribute(s) of the venue or an event that occurred during the show, then don't use **the**. Use **a** or **an** if you are referring to a particular concert or to an event *or* nothing if it is generic (such as referring to the attributes).

Examples:

I went to **a** concert in Hammersmith Odeon last night (when).

__Concerts should take place in venues with good acoustics (attributes).

I was going to **an** open air concert last night but it rained so it was cancelled (event).

Notes and examples

RECORDINGS AND PLAYBACK

<u>Musical recordings</u> can either be made in a studio or at a live concert and whatever method is used it is prefaced with **a** or **an**. If more than one recording is being discussed a null determiner would be used.

Example: Their first album was **a** studio recording; whereas, their second and third albums were taken from __ live concerts.

Exception: When certain aspects of a recording are being discussed then it would be prefaced with **the**.

Example: The recording is very old so it is not high quality. (The age is the aspect that is being highlighted).

<u>Playback</u> is achieved through a number of methods each of which would be prefaced with a or an.

Examples:

I used to have **a** record player when I was a teenager.

Nowadays most mobile phones have **a** built in MP3 player.

The **<u>playback media</u>** would be prefaced with **a** or **an** for single recordings or a null or numerical determiner for multiple (different) recordings.

Examples:

Many music purists prefer the sound from **a** vinyl record (single recording)

__ MP3 files are compressed to save space in memory but often lack fidelity due to the compressed frequency response (multiple recordings).

Notes and examples

MEDIA

GOOGLE+ FACEBOOK
YOUTUBE COMMUNICATION
POPULAR WORDPRESS WEB
FRIENDS MEDIA GLOB
MOBILE FLICKR SEA
COMMUNITY PEOPLE
INFORMATION CONTENT
KE SHARE
INTERNET MONEY
LINE RADIO NETWO
OCIAL DATA
FACEBOOK YOUTUBE
WEB POPULAR
FRIEN

NAMES OF NEWSPAPERS

The is generally used to preface the name of a newspaper.

Examples:

The New York Times

The Daily Mail

The Guardian

Exception: The is generally not used to preface the name of a magazine, unless it is targeted at a specific sector or viewpoint.

Examples:

Electronics Weekly

Time

The Engineer (targeted at a specific sector, in this case Engineers).

The Economist (aimed at pushing classical and economic liberalism).

Notes and examples

NEWSPAPER HEADLINES

Generally articles are not used in headlines, signs, labels or anywhere where concise English needs to be used. Note that verbs are often omitted in headlines too.

Examples:

Politician in corruption shock
Coffee bad for you says scientist

Exception: If the headline writer wants to draw specific attention, or add emphasis, to something then **the** can be used.

Example: Apple's iPhone 5 is **the** most hated handset (Daily Mail, 7th July 2013) – this would use the pronunciation /ði:/ when spoken out loud.

Notes and examples

BROADCAST SERVICES

The is generally not used to preface the name of broadcast services.

Examples:

CNN

ABC

Fox News

Exception: The is often used when talking about a service that is either provided for or on behalf of a government (although it may exercise editorial freedom away from government control) or is targeted at a specific sector.

Examples:

The BBC (provided on behalf of a government)

The Canadian Broadcasting Corporation (targeted at Canadians)

Notes and examples

TELEVISION

The can be used to preface the word television or the more commonly spoken acronym T.V. (pronounced /**ti.vi**/) when talking about either the device itself or a program that the person viewed on it. The acronym (either as un-punctuated letters (TV) or, more correctly, suffixed with periods (T.V.) should always be capitalised.

Example: Did you see the documentary on **the** TV last night?

Exception 1: In earlier times when televisions were so rare that they would only be present in the main room of the house it was always referred to as **the TV**; however, nowadays televisions (or TV programs streamed via the Internet) are found everywhere so it has changed into a more generic term (with no article). So either method of referring to them is acceptable (with ~~the~~ or without **the**).

Examples:

I watched a really interesting wildlife program on **(the)** TV last night.

Do you watch **much** TV? (Note the use of the indefinite quantifying determiner '**much**' that indicates some amount of something uncountable. This is because it is a generic reference to the actual act of watching it, which cannot be quantified as it is an abstract concept, rather than what was appearing on it).

Exception 2: When making a general reference about the device itself **the** is not used, use **a** or **an** instead as it is referring to one of many.

Example: Do you have **a** TV at home?

Exception 3: When discussing watching the TV as a leisure activity, the amount of time spent viewing is uncountable so in the US they often use **some**; whereas, in the UK they tend to use **the** as it refers to the device rather than the content and the time spent watching it.

Examples:
I think I'll watch **some** TV (US).
I think I'll watch **the** TV (UK).

Notes and examples

WEBSITE NAMES

The is generally not used to preface the name of a website, usually because it doesn't match the website URL (Uniform Resource Locator aka the address), or if it takes someone's name.

Examples:

Core English language learning Books (www.englishbook.shop)
Indgenius technology (indegenius.com - describing the theme)
Breitbart (www.breitbart.com – taking someone's name)

Exception: The is often used when the website provides or promotes a certain philosophy or it is providing an online news service.

Examples:

The American Thinker (americanthinker.com - Conservative philosophy)
The Atlantic (theatlantic.com - Liberal philosophy)
The Huffington Post (huffingtonpost.com - online news service)
The Daily Mash (thedailymash.co.uk - satirical news site)

Notes and examples

INTERNET STREAMING SERVICES

The is generally not used to preface the name of an <u>Internet streaming service</u> (providing an instantly viewable continuous video stream).

Examples:

Is the movie available on <u>Netflix</u> yet? (Providing online movies on demand).

I put my video on Vimeo (providing general videos on demand).

Exception: The may be used when referring to where the service can be found as part of a <u>compound noun</u>; however, it is more common to use either **a** or **an**, when referring to something associated with the site, or **my** to show that you have a personal account onto which you place your own material.

Examples:

I saw a movie on **the** <u>Hulu website</u> (specific compound noun).

I have **an** <u>Amazon account</u> (one of many such accounts).

I put the video on **my** <u>Youtube channel</u> (it is personal and specific to me as I can upload videos to it for others to watch. If you only have one video on the site you would more likely say – I put **my** video on Youtube – with the emphasis on your work rather than the channel).

Notes and examples

MOVIES

The names of movies are usually preceded by **the** as long as they are either named or are at a specific time and at a specific place. The generic US English term 'movies' is used to describe a leisure activity that is usually prefaced with **the** (note, in the UK the word cinema would be used instead of movies and film would be used instead of the singular movie).

Examples:

I saw **the** new James Bond movie (specific movie).

I was bored so I went to **the** movie (Generic leisure activity).

Did you see **the** film on TV last night? (Specific time and place).

Exception: If the general generic term is used to describe the movies themselves (or itself) rather than the action of watching it, then **the** is not used, but **a** or **an** are used to describe a particular movie (at a particular time and or place) or a null determiner is used if referring to the generally descriptive term).

Examples:

I went to see **a** movie at the local cinema last night.

Do you like to watch __movies? (General descriptive term in a question)

Watching __movies is a waste of time (descriptive term in a statement).

Notes and examples

PHENOMENA

A phenomenon (the plural is phenomena) is a term used to talk about something that is interesting or unusual and is generally regarded as something that can be experienced using the senses.

COLOURS (COLORS - US)

Colours are generally used as adjectives; therefore, they wouldn't normally be prefaced with **the**. They would use **a** or **an** when used as an adjective preceding a noun and a null determiner when used as an adjective serving as an abstract noun.

Examples:

He wore a **blue** shirt. (Adjective preceding a noun).
His shirt was **blue**. (Adjective used as the abstract noun object of a linking verb).

Exception: When referring to a specific feature that is specified using its colour, either using an adjective or a noun, then **the** would be used.

Examples:

The *purple* streak in her hair gave her a wild look. (*Adjective*)
I think **the** <u>blue</u> matches your eyes. (<u>Noun</u>).

Notes and examples

SHADES OF LIGHT

Shades of light are generally referred to using <u>adjectives</u> as they refer to the effect of something (<u>dark</u> room, <u>bright</u> screen, <u>gloomy</u> building). They are generally subjective in that they are determined by the speaker/observer and are often used as literary devices in fiction to provide atmosphere, in which case they are commonly prefaced with **the** as they are specific to the storyline in that they are used to set the scene. They tend to be used as sentence subjects (the focus of the scene) or in <u>prepositiona</u>l phrases (mood setters or contrasts).

Examples:

The gloom in the room made it depressing. (Subject).

I could make very little progress <u>in</u> **the** murk. (Mood setter).

She peered out <u>into</u> **the** dark. (In contrast - *peer out* is a phrasal verb).

Exception: When referencing the shade(s) in general terms **the** wouldn't be used as it is being used as a generic reference and refers to everywhere rather than a specific place or a contrast to a specific place.

Example: <u>Darkness</u> settled over the land. (All of the land).

Notes and examples

NATURAL PHENOMENA

Natural phenomena include such things as: aurora borealis, earthquakes, erosion, germination, storms, sunrise, sunset, tides, tornadoes, decomposition, tsunamis and volcanic eruptions. Natural phenomena tend to be very specific when being referred to so they are generally prefaced with **the** in order to highlight the fact that they are known about.

Examples:

Houston was damaged by **the** storm. (Object).

The erosion has endangered the houses on the cliff. (Subject)

Exception: When referring to the *phenomena* in general terms (such as when describing <u>all</u> instances of it) then **the** is not generally used, a null determiner is used instead.

Examples:

__ *Tsunamis* are generally caused by undersea earthquakes. (Most tsunamis).

__ *Volcanic eruptions* happen in places where the Earth's crust is at its weakest. (All volcanic eruptions).

Notes and examples

PHYSICAL PHENOMENA

Physical phenomena include both manmade and naturally occurring dynamic functions such as biological, chemical and physical processes, electromagnetic pulses, light waves, laser beams, microwaves and wireless propagation. *Physical phenomena* are generally referred to in general terms so they are usually not prefaced with **the.**

Examples:

The food is heated using __ *microwaves.* (Object).

__ *Wireless propagation* is a complicated subject to study (Subject).

Exception: When the reason for an effect is required in the sentence then **the** would generally be used.

Examples:

The heat was caused by **the** chemical reaction between the sodium and the water. (Object).

The laser beam burned a hole in a brick. (Subject).

Notes and examples

WEATHER

Weather is commonly described in terms of adjectives (cloudy, sunny, wet and hot) and so the noun they are helping to define is what the article would be applied to; for instance, the word weather is often used (i.e. stormy weather). If the sentence is specific, in that the weather has or had a specific effect or is out of the ordinary, then it would be prefaced with **the**. If a specific type of weather phenomena is being discussed using a noun (rain, heat and clouds) then it would normally be prefaced with **the**.

Examples:

The <u>sunny</u> weather is wonderful. (Prefacing a weather <u>adjective</u> talking about the current weather).

The *rain* we are having is depressing. (Using a weather *noun*).

It is difficult to see in **the** *fog* (Object *noun* – specific weather happening now).

Exception: When making a general reference to a type of weather then **a** or **an** would be used, particularly when it is the subject object; however, this will apply to weather adjectives but not with nouns (general references wouldn't have an article at all – see the 2nd example).

Examples:

It was **a** <u>sunny</u> day. (General adjective based reference).

I walked in __ sunshine. (General reference, so no article is needed).

Notes and examples

ABSTRACT PHENOMENA

An abstraction is theoretical and so it cannot be sensed using the human senses, as it has no form or substance. Examples of abstract concepts include things such as time, infinity, negative numbers, zero and gravity. As they are not tangible they are usually referred to in general terms and so they are not prefaced with **the**, instead they would usually be prefaced with a <u>null determiner</u> or an interrogative determiner when asking questions about it.

Examples:

The concept of __ zero is generally thought to have originated in India. (General reference with a <u>null determiner</u>).

What time is it? (Interrogative determiner used to ask a question)

Exception: When discussing specific instances of phenomena then **the** would be used.

Examples:

The time is 8 o clock exactly. (A specific instance of the phenomena).

The gravity *on the moon* is less than that on Earth. (Phenomena specified using a *prepositional phrase*).

Notes and examples

PARANORMAL PHENOMENA

Paranormal things are phenomena whose existence cannot be explained by normal experience or scientific explanation. These include such things as ghosts, extraterrestrial life, unidentified flying objects and cryptids (mythical creatures). When referring to a specific thing, or some particular aspect of it that makes it interesting, then **the** would be used.

Examples:

Well known mythical creatures include **the** Yeti and **the** Loch Ness Monster. (Specific things).

The ghost in Kimbolton Castle is said to be that of Catherine of Aragon who died there. (Interesting fact appertaining to a specific thing).

Exception 1: They would generally be referred to using **a** or **an** when someone is claiming to have been affected by or has come in contact with one. This is particularly true when the person being told or is telling the story doesn't believe it.

Examples:

She said she was frightened by **a** ghost in her bedroom (affected by).

He said was taken up in **a** flying saucer and probed (have an unwanted intimate contact with).

Exception 2: When referring to them in general a null determiner would be used.

Examples:

In an infinite universe __ extraterrestrial life is very possible.

A lot of people believe in __ evil spirits.

Notes and examples

ACCIDENTS AND DISASTERS

ACCIDENTS

Accidents tend to be very specific to a person, group, vehicle, area, building or plant. **The** would be used to preface the things involved in the accident and/or it would be used to preface a previously described accident as a continuation of a discussion, report or train of thought. Note that people involved in accidents are not generally prefaced with **the** unless it is in the context of the consequence of an accident or as an unknown victim who is of particular interest.

Examples:

The *truck* ran into **the** *car* and crushed it. (The *things involved* in the specific accident are prefaced with **the**).

The accident was caused by excessive speed. (The details of the accident have been described previously as a continuation).

The victim <u>of the accident</u> died last night. (Consequence of the accident with the context and specificity being supplied by a <u>prepositional phrase</u>).

The woman fished out of the canal was described as around 25 years old with blond hair. (Where the victim is a person of interest).

Exception 1: When discussing an accident where the events leading up to it or the context (where, when, how etc.) are more important than the accident itself then **a** or **an** would be used to refer to the people or things involved.

Examples:

A woman was knocked over by **a** bus yesterday. (General reference to a person and the object involved in an accident).

A tree branch fell on to my car. (General reference to **a** thing that caused the accident).

A car ran into **a** truck <u>on the highway</u> *today* **because of brake failure**. (The context is <u>where</u> [using a prepositional phrase], *when* [using an adverb] and <u>how</u> [using a prepositional phrase] it happened)

Exception 2: When the accident is personalised, for example when describing your own or a third person's accident, then a **possessive determiner** would be used.

Examples:

My accident was caused by me being careless. (First person narrative).

Her fall was caused by black ice. (Commenting on a third person).

MANMADE DISASTERS

Man-made disasters are usually very specific; therefore they are generally prefaced with **the**.

Examples:

The Piper Alpha disaster was caused by poor maintenance procedures. (Named disaster).

The sinking was caused by a collision. (Previously known disaster that is being further discussed).

Exception 1: When grouping particular types of disaster, for example to discuss causes, effects or preventions, a *comparative*, **superlative** or *inclusive* determiner would be used.

Examples:

Many airline disasters are caused by faulty pitot tubes. (*Comparative determiner* describing the cause of a type of disaster).

Most disasters could have been prevented with some forethought. (*Superlative determiner* describing preventative measures).

All nuclear disasters have some long term effects on people and the environment. (*Inclusive determiner* describing the effects of a certain type of disaster).

Exception 2: When discussing a disaster that has not or may not happen **a** or **an** are often used.

Example: *The* overcrowded ferry was **a** disaster waiting to happen. (Note the emphasis is on the overcrowded ferry, prefaced with *the*, rather than the potential disaster).

Notes and examples

NATURAL DISASTERS

Natural disasters are caused by nature and these include floods, hurricanes, volcanic eruptions and earthquakes. If the disaster is underway (happening now) or is expected then it would normally be prefaced with **a** or **an**. When discussing disasters in general a <u>null determiner</u> would be used.

Examples:

According to local sources **a** volcanic eruption is taking place in Indonesia. (The disaster is happening now using continuous tense).

An earthquake is expected in California at any time. (Expected disaster with the passive voice).

_____Floods are an annual event in Bangkok. (General reference to recurring disasters using a <u>null determiner</u> and present simple tense).

Exception: It would often be prefaced with **the** when discussing the cause(s) or the effects of a disaster.

Examples:

The tsunami was caused by <u>an</u> undersea earthquake. (Note the cause is prefaced with <u>an</u> as the focus is on the tsunami rather than its cause).

Extensive flooding was caused by **the** tsunami. (The effect - extensive flooding – is not prefaced with **the** when talking of a general effect, flooding everywhere for example. If the effect was focused on a specific thing, such as flooding in a particular area, then it would be prefaced with the – **The** flooding here was caused by **the** tsunami).

Notes and examples

AVERTED DISASTERS

If an accident or a disaster has been avoided or prevented then it would usually be prefaced with **a** or **an** because they don't actually exist and so they can't be specified.

Examples:

A crash was avoided when she violently twisted the wheel. (Avoided accident).
A collision between the two supertankers was averted at the very last minute. (Avoided disaster).

Exception: When taking or awarding credit for avoiding a disaster then **the** would generally be used to describe the disaster.

Example: The pilot stayed at the controls to avoid <u>**the** plane crashing into the town</u>. (The disaster is described using the <u>underlined noun</u> [what could have crashed - the plane] + <u>clause</u> [what could have happened - crashing into the town]).

Notes and examples

SOCIETAL DISASTERS

Societal disasters can be things like economic collapses or invasions. As they are often viewed as very specific individual events they are usually prefaced with **the**.

Examples:

The Great Depression (Economic disaster).

The Fall of Rome (Societal collapse).

The Black Death (Plague).

The Dust Bowl (Agricultural collapse).

Exception 1: When discussing the causes of a specific type of disaster then **a** or **an** would be used.

Example: An economic collapse is mainly caused by a lack of confidence in the economic system.

Exception 2: When discussing disasters overall then a null determiner is generally used.

Examples:

__ Bacterial plagues caused a huge loss of life in the middle ages.

__ Revolutions generally lead to reduced living standards and are usually caused by a loss of confidence in the ruling classes.

Notes and examples

MISCELLANEOUS

LANGUAGES

Null determiners are generally used to preface the names of languages.

Examples:

She can speak __English.

__ Mandarin Chinese is the most commonly spoken language in the world.

Exception: If the adjective version of the language is used (preceding a noun) then **the** can be used.

Examples:

The *Japanese* <u>language</u> is very difficult to learn. (*Japanese* is being used as an adjective, <u>language</u> is the noun).

The *English* class will be postponed this week due to illness.

Notes and examples

EMOTIONS

Emotions are essentially abstract, because they can't be sensed using any on the senses - such as taste, smell, sight or touch - they can only be described or deduced. These include things such as motivation, resourcefulness, love, justice, friendship, fairness, hate, dislikes, happiness, sadness, depression, dreams, arousal, intuition, common sense, understanding, imagination, thoughts, conceptualisation, deductions and axioms. As they are difficult to specify they usually are not prefaced with **the**. When talking about them in general they are prefaced with a <u>null determiner.</u>

Example: __ Love is difficult to describe. (General concept prefaced with a <u>null determiner</u>).

Exception 1: A possessive determiner would be used when they are personal to a particular person.

My intuition tells me that this will go wrong. (Personal emotion expressed using a **possessive determiner**).

Exception 2: The is used to preface an emotion if it is being emphasised using an adjective clause or a prepositional phrase.

Examples:

The hate <u>that I feel for him</u> is boundless. (Emphasized using an adjective clause).

The motivation *of the team* needs improving. (Emphasized using a *prepositional phrase*).

Notes and examples

ART AND ARTWORKS

The production of art is generally regarded in speech as an abstract concept; therefore, it would generally be preceded by a null determiner.

Examples:

My daughter is good at __drawing.

__Pottery is a very common pastime for those that can afford it.

Exception 1: General artworks are usually preceded by a null determiner.

Examples:

__ Paintings are on display throughout the great hall.

__ Statues are common in town centres.

Exception 2: Where a particular person's work is being discussed it would be preceded by a possessive determiner if the artist had previously been discussed or by a possessive noun.

Examples:

Her architecture featured bold styles.

Constable's paintings generally feature English pastoral scenes.

Exception: When a particular artwork or an exhibition of an artists work is being discussed it would be preceded by the.

Examples:

The Mona Lisa is probably the world's most famous painting. (Individual artwork).

The Van Gogh exhibition will take place at **the** National Gallery in June. (Exhibition of an artist's work at a specific place).

Notes and examples

SPORT

The is not generally used when naming sports as they are regarded as generic (referring to that sport as whole) so they would be prefaced with a null determiner.

Example: __ Cricket is played in many countries and so is __ tennis.

Exception 1: When the sport's name is used in the adjective (descriptive) form or as part of a compound noun **the** may be used.

Example: I watched **the** cricket match.

Exception 2: When the sport's name is used in relation to a specified place then **the** would be used.

Example: I watched **the** tennis at Wimbledon.

Notes and examples

CLOTHES

As a general rule, clothes are referred to in a specific way, for example to draw attention to a person's specific clothing in a given situation. Whether they are referred to using the definite article usually depends on whether the clothing is the subject of the sentence, particularly in noun clauses, or a comparative object.

Examples:

<u>**The**</u> <u>skirt she was wearing</u> was considered to be too short for school. (Sentence subject using a <u>noun clause</u>).

This shirt is silk unlike **the** last one. (Sentence Object using <u>noun phrase</u>)

Exception 1: It is more common to refer to items of clothing in terms of personal possessions, using a possessive determiner, or to the merits of a particular item using an indicative determiner, or, when referring to a sentence object (usually about particular features about an item described using an adjective) an indefinite article is used.

Examples:

Her dress was very colourful. (Possessive determiner).

This shirt is too garish for the office. (Indicative).

She is wearing **a** black dress. (Indefinite article that is highlighting the colour of the dress – taking out the 'black' would indicate that she was wearing a dress instead of something else like a skirt or trousers).

He has bought **some** pink socks. (Using **some** to act as an indefinite article for plural/paired items).

Exception 2: When referring to all such items then a null article would be used and the noun would generally be plural. The items can apply in general to all items of that type or be specified using adjectives.

Examples:

__ **Skirts** worn in school should be around knee length. (All skirts - note, it would be more common to use 'school' as an adjective, again with a null determiner - see below).

__ *School* **trousers** should be black. (Specified using an *adjective*)

MATERIALS USED IN CLOTHES

The materials that clothes are made from aren't generally prefaced with **the** as they tend to be referred to in a generic, non-specific, way. The emphasis is on the type of clothing, using a determiner such as 'my' (possessive) or '**that**', (indicative). Note, the <u>object</u> describes the material and is generally prefaced with a null determiner.

Examples:

My Tie is ___ <u>pure Thai silk</u>. (Possessive determiner).

These socks are made from ___ <u>polyester</u> (Indicative determiner).

Exception 1: If the material is described using an <u>adjective</u> then **the** can be used, especially if referring to an article of clothing not being worn at that time. When referring to clothing currently being worn an indicative determiner would be used.

Examples:

The <u>cotton</u> shirt was very cool. (The shirt is not being worn presently; however, it has been worn so the speaker is able to recount the experience of wearing it).

This <u>polyester</u> shirt is very hot. (Shirt currently being worn - note, if the material is not mentioned then a possessive determiner would be used - **My** shirt is very hot).

Exception 2:   If the noun being referred to is generic (it applies to all clothing made out of <u>that material</u>, usually specified using plural nouns) then no determiner is needed.

Example: __ <u>Silk</u> clothes feel nice on the skin.

Notes and examples

HOBBIES AND PASTIMES

The is not used to preface the names of hobbies or pastimes as they are generally proper nouns (names) and they are generally referred to in generic terms.

Examples:

He likes __ train-spotting. (Train-spotting is a generic pastime where enthusiasts stand near railways and take down train and/or rolling stock numbers).

__ Stamp collecting can be done by anybody (Stamp collecting is the compound noun naming the hobby).

Exception: When something is needed or used in order to undertake the hobby or pastime then this medium would normally be prefaced with **the.**

Examples:

Surfing **the** Internet is the most popular hobby (Surfing is the hobby and the Internet is the medium).

Watching **the** television is a pastime commonly undertaken by older people. (Watching is the pastime and television is the medium).

Notes and examples

NATIONALITIES

When describing the race of a person, or group of people, then **the** is not generally used. The main reason is that most of the descriptors are used as adjectives and they tend to be making abstract references

Examples: He is __ Japanese (Nationality preceded by a null determiner).

Exception 1: Where the population of a nation is being spoken about then **the** can be used.

Example: **The** Chinese work very hard.

Exception 2: When the nationality of a person is being supplied in the form of an adjective a or an would be used.

Example: Anna is **a** Polish woman.

Notes and examples

PROCEDURES AND TASKS

The would be used to highlight a specific procedure or way of doing things. **The** would also be used if the person doing the task is identifiably different or specific.

Examples:

The injection was given by **the** nurse (both the procedure and the person doing it were specific).

The test was very hard. (The test we just did).

Note, we could have used **that** instead, for example when talking about a test that was just finished (**That** test was very hard) in order to emphasise the quality of the immediate thing.

Exception: Don't use **the** if the procedure is generic or routine; use a null determiner instead.

Examples:

__ Injections are given by __ nurses.

__ Tests are meant to be hard.

Notes and examples

SOMETHING SPECIAL TO A PLACE

The is used to the name of something that is unique or of special interest.

Example: The Mona Lisa is a famous portrait by Leonardo Da Vinci. (Note: by using the indefinite article **a** in the sentence we are saying that it was one of the famous portraits by the artist; however, if we wanted to say it was his most famous work we'd use <u>the</u> and the superlative <u>most</u>: **The** Mona Lisa is <u>the</u> most famous portrait by Leonardo Da Vinci).

Exception: If you don't know the name or don't consider it to be of interest then use '**a**' or '**an**' or we want to place the emphasis somewhere else in the sentence.

Example: I saw **a** famous painting hanging in **the** Louvre in Paris (the painting was not important but the place where I saw it was).

Notes and examples

WHEN THE PLACE IS KNOWN

The is used to refer to something that either both parties know about or where the speaker/writer has the expectation that the listener or reader would know about it.

Examples:

I will meet you in **the** coffee shop. (The one we both know)

I picked her up at **the** station (the local one, so the assumption is that the listener knows which station; however, if I were to go to another station, out of town say, I'd either use a <u>prepositional phrase</u> to say where that station was - for example: I picked her up at **the** station <u>in Cambridge</u>, using **the**, or I'd use a compound noun - I picked her up at __Cambridge station - using a null determiner and not **the**.

Exception: If the speaker/writer doesn't want to be specific or the location doesn't matter, then use **a** or **an**.

Examples:

We need to find **a** coffee shop as I need some caffeine (any coffee shop).
I visited **a** farmer's market once to buy turnips (unspecified location).

Notes and examples

ASKING FOR LOCATION OR NAME

The is used to refer to something that one party, the one speaking or writing, isn't sure about what is being discussed. In other words the person wants to know exactly where something is or what it is called; or both. This structure is used where something has been referred to previously in the conversation. For example, the conversation prior to the question in the first example below might have gone something like: 'You need to catch a bus'.

Examples:

Where is **the** bus station? (Wanting to know the location).

What is **the** bookshop called? (Wanting to know the name of the thing being referred to in the conversation).

Exception 1: If you are enquiring about a previously mentioned place then you'd use a noun clause to ask about it. Note, in the second sentence of the example, the possessive determiner **its** would be used.

Example: Where is <u>that restaurant you told me about</u>? Can you remind me of <u>its</u> name again? (Note, if you use an *adjective clause* instead, you can use '**the**' as the adjective clause is specifying the noun - Where is **the** restaurant *that you told me about*?).

Exception 2: If the speaker/writer wants to know something personal, like a person's name, then **the** is not used; a possessive determiner, like **your** or **its**, is used instead.

Example:

May I have **your** name please?

I like your dog; what's **its** name?

Notes and examples

PERSONAL PROPERTY

As you would expect personal items belonging to the speaker would normally be prefaced with a possessive determiner in most instances. This is especially true if the items are being carried by the person.

Examples:

My pen has leaked into my pocket.

She said it was **her** bag.

Exception 1: When questioning the ownership of something then an indicative determiner is normally used.

Is **this** your bag Sir?

Is **that** car yours?

Exception 2: If you are being very specific about an item of property to ensure that there is no doubt then the would be used; usually, in conjunction with a prepositional phrase or an adjective.

Examples:

The mobile phone <u>on the table</u> is mine (Specified with a <u>prepositional phrase</u>).

The *tablet* computer is his. (*Tablet* is used as an adjective - note that in this case 'his' is being used as an indicative pronoun).

The car *<u>than you ran into</u>* is mine (Using an *<u>adjective clause</u>* to specify the possession).

Notes and examples

TRANSPORTATION SERVICES

The is used when talking about a specific transportation service that is undertaken by the thing the <u>noun</u> describes. Note that it refers to a specific service on a specific route, usually by a specific service provider.

Examples: I came on **the** <u>bus</u> (The service was transportation and the noun representing it was the bus on that route).

Exception 1: If the service is represented by one of many such services then don't use **the**, use **a** or **an** instead.

Example: I came here on **an** airline.

Exception 2: If the service is represented in general terms (such as by the type of transport rather than a particular vehicle on a particular route) then don't use **the**. Either use **a** or **an** (as they represent one of many of that type) or **by** (as it represents the method).

Examples:

I came here on **a** ferry (one of that type).

I came here **by** bus (this was the method I used).

Notes and examples

REFER TO A PUBLIC SERVICE

The is used when talking about a specific service that is provided to serve the community as a whole.

Examples:

He joined **the** army when he left school.

If you don't leave I'll call **the** police.

Exception: If the service is represented by unspecified individual members from within the group providing the service, then don't use **the.** Note that the overall group or its action(s) are specific and use **the,** even if the action(s) may have been undertaken by certain individuals, as the whole group is taking responsibility; whereas, individuals that are described collectively as belonging to a group are not specified and will not, collectively, carry out the task(s) so they use a null (i.e. no word) determiner. Study the following examples:

Examples:

The government creates policies and __ civil servants carry them out. (The government is a specific group and civil servants are unspecified individuals within the civil service group).

The government creates policies and **the** public sector carry them out (**the public sector** is a distinct, specified group).

The government creates laws and **the** police enforce them (in this case the whole of the police group is responsible for carrying out the tasks).

Notes and examples

Website: www.englishbook.shop

WHEN EXPRESSING SURPRISE

The is used in a question form to ask, usually informally, about what had just been said. It wouldn't follow a recognised question form (such as being preceded by a 'wh' question word or using subject/verb inversion), but is still recognisable as a question by a native speaker.

Example: if the preceding sentence asked is something like:

Where is **the** sphygmomanometer? (The only one we have)

The answer might be: **The** what? (What is a sphygmomanometer?)

Exception 1: If the whole sentence has been misunderstood then **the** would not be used, but the pronoun 'that' would be used instead to refer to the whole sentence.

Example: Sorry, could you repeat **that** please? (The whole sentence was misunderstood or misheard).

Exception 2: If something unspecific is being referred to, or there is the possibility that there isn't one at this location, then **the** would not be used - **a** or **an** would be used instead, particularly if the question itself used **a** or **an**.

Example:

Question: Have we got **a** sphygmomanometer? (Unlikely to have one)
Answer: **A** what?

Notes and examples

HOTEL ITEMS

Items used and consumed by guests staying in hotels are generally unspecified as they are just one of many. If referring to an item using a countable noun then **a** or **an**, or a numeric determiner if there are more than one, are used, whereas **any** or **some** are used with uncountable nouns.

Examples:

Can I have **a** clean towel? (Question about countable noun).

There are **three** clean towels in your closet (numeric determiner).

There is **a** bathrobe in the hotel closet (countable noun statement).

There is **some** soap in the bathroom (uncountable noun).

There isn't **any** toilet paper (refer to negative or zero amount of uncountable nouns).

Can you let me have **some** toothpaste? (Question about uncountable noun).

Exception: When referring to a specific item or items, often as part of a complaint, then **the** is generally used (usually with a prepositional phrase) as they are specific to the speaker. This applies to both countable - both singular and plural - and uncountable nouns.

Examples:

The light next to my bed doesn't work (singular countable)

The towels in my room are damp (plural countable noun).

The shampoo is missing from the bathroom (uncountable).

Notes and examples

OTHER DETERMINERS

OTHER DETERMINERS

The following tables contain the important information about all of the commonly used determiners. The definitions used in the tables are as follows.

Determiner: this is the actual determiner, which can be either a single word or a phrase. Note that the articles are not included in the list as they have been covered previously; however, they may appear here if they form part of a determiner phrase.

General Definition: this could be regarded as the overall definition, such as the sort of thing you would find in a dictionary.

Pronunciation: pronunciation is an important component in using a determiner. The symbols used are from the IPA (International Phonetic Alphabet); there is a pronunciation exercise at the start of the book to help you to make the right sounds.

Number of things being referred to: this tells you how many people or things are being indicated or referred to by the determiner. In some cases the number is unquantifiable as it is an abstract reference.

Noun is Countable, Uncountable or Both: this refers to what type of noun the determiner can be used with, if it is both then it means it can be used with either countable or uncountable nouns.

Noun is Concrete, Abstract or Both: this refers to whether the noun describes something concrete, which generally means something you can touch, or abstract, which refers to a concept or feeling.

Specific definitions: In many cases a determiner has more than one meaning or use in which case the use definitions are listed one below the other.

Examples of use: Each meaning has a sample sentence shown next to it showing the determiners in use. The determiners are in **bold** in the sentence so they can be seen easily.

Comments and points of interest: the differences between certain determiners can be very subtle, with two similar looking determiners having entirely different meanings or uses. In this table section the differences are discussed together with any other points of interest in the use or meaning and how the determiner can be used to influence the thinking of the reader.

DETERMINER TABLE KEY

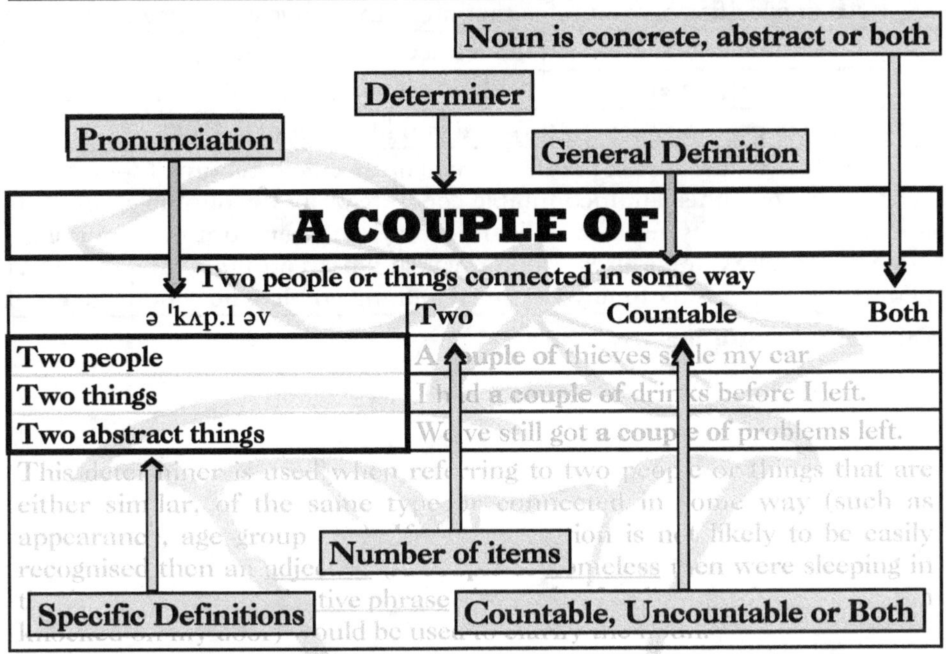

The determiner tables contain the information needed to both use and understand the various determiners. The technical information about the determiner is contained in the cells outlined above and the examples of use and informational notes (together with further examples) are shown in the cells outlined below.

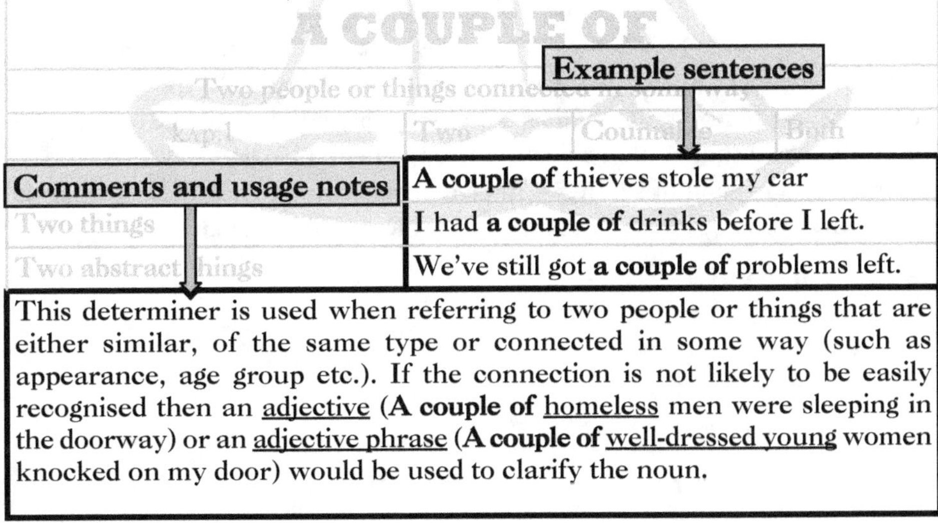

This determiner is used when referring to two people or things that are either similar, of the same type or connected in some way (such as appearance, age group etc.). If the connection is not likely to be easily recognised then an <u>adjective</u> (**A couple of** <u>homeless</u> men were sleeping in the doorway) or an <u>adjective phrase</u> (**A couple of** <u>well-dressed young</u> women knocked on my door) would be used to clarify the noun.

A BIT OF

An unspecified amount of something either physical or abstract			
ə bit əv	Undefined	Uncountable	Both
Unspecified abstract amount	**A bit of** what you fancy does you good.		
Offer a small part (physical)	Would you like **a bit of** cake?		

Use this determiner to seek or offer a small unspecified amount of something represented by either an uncountable concrete or an uncountable abstract noun. It is primarily used to indicate a very small amount of something. Note, the first example uses a noun clause **what you fancy** and is a UK idiom, meaning it is ok to have or do something you like but not to excess.

Notes and examples

A BIT OF A(N)

An abstract reference to something with no known extent			
ə bit əv ə (ən)	Un-quantifiable	Uncountable	Both
Abstract reference	We seem to have **a bit of a** problem		

Whether you use **an** or **a** as the suffix word depends on the first syllable of the following word. This determiner is most often used to refer to an abstract concept (such as a problem or issue) in order to indicate that the extent, and the cause, is unknown (it could be a major problem that could be unsolvable or a minor one that could be easily solved). It can also be used to 'soften' a rejection; so instead of saying "I have a problem with your idea", which is quite harsh, you say "I have **a bit of a** problem with your idea".

Notes and examples

A COUPLE OF

Two people or things connected in some way		
ə ˈkʌp.l əv	Two | Countable | Both	
Two people	A couple of thieves stole my car	
Two things	I had a couple of drinks before I left.	
Two abstract things	We've still got a couple of problems left.	

This determiner is used when referring to two people or things that are either similar, of the same type or connected in some way (such as appearance, age group etc.). If the connection is not likely to be easily recognised then an <u>adjective</u> (**A couple of** <u>homeless</u> men were sleeping in the doorway) or an <u>adjective phrase</u> (**A couple of** <u>well-dressed young</u> women knocked on my door) would be used to clarify the noun.

Notes and examples

A FEW

Refers to a small uncountable number of people or things		
ə fju:	A small number | Both | Both	
Small uncountable number	A few people have reservations about it.	
Small number of parts	A few bits of broken glass are on the floor.	

Using the determiner **few** prefaced with an indefinite article (**a**) is used to draw attention to that we are referring to a smaller group from within a much larger group or a whole, which could, like in the example above, consist of the whole population or thing. It is generally used to minimise the number being referred to, for example to say that most people agree with only a very small number not agreeing (The majority of people agreed; however, **a few** people didn't), if we minimise this sentence then **a few** becomes a noun (Most agreed **a few** didn't).

Notes and examples

A FEW OF

An unspecified amount of something either physical or abstract	
ə fjuː əv	A small number | Countable | Concrete
Small number from a group	A few of us like eating boiled lamb.
Different subgroup	A few of the crowd left early.

The difference between this compound determiner and the previous one is that this one specifically refers to a smaller sub-group within a specific overall group, which needn't, itself, be particularly large, and, unlike the previous determiner, it can be used with pronouns representing the whole group, like in the example above (**us**). In this case the group referred to would have been mentioned previously or is known already. The number referred to could, by implication, represent a significant number as long as it is lower than half the larger group. Note: **a few** can be used as a pronoun, with no following noun; whereas, **a few of** needs a following noun or pronoun (see the example above). It can also preface **the** when highlighting how the named sub group was perceived or behaved in a different way.

Notes and examples

A GOOD DEAL OF

A significant part of	
ə gʊd dɪəl əv	A big part | Uncountable | Normally abstract
A significant part	A good deal of my time is spent fixing problems

This determiner is generally used to say that a significant part of something else is devoted to a particular issue. It differs from the following determiner (a great deal of) in that it generally refers to a smaller amount of something than **a great deal of.** You could also use it as an idiom to state that something is unaccountably larger than expected, for example "It would cost **a good deal of** money for the holiday we liked. So we chose something else." It tends to be used more in UK English than US English. It is often followed by another determiner like **my** or **the** (**A good deal of the** day was spent eating).

Notes and examples

A GREAT DEAL OF

Significant number of people or things connected in some way		
ə greɪt dɪəl əv	A large amount | Uncountable | Both	
A very significant part	It cost **a great deal of** money to buy.	
A long time	**A great deal of** time was spent fixing it.	

This determiner is generally used to imply that the amount referred to, although uncountable, is very significant and may be out of proportion to what was either expected or what it was worth. When used to refer to things like time the implication is that the majority of time is spent on this issue when measured against other tasks. Unlike the previous determiner (A good deal of) it is generally NOT followed by another determiner like **my** or **the** but instead it is followed directly by a noun, noun phrase or noun clause.

Notes and examples

A GREATER NUMBER OF

Refers to a very significant part of a group			
ə greɪtər ˈnʌm.bə əv	A majority	Both	Both
A more significant part of	A greater number of us liked it this time.		

This determiner is generally used with pronouns to state that a much larger number of some people or things took an opposite view/posture to those people or things that had previously been mentioned. So the sentence construction would be: People or things + did or believed something + but + **a greater number of** + <u>pronoun</u> + didn't (A few people shouted but **a greater number of** <u>them</u> stood silently), you could use **the greater number of** if you wanted to place particular emphasis on the latter group. You can you also use it to show popular progression - see the example above.

Notes and examples

A GREATER NUMBER OF THE

A majority of something either physical or abstract		
ə greɪtər ˈnʌm.bə əv ðə	A majority | Countable | Concrete	
Majority from a a group	A few of us like eating boiled lamb.	

This determiner is generally used with a noun to state that a larger group did or believed something in comparison to another group. The definite article, **the**, means that the group is specific, although still uncountable, and so care must be given to ensure that it is recognisable either by using <u>adjective phrases</u> (**A greater number of the** <u>tall, thin</u> people...), a <u>prepositional phrase</u> (**A greater number of the** people <u>at the event</u>...), an <u>adverb</u> (**A greater number of the** people <u>there</u>...) or an adjective clause (**A greater number of the** people <u>who attended</u>...). It would generally be used with the conjunction, <u>than</u>, to refer to the smaller group (**A greater number of the** people invited stayed at home <u>than</u> the ones who attended). Note: the word, **invited**, is a trailing adjective.

Notes and examples

A LACK OF

Zero/no or a very low number of countable or uncountable things	
ə læk əv	Zero or a very low amount | Both | Both
Zero/few countable	There was **a lack of** students in the class today
No/little uncountable	**A lack of** rain killed my lawn.

Comments: This determiner is generally used to imply that something that was either expected or required. It is different from, say, saying **zero** in that it implies more expectation; in other word **a lack of** would imply there were none, or very little, of whatever is needed, but it generally wasn't a problem - however, with **zero** the implication is that the fact that there were none at all has created a problem. It can also be used to say that there may be some of whatever the things are but not enough and they are running out, implying problems later (**A lack of** parts is threatening production).

Notes and examples

A LITTLE

A small value or amount		
ə ˈlɪt.l	Small amount | Uncountable |	Both
A small value	I feel **a little** tired.	
Emphasize small amount	She takes **a little** sugar in her coffee.	

This determiner is generally used to refer to and emphasize a very small amount or the value of something uncountable. It differs from the bare determiner, **little**, in that **a little** emphasizes a very small amount of a defined available group; whereas, **little** is generally used to be used in a more general sense, where the group that the noun refers to is not specified as being part of a larger group. It is generally used with abstract concepts or uncountable things.

Notes and examples

A LITTLE OF

Used to emphasize how small an amount of something specific is		
ə ˈlɪt.l əv	A small number | Both |	Both
A small amount of property	She only drank **a little of** *my* wine.	
A small amount	Only **a little of** *the* food was still edible.	

The difference between this determiner and the previous one, **a little**, is that this one would generally be followed by another determiner such as a possessive determiner (**my, your, her, his, our, their**) or the definite article, **the**, and would imply that it is more specific than **a little**. It is often used with an adverb like **just** or **only** to emphasize the fact that the amount is very small with the possible expectation that there should be more [only], it was not a big burden (see abstract example below) or as an apology [just]. It can be used with both abstract (It only took up **a little of my** time) or concrete ([Just] a **little of the** stew is still left in the pot) nouns. Note, in the previous (concrete) sentence using 'just' implies 'Sorry, there should be more'; whereas, without 'just' it implies that there may be enough.

Notes and examples

A LOT OF

There is enough or a surplus of something			
ə lɒt əv	A significant amount	Both	Both
Many countable things	A lot of the students were absent today.		
Lots of uncountable stuff	A lot of my time is spent waiting.		

Comments: This determiner is generally used to refer to a significant number of uncounted things or people. It can be followed by another determiner such as a possessive determiner (**my, your, her, his, our, their**) to state that a lot of personal possessions are being referred to (**A lot of my** money is in a savings account in the bank) or the definite article, **the**, to state that a large part of a specific group is being referred to (**A lot of the** people *in my office* come in early to miss the traffic) note the *prepositional phrase* being used to specify the main group. It is used in both abstract (He exerted **a lot of** energy on his run today) or concrete (There is **a lot of** litter in the park) objects.

Notes and examples

A MINORITY OF (THE)

Lesser number or percentage of countable or uncountable things			
ə maɪˈnɒr.ɪ.ti əv (ðə)	Small percentage of	Countable	Both
Small percentage of	A minority of voters were still undecided.		
Small number of	A minority of the people in cities own car.		

This determiner is generally used to imply that a small number or percentage of a particular group are taking an opposing stance to most of the rest of the group. It can be used with both plural pronouns (**A minority of** them are in favour) and with both abstract (**A minority of** plans work out well) and concrete nouns (**A minority of** consumers prefer quality products). It can also be suffixed with **the** to highlight a previously mentioned specific (usually specified with a *prepositional phrase*) or known group (**A minority of the** people *in London* live in the city centre).

Notes and examples

A NUMBER OF

An unknown or uncounted number

ə ˈnʌm.bər əv	Unknown quantity | Countable | Both
Unknown quantity	**A number of** my students will fail.
Uncounted quantity	There were **a number of** protesters present.

This determiner is used to indicate that an unknown quantity **will** <u>do</u> or <u>be</u> something (future) or an uncounted quantity <u>did</u> or <u>were</u> (past). It can be followed with possessive determiners (**A number of** *her* dogs escaped) or articles (**A number of** *the* people there didn't drink). It can also be used with plural pronouns (**A number of** us hate it) or abstract (**A number of** ideas come to mind) or concrete nouns (**A number of the** books have been stolen - note, the use of '**the**' which states the stolen books were from a specific group; whereas, without '**the**' it means some unspecified books). It can be used to refer to something that happened too many times (The software used to lay out parts of this book crashed **a number of** times and I lost all my work). Note, the number could be counted but wasn't.

Notes and examples

A PERCENTAGE OF

An unknown or assumed amount

ə pəˈsen.tɪdʒ əv	Amount out of 100 | Both | Concrete
Unknown amount	**A percentage of** them will vote against it.
Assumed amount	**A percentage of** us will be successful.

This is used to indicate a number expressed as a number out of 100. It is commonly used to talk about things like votes or support/opposition for someone/something because it is easy for people to visualise. It can be used with a <u>quantifying adjective</u> (**a** <u>small</u> **percentage of...** *or* **a** <u>huge</u> **percentage of...**) to provide an instant 'picture' in the listener or reader's mind as to the magnitude of something. It is often used in the press to sway public opinion towards or away from a particular viewpoint; where the reporter will give **<u>their opinion</u>**, but not proof, as to how large the number is: "It is believed that **a** large **percentage of** MPs oppose it, **<u>possibly up to 75%</u>** according to reports". It can be used with <u>pronouns</u> (**A percentage of** <u>them</u>) and <u>nouns</u>, with *the* (**A percentage of** *the* <u>independent voters...</u>).

Notes and examples

A PIECE OF

Referring to an unquantified and cut out part of something	
ə piːs əv	Undefined amount | Both | Both
A part of a concrete thing	Would you like **a piece of** cake?
A part of something abstract	I gave her **a piece of** my heart (= love)

This determiner is generally used to talk about a specific but undefined (in terms of the size, weight, etc.) part of something. It can be followed by another determiner such as a possessive determiner (**my, your, her, his, our, their** – see the 2nd example sentence above), an indicative determiner (**this, that, those, these** – I'd like **a piece of** <u>that</u> pie), the definite article, **the**, or with no determiner (see the 1st example sentence above). It is also used in US idioms meaning do you want to fight? (Do you want **a piece of** me?) or I want to be (intimately) involved (I want **a piece of** that). In UK English it forms part of idioms like, "It was **a piece of** cake", meaning some task was easy and "I gave her **a piece of** my mind", meaning I shouted at her.

Notes and examples

A PROPORTION OF (THE)

An unspecified number or amount that is compared to the whole	
ə prəˈpɔː.ʃən əv (ðə)	Comparable amount | Countable | Both
Comparative number	A tiny **proportion of** the class were sick today.
Comparative amount	A **proportion of** his pay is used to buy shares.

This is used to express an amount compared to a whole and is often used with *adjectives* like *small, large* or *fair*. It can be used with <u>pronouns</u> (a *fair* **proportion of** <u>it</u> was saved for later) or <u>nouns</u>, with **the**, (a *large* **proportion of the** <u>group</u> wanted him fired). It can also be used with possessive determiners (**A proportion of** *her* flowers are really weeds) and indicative determiners (**A proportion of** *this* money is going to charity).

Notes and examples

A SECTION OF (THE)

A prominent part of *or* a slice of			
ə ˈsek.ʃən əv (ðə)	One part of	Countable	Both
A prominent part of	**A section of the** boat was replaced.		
A slice of	**A** thin **section of the** tumour was biopsied.		

This determiner is used to identify a prominent, and usually contiguous, part of something. It is used with *pronouns* when a single small contiguous part is specified (**A section of** *it* was used to support the ceiling); however, when it may be made up of a larger part of a thing use **a part of** instead. When it prefaces a noun or noun phrase it is suffixed with **the** in order to define the <u>group</u> from which the particular part came from (**A section of the** <u>crowd</u> started cheering - note, when **a section of** is used in the context of a crowd of people it normally refers to the group in a particular area behaving in a certain way).   In order to give a better idea of the magnitude of the section's size an <u>adjective</u> may be used between the indefinite article and the noun (**A** <u>huge</u> **section of…** or **a** <u>large</u> **section of…** or **a** <u>small</u> **section of…**). If a crucial part is involved - **a significant section of…** would be used..

Notes and examples

A SEGMENT OF

A defined portion of something linear			
ə ˈseg.mənt əv	A linear part	Both	Concrete
Abstract linear part	**A segment of** time was set aside for rest.		
Concrete linear part	**A segment of** rope was cut off.		

This determiner is used to refer to part of a single dimensional contiguous <u>concrete object</u>, like <u>string</u> or <u>thread</u>, or an <u>abstract concept</u> like <u>time</u> or <u>space</u>. It can be used to refer to an uncountable portion of something countable like the time involved in a news broadcast (**A segment of** the show will be given over to the plane crash). It is commonly misused referring to things like crowd (A segment of the crowd – use something like "a section of the" crowd instead). It isn't often used with pronouns; however, it can be used with previously known nouns (**A segment of the** chain was judged to have weakened over time).

Notes and examples

A SPOT OF

Referring to a very small and almost insignificant amount of something			
ə spɒt əv	Tiny amount	Uncountable	Both
Very small amount (concrete)	Would you like **a spot of** milk in your tea?		
Very small amount (abstract)	I have **a spot of** leave so I'll go to Paris.		

This determiner is most commonly used in UK English and is used to refer to a, usually small, amount of something uncountable, commonly a liquid. The amount of the concrete noun is completely unspecified and would often require the other person in the conversation to guess how much is present, is required or is being offered (I had **a spot of** blood on my shirt *or* I need to put **a spot of** oil in my car *or* Would you like **a spot of** tea?). It is also used in British understatement to say that problems were encountered when doing something (I had **a spot of** bother with the car today = It broke down completely *or* I had **a spot of** trouble reading your writing = I couldn't understand it at all). It is generally not used with pronouns or other determiners, except in idioms (**A spot of** the other = sex in UK English).

Notes and examples

ALL

Every member of a group *or* happening frequently			
ɔːl	Every one of	Countable	Both
Every one	**All** faculty members will be there		
Almost constantly	I go to the cafe **all the** time.		

This determiner is used to state that the entirety of a group is represented in some way. It can only refer to a countable noun phrase (adjectives + noun) or noun clause – it cannot be followed by a pronoun (use '**all of**' to do that – see below). The size of the group it refers to is not generally specified, possibly because the extent is unknown. In spoken English it is often used incorrectly with a following determiner: for example "All my friends are coming" where the correct thing to say is "All **of** my friends are coming." It can also be used with **the** to mean frequently (**all the** time) or at the same time (**All the** while I was talking she was looking at her phone).

Notes and examples

ALL OF (THE)

Every one or every part of a specific group			
ɔːl əv (ðə)	Every part of	Both	Both
Every one (concrete)	All of my friends like Sushi.		
Every part (abstract)	All of the fog was gone by noon.		

This determiner is used to state that the entirety of a specific group is represented in some way. It can be followed by another determiner such as a possessive determiner (**my, your, her, his, our, their** – **All of <u>my</u>** students got A+ in the exam), an indicative determiner (**this, that, those, these** – I'd like **all of <u>that</u>** pie), the definite article, **the**, (**All of <u>the</u>** students arrived on time), an <u>indefinite article</u> – usually as an idiom with an abstract noun (I'm **all in <u>a</u>** dither today – idiom = I am not organised) or with no determiner, such as with a <u>pronoun</u> (**All of <u>us</u>** went to see the movie). It can be used with either countable or uncountable nouns. **All of** refers to a specific group with a known size; whereas, with plain **all**, the size of the group isn't specified.

Notes and examples

AN ABUNDANCE OF

An extremely plentiful amount *or* too much *or* more than enough			
æn əˈbʌn.dənts əv	Too many	Both	Both
Too many (countable)	There is **an abundance of** apples on my tree		
Too much (uncountable)	We've had **an abundance of** rain this year		

Use this determiner to state that there is such a plentiful supply that it is too much and may lead to problems (fruit going rotten, floods, etc.). If you need to highlight the fact that there is far too much of something then you can use an <u>adjective</u> between the indefinite article and the noun, (There is **a <u>significant</u> abundance of**...) The word **overabundance** can be used instead (There is **a <u>huge</u> overabundance of**...). It is not commonly followed by another determiner nor pronouns. It can be used with abstract nouns to show that there was significant support for a person (The church members provided **an abundance of** support to help her overcome her hardship) or concept (There was **an abundance of** grief among his subjects when he died). Note, another determiner '**an outpouring of**' could be used to express extreme emotions (There was **an outpouring of** grief when he died).

Notes and examples

ANOTHER

An additional one *or* A different one			
əˈnʌð.ə	**One** |	**Countable** |	**Both**
Additional one	Would you like **another** cup of tea?		
A different one	**Another** way of getting there is by bus.		

This determiner is used to talk about an additional person or thing, which is similar, or the same, as one referred to earlier (usually concrete), or to refer to a different method (usually abstract). It can also be used to politely decline an invitation (**Another** time perhaps - where perhaps indicates that it is possible but implies it is not likely) or to ask for an an alternative (Can we go to **another** restaurant as I really don't like their food). It is only used when the thing or person being talked about is already known. It would only preface singular nouns, noun phrases or noun clauses. Use **another of** (see below) to preface determiners, plural nouns or pronouns. It can be used as a pronoun when pointing to something (Would you like **another**? - said while pointing towards an empty glass or cup).

Notes and examples

ANOTHER OF

Additional or different one from within a defined group			
əˈnʌð.ə əv	**Singular or plural** |	**Countable** |	**Both**
A defined addition	Would you like **another of** these cakes?		
An additional example	**Another of** my inventions is used worldwide.		

Use this to talk about an additional or different one from within a specific group. It can be followed by another determiner such as a possessive determiner (**my, your, her, his, our, their** – Another of <u>my</u> students got a scholarship to Oxford), an indicative determiner (**this, that, those, these** – **Another of** <u>those</u> pies would be nice), the definite article, **the**, (Another of <u>the</u> ways to get cheap tickets is online) or with no determiner, such as with a <u>pronoun</u> (**Another of** <u>them</u> sold his book to Hollywood). Unlike plain **another** it can be used to preface <u>plural nouns</u> representing a choice from within the same group (**Another of** my <u>friends</u>); whereas, the simple 'another' would refer to something of the same type but from a different group (**Another** choice is an SUV - where the different group is other types of vehicle but it is the same type i.e. personal transport, note that it refers to a singular item, in this case a group of vehicles). It can also be used with abstract nouns (It was **another of** those crazy ideas that might just work).

ANOTHER ONE OF (THE)

Highlight qualities of additional one from within a group

əˈnʌð.ə wʌn əv (ðə)	One more | Countable | Usually concrete
One more	I saw **another one of** those rare birds today.
Next one	**Another one of the** guests has just arrived.

This is usually used to highlight certain aspects of the individuals or singular things being mentioned. In particular it is used to highlight positive things (One of my ex-students went on to study at Cambridge and **another one of** *them* went on to study at Harvard). It is commonly used with *pronoun objects* as it is referring to a group that has already been mentioned. It can also be used with *indicative determiners* (I'll have **another one of** *those* chocolate cakes, please) and the (**Another one of the** things I like are Thai massages - note the abstract reference to plural actions). It doesn't tend to get used with indefinite articles (a,an, some or any). It can also be used to highlight the fact that it refers to a singular individual or thing, while still referring to certain shared qualities. It is used in the UK idiom 'It's been **another one of** those days' to say that everything has gone wrong today.

Notes and examples

ANY OF

Choice of one or more people or things from a known group

ˈen.i əv	One or more|Countable|Usually Concrete
More than zero	Do **any of** you know how this works?
Multiple	Do **any of** you want to help me?

This determiner is normally followed by a pronoun. When using the pronoun, **you**, it refers to the plural version as it relates to one or more people or things from a specified, known group. It is most commonly used in questions, particularly those that ask for people to come forward or volunteer, and is usually used to enquire about more than one item from a group, for example: Do **any of** you know the answer? (Asking for any number > 0) *or* <u>Are</u> **any of** you ready to take the test? (Asking for plural entities – note the plural auxiliary verb <u>are</u>). The word '**any**' has it's own page in the articles section of this book.

Notes and examples

ANY OF THE

Highlight equality within a group

'en.i əv ðə	One or all	Countable	Both
Ease of doing something	**Any of the** ways I taught you can be used
Equality of people or things	You can choose **any of the** prizes here.

This determiner is commonly used to indicate that all members or parts of a group, or objects within a group, are more or less of equal status. It is often used when more than one thing with equal status are being compared; **either (of the)** is used when only two things are being compared. If it indirectly refers to a task then it is taken to mean that any previously known method can be used to undertake a task; however, a *qualifier* is normally added to highlight the best method (**Any of the** roads will take you there; *but, this one is quicker*). It can also be used in questions to enquire about the possibility of something positive existing (Did **any of the** students pass?)

Notes and examples

ANY NUMBER OF

Refer to an unknown number of choices

ɔːl	Unknown number	Uncountable	Both
Lots of ways	There are **any number of** ways to fix that.
Lots of objects	There are **any number of** prizes on offer.

This determiner tends to be used (often in an idiomatic way) to say that there are likely to be a large number of different ways of achieving, or causes of, something or there are a multitude of tools/items that could be used to attain a specific goal. The overall indication is that the methods/items are likely to be of equal weight or validity but with the implicit meaning that the speaker has no way of knowing whether they are or not. It can also mean that an unknown quantity of things available but the speaker is not sure how many. Note, that there is no indication of the quantity available and therefore it tends to be used to refer to an uncounted number of countable items (things that could be counted but weren't).

Notes and examples

ANY ONE OF (THE)

Offer a choice of equal things or people from within a group			
'en.i wʌn əv (ðə)	One	Countable	Concrete
Equality of choice	**Any one of** them could have fired the gun.		
Show and/or offer choices	I will buy you **any one of** these rings.		

This determiner is commonly used to indicate that any item or every member of a group is of equal worth or have equal capabilities regarding their suitability. It differs from '**any of the**' in that this compound article highlights that face that each individual item or person is known to have complete equality therefore there would generally not be a better option out of those on offer. It is also used to highlight the fact that only one thing or person can be chosen. Without '**the**' it can be used to preface a *pronoun* (**Any one of** *us* could drive there) or an *indicative determiner* (You can choose **any one of** *those* prizes on the shelf). When suffixed with '**the**' it is used to preface nouns to name the group from among which the choice could be, or could have been, made (**Any one of the** porters can carry your bag [could be] or **Any one of the** choir could have sung it [could have been]).

Notes and examples

BOTH

Treating two people or things as a set			
bəʊθ	Two	Countable	Usually Concrete
Similarities of two things	**Both** cars run on gas.		
Difference between 2 things	**Both** good and bad can be found in anybody		

This determiner is usually followed by a **noun**, often after previously introducing the two items or people in the group. It is often used to indicate their joint attributes or capabilities, particularly when used or working together (**Both** dogs loved to go for walks). It can be used with an *adjective* to show that the two people or things being described differ in some way from the rest of a larger group (**Both** *male* students were late but the female students were all on time).

Notes and examples

BOTH OF

Two things or people referred to as one	
bəʊθ əv	Two | Countable | Concrete
Common attributes	**Both of** us like classical music.
Common capabilities	**Both of** them speak fluent English.

This determiner is usually followed by a plural **pronoun**, usually after previously introducing the two items or people in the group. It is often used to indicate their particular attributes or capabilities, such as mutual likes/dislikes and very similar abilities. It can also be used with a *possessive determiner* and a plural noun to describe a pair of unnamed people or items that are special in some way (**both of** *my* students earned a GPA of 4.0). In US English the 'of' is often left out of speech when used in this context (Both my kids have blond hair [US] ~ both **of** my kids have blond hair).

Notes and examples

BOTH OF THE

Refer to an unknown pair that were previously referred to	
bəʊθ əv ðə	Two | Countable | Usually concrete
Clarify specific attributes	Both of the cars have alloy wheels.
Add a further description	Both of the suspects wore face masks.

This determiner is usually followed by a **noun** that refers to a pair of people or things that have been previously described and that share strong similarities. For instance look at the following sentences where the arrow shows the reference to the same subjects:

<u>Two men</u> were seen escorting the missing girl out of the club.

Both of the <u>men</u> were wearing hoods to hide their faces.

This article is often used by law enforcement to give further descriptions to wanted subjects when both subjects had similar attributes or were seen to act in the same way, in which case it used to highlight the similarities. When referring to two intimate groups of two, it is common to refer to them as <u>couples</u> (**Both of the** <u>couples</u> live near me); whereas, non-intimate or unknown groups of two are often referred to as pairs of individuals (**Both of the** pairs of individuals looked shady).

EACH

Every thing or person in a group of two or more, considered separately

iːtʃ	One | Countable | Concrete
Collective attributes	**Each** teacher is given a red pen.
Individual actions	**Each** student must study alone.
Individual traits	**Each** person in the group had a different skill.

This determiner is usually followed by a <u>singular</u> **noun** (and a 3rd person verb tense) and is used to refer to individual actions, traits or attributes that are commonly shared between other individual members of the group to which they belong. It can also be used to highlight the differences in their actions, traits, attributes or skills (**Each** dog has its own personality - attribute) or (**Each** engineer solved the problem in their own way - action).

Notes and examples

EACH AND EVERY

All members of a group treated, acting or viewed in the same way

iːtʃ ænd ˈev.ri	Every one | Countable | Both
All members act the same	**Each and every** member attended the play.
All members are the same	**Each and every** student is a genius.

This determiner is used to state that every individual with a group has an equal responsibility to act, or have already acted, in the same way. It could also mean that they share the same characteristics. It is often followed by a prepositional phrase preceded by '*one of*' (**Each and every** *one of* the visitors is required to register at the front desk). The general principle is that they are referred as equally valid individuals within a group with no exceptions. It can also be used to describe the same result each time something is tried (**Each and every** time I come here I manage to get lost).

Notes and examples

EACH OF

Highlight equality within a group			
iːtʃ əv	Any or All	Both	Both
Collective attributes	**Each of** them has a car.		
Collective actions	**Each of** us brought a packed lunch.		

This determiner could be used with a noun together with an *indicative determiner* (**Each of** *those* firemen deserves a medal), '*the*' (**Each of** *the* students did well on the exam) or a *possessive determiner* (**Each of** *his* ideas were considered on their merits [abstract]). Note that it is followed by a plural noun but the verb is singular. It can also be used with a plural object pronoun as a sentence subject (**Each of** *us* has a vice or a shameful habit). It can also be used with the pronoun '*which*' to refer to a choice from people or things that are already known (**Each of** *which* can be used to fix the car).

Notes and examples

EITHER

Choice of two people, things or possibilities			
ˈaɪ.ðər	One of two	Countable	Both
Choice of two things	You can have **either** tea or coffee, but not both		
Choice of two people	**Either** job applicant could do the job.		

This determiner is generally used to indicate a choice of one person or thing from a group of two. It is generally followed by a noun, noun phrase or a noun clause that is used to describe which of the two objects or people are being considered. It is used where the two entities have not been previously described, therefore a description of them in a noun form is needed so the listener/reader knows who or what is being talked about. It is very close in meaning to **each**, the difference being that '**either**' is only applied to a group of two; whereas, **each** can apply to any sized group and is generally not used for groups of two. It can also be used to describe both when describing time or space, the difference being that **either** would preface a *singular noun*; whereas, **both** would use a <u>plural noun</u> (Noisy eaters sat **either** *side* of me in the cafe *or* Noisy eaters sat **both** <u>sides</u> of me in the cafe). Do not confuse it with the adverb either, which is normally used at the end of a sentence to mean an additional thing (I don't like her and I don't like him **either**).

EITHER OF

A choice from two described people or things

ˈaɪ.ðər əv	One of two | Countable | Concrete
Choice from a known pair	**Either of** us can drive you home.
Choice of things	**Either of** those tops will look great on you.

This determiner is usually followed by a plural pronoun, such as **us** or **them**, and is used to indicate that one of the two previously mentioned people or things can either act or be considered for something. If this determiner is followed by the definite article (**either of the**) then it is generally used to refer to nouns rather than pronouns. Its main use is to highlight **specific attributes** that the entities or items, that can be chosen, have that set them apart from others of that type (**Either of the <u>tall</u> men can reach that shelf [people] or Either of the <u>blue</u> pens can be used [things]**). It can also be followed by a *plural indicative determiner* to help to specify the choice (**Either of** *these* computers can be used for word processing.)

Notes and examples

EITHER ONE OF

Specifying that only a single choice can be made from two options

ˈaɪ.ðər wʌn əv	One of Two | Countable | Both
Choice of two things	**Either one of** us can write your code.
Compare similarities	**Either one of** them will lie to get elected.

This determiner is usually followed by a plural pronoun, such as **us** or **them**, and is generally used to indicate that one of the two previously mentioned people or things can either act or be considered for something. It is mainly used to specify that only one person or thing can be selected. Note, it would use a <u>third person singular verb</u> (**Either one of** *them* <u>is</u> a strong candidate for the post). It can also be followed by a plural indicative determiner for newly introduced things (**Either one of** <u>these</u> bags can be used) or an *indicative pronoun* for known things (**Either one of** *these* can be used).

Notes and examples

EITHER ONE OF THE

A choice of one of two previously unknown things			
ˈaɪ.ðər wʌn əv ðə	Two	Countable	Concrete
One of two physical choices	Either one of the trains will get you there.		

The difference between this determiner and the previous one (either one of) is that this one would be used with a specifying plural noun instead of a pronoun. By way of contrast, the simple '**either**' would be followed by a singular noun. '**Either of (the)**' is very similar in use to '**either one of the**', but doesn't place an emphasis on the fact that only one choice is possible. '**Either one of the**' can be used with *concrete nouns* specified with a <u>prepositional phrase</u> or an adjective (Take **either one of the** *cakes* <u>on the plate</u>) and with known or previously referred to *abstract plural nouns* (**Either one of the** *schemes* could be chosen by the mayor).

Notes and examples

ENOUGH

As much as necessary			
ɪˈnʌf	Adequate amount	Both	Both
As much as necessary	I have **enough** money to buy a car.		
To the degree needed	**Enough** time was allocated for the task.		

This determiner is used to indicate that an adequate amount or number of things or people are available to achieve an end goal. It may be used with abstract nouns (Do you have *enough* energy to run a marathon?) or *concrete nouns* (Do you have **enough** *application forms* for everybody?) and with *countable nouns* (We have **enough** *seats* booked to take anybody who wants to go) or *uncountable nouns* (I have **enough** *rice* to feed everybody). It would not be used to directly precede a pronoun. There is also an adverb version of this word (Have you eaten **enough**?)

Notes and examples

ENOUGH OF (THE)

Indicate the extent of adequacy			
ɪˈnʌf əv (ðə)	Indicated extent	Both	Both
Adequate *nouns*	Enough of the *food* was left to feed the dog.		
Adequate *pronouns*	Enough of *us* liked the idea of a barbeque.		

This determiner can be used to precede pronouns (**Enough of** *us* were in favour that the proposition carried). It is commonly used to indicate that a quorum or a limit has been reached (I have had **enough of** this shouting over each other so I am calling an end to this meeting). It is used with '**the**' followed by a noun to specify exactly what there is an adequate supply of, usually followed by *a reason for wanting it* (We have stored **enough of the** wheat we harvested *to last us through the winter*).

Notes and examples

EVERY

Refer to all members of a group of three or more			
ˈev.ri	All in a group > 2	Countable	Both
All members of a group	Every student attended the ceremony.		
Treated equally (abstract)	Every idea is considered on its merits.		

This determiner is generally followed by a noun or a noun phrase and is used to indicate that every member of a group, comprising of 3 or more people or things, is included within the explanation. When this determiner is followed by **body** (everybody), **thing** (everything), or **where** (everywhere), the words join together to form a pronoun. If it followed by **one** on its own it will create a pronoun **everyone**; however, if it used with **one** and **of** it creates a compound determiner (see below). This determiner is similar to '**all**' in use: the difference being that '**every**' prefaces <u>single countable nouns</u> and '**all**' prefaces *plural [group] nouns* (**Every** <u>child</u> deserves a happy childhood - **All** *children* deserve a happy childhood - note the verb tenses).

Notes and examples

EVERY ONE OF (THE)

All parts of a specified group of three or more

'ev.ri. wʌn əv (ðə)	All in a group > 2 | Countable | Both
All in a specified group	**Each and every one of** them loved the idea.
All in an unknown group	**Each and every one of the** crew survived.

This determiner is generally followed by a plural pronoun that refers to all members of a previously introduced or known group. It can also be followed with the definite article - **every one of the** – in which case it is used with a plural noun and a singular, third person, verb. It differs from the previous determiner 'every' in that it uses a plural noun and can be used to preface pronouns; whereas, **every** can only preface singular nouns and not pronouns. Note it is pronounced differently to the pronoun everyone (every one = 'ev.ri. wʌn with a pause between every and one; whereas, **everyone** is pronounced 'ev.riwʌn with no pause).

Notes and examples

FEW

A small number of

fjuː	A small number | Countable | Both
A small number of	**Few** ideas are good enough to manufacture.
Not many	**Few** people enjoy war.

This determiner is generally followed by a plural noun, noun phrase or a noun clause and refers to a small but unknown number of things or people. It is used as an alternative to a cardinal number used as a determiner to indicate that the number of people/things being discussed were either unknown, not counted or not of concern. However, the things/people being referred to are generally countable, even though they haven't actually been counted, as the actual number is not regarded as being useful or pertinent. In this context it is often used to express disappointment (**Few** people attended) or shock (**Few** students passed) with positive verbs, or satisfaction (**Few** people didn't like her) with negative verbs. If this word is preceded by an indefinite article it is an adjective (A **few** people protested!) or if it precedes a verb it is a pronoun (**Few** came to the party).

Notes and examples

FEW OF (THE)

A comparatively small number	
fju: əv ðə	A small number | Countable | Concrete
In a known group	**Few of** us agree with you.
In an unknown group	**Few of the** party guests left early

This comparative determiner can be followed by a plural pronoun that refers to a smaller number of members of a previously named group that have a contrary view or have taken different actions than most of the other members. It can also be followed with the definite article - **few of the** – in which case it is used with a plural noun and a plural, third person, verb. This compound determiner can by prefaced with an indefinite **article**, (**A few of the** members voted against the new rule), in order to further minimise the size and importance of the dissenting group and highlight the fact that they are an indeterminate number, even though they are able to counted, so it can be used to minimise the number of dissenters in, say, a newspaper article where the editorial stance is generally in favour.

Notes and examples

FEWER

A decreasing number from within a group	
fjuː.ə	Decreasing number | Countable | Both
A smaller number of	**Fewer** voters are for him than against him
A decreasing number of	**Fewer** people come in the shop every day.

This determiner is generally followed by a plural noun that refers to a smaller or diminishing number of members of a previously named group. This determiner is often confused with the determiner '**less**'; whereas, **fewer** is used for countable nouns (There are **fewer** bottles of water on sale in the shop today), **less** is used for uncountable nouns (There is **less** water in the tank today). It can be used in the compound determiner '**fewer and fewer**' to emphasize that the numbers are decreasingly rapidly and could *lead to an effect* (**Fewer and fewer** people are buying the products so *the factory may be forced to close* - note the conjunction 'so' used to preface the effect).

Notes and examples

HER

A singular known female's possessions, skills or attributes	
hɜːr	Any number > 0 | Both | Both
Possessions	**Her** dog was a nuisance.
Skills	**Her** expertise with computers helped us.
Attributes	**Her** beauty was legendary.

This determiner can be followed by either a singular or a plural noun and refers to people (**Her** brother is a doctor) or things; either abstract (**her** mood swings were wild and erratic) or concrete (**her** new shoes hurt her feet). It is often referred to in many grammar books as a possessive pronoun, even though it appears before a noun or noun phrase. It can also refer to things that are connected to but not possessed by the female (**Her** support was crucial). It can also be used as an object pronoun (I saw **her** yesterday).

Notes and examples

HIS

A singular known male's possessions, skills or attributes	
hiz	Any number > 0 | Both | Both
Possessions	**His** car broke down on the way to work.
Skills	**His** electronics skills got him a good job.
Attributes	**His** IQ is thought to be over 180.

This determiner can be followed by either a singular or a plural noun and refers to people (**His** sister is a mathematician) or things; either abstract (**his** temper was vicious) or concrete (**his** computer was full of viruses). It is often referred to in many grammar books as a possessive pronoun, even though it appears before a noun or noun phrase. It can also refer to things that are connected to but not possessed by the male (**His** application is in the pile). Unlike **her** (see above) it cannot be used as an object pronoun - you should use **him** instead (I met **him** at work). **Her** was derived from Dutch (hora); whereas, **his** was derived from Anglo-Saxon (is) and **him** was later (from around 1000 to 1500) derived from German (ihm - as both the masculine and neuter versions of hi [he]). Hence the differences in use.

Notes and examples

ITS

A singular known thing's possessions, skills or attributes	
its	**Any number > 0 | Both | Both**
Possessions	**Its** bone is buried in the garden.
Skills	**Its** ability to detect smells helps its owner.
Attributes	**Its** unreliability is well known.

This determiner can be followed by either a singular or a plural noun and refers to people or things that are either abstract (**Its** bark is worse than **its** bite) or concrete (**Its** main feature is permanent four wheel drive). It is often referred to in many grammar books as a possessive pronoun, even though it appears before a noun or noun phrase. This word isn't often used as an object pronoun – use **it** instead (I fed **it** this morning), it can, however, be used as a subject pronoun (**Its** a Toyota). This word is often confused with the abbreviation of **it is** (**it's** a boy) or **it has** (**it's** got brown fur) – if it appears before a noun then it's the determiner **its**, if it appears before a determiner, adjective or verb it is the pronoun & verb abbreviation **it's**.

Notes and examples

LESS (OF)

A comparatively smaller or diminishing amount	
les (ev)	**Smaller amount | Both** (with of) **| Both**
Smaller amount	**Less** cola was drunk than I thought.
Decreasing amount	**Less** tobacco is being grown every year.

This determiner is used to refer to a smaller or diminishing amount of some uncountable people *or* people or things that could be counted but weren't. It can also be followed by the word 'of' and used as a comparative with a countable <u>pronoun</u> or *noun* (<u>Pronoun</u>: There were **less of** <u>us</u> than before - *noun*: I spend **less of** *my money* on food now). It is often confused with the word **fewer**, which is used with countable (and generally counted) nouns In addition, 'less' usually means that the decreasing amount is not necessarily a problem; whereas, 'fewer' normally implies that it is. There are comparative adverb (He speaks **less** than his wife) and preposition (The price is $10 **less** tax) versions of this word. It can be used with 'no' and 'than' to say that something is larger than expected (**no less than** three quarters of the crowd went home after the first half) or to emphasize that someone important was present (Presenting the prizes for the speaking contest was **no less than** the President of the University himself).

LITTLE

Not much *or* a tiny amount of		
'lɪt.l	**Not much** | **Uncountable** | **Both**	
Not much	**Little** fuel is left in my car.	
A tiny amount	**Little** wealth finds its way to the poor.	

This determiner is used to refer to a very small amount of some uncountable items. It can be used with concrete (There is **little** milk left) or abstract (there is **little** joy in their house) nouns. It is sometimes used to preface an <u>infinitive</u> (there was **little** <u>to do</u> as it had mainly been done by others). There are adjective (He is the **little** boy over there), adverb (He knew **little** about the subject) and noun (They took the **little** he had) versions. It can be used together with 'enough' to complain of a lack of something from others (There was **little enough** support for me from my colleagues when I complained). It can also be used with 'of' to highlight the fact that a much smaller amount than expected (**Little of** the money I was owed was repaid).

Notes and examples

MANY

A large number of people or things		
'men.i	**A lot** | **Countable** | **Concrete**	
A large number of	**Many** people believe in God.	
A collective mass of	**Many** roads lead to London.	

This determiner is used to refer to an indeterminate number of some countable items or people. It can be used with concrete (There are **many** cars in the car park) or abstract (**Many** happy returns on your birthday) nouns. It is often confused with the determiner much, which is used to preface uncountable nouns. There are adjective (A great **many** readers like detective books), noun (Great wealth often goes to the few not the **many**) and pronoun (**Many** are the reasons for not doing it) versions of this word.

Notes and examples

MANY OF (THE)

A great number of defined things	
ˈmen.i əv (ðə)	Large number | Countable | Both
A lot of the known things	**Many of** them said they would come.
A lot of a connected group	**Many of** her class have caught the flu.

This determiner is used to refer to an indeterminate number of some countable items or people and is used to preface a plural pronoun. If it is followed by the definite article 'the' it is used to highlight the fact that the collective mass that is being referred to is from a very specific group. It can also be followed by a possessive determiner or noun in order to show that the mass of people or things being referred to is connected in some way to either the speaker (**Many of** my...) or someone else (**Many of** Peter's...). It can be prefaced with 'too' to show that something is unacceptably large (**Too many of** our children are obese *or* **too many of** the voters didn't vote).

Notes and examples

MORE

A comparatively larger number or amount of	
mɔːr	Comparatively bigger | Both | Both
A larger number of	**More** people are diagnosed as obese now.
A larger amount of	There is **more** algae in my pond this year.

This determiner is used to refer to an increasing or comparatively larger number or amount of people or things. It can be used with concrete (There are **more** people coming) or abstract (there is **more** happiness now that he has returned) nouns. It can be used with both uncountable (There is **more** juice in the fridge if you need it) and countable (There are **more** cars in the car park today) nouns. It is sometimes used to preface an <u>infinitive</u> (There is **more** <u>to do</u> now that my daughter has moved back home). There are adverb (She knew **more** about physics than he did) and noun (The **more** the merrier - idiom meaning that everyone is welcome) versions of this word.

Notes and examples

MOST

The majority of *or* much of			
məʊst	Majority of	Both	Both
Majority of (countable)	**Most** people love their family members.		
Larger amount	**Most** milk comes from cows.		

This superlative determiner is used to refer to either the majority of some people or things, but not all, represented by a countable noun (**Most** dogs like going for walks) or the greater amount of, represented by an uncountable noun (**Most** work is done during the day). It can be used to preface concrete nouns (**Most** modern cars can be converted to run on gas) or abstract nouns (**Most** anger is misdirected and destructive). As it is a determiner it does not need to be prefaced with the definite article 'the' unlike the adjective version (<u>The</u> **most** famous person at my school is now an actor). There are also noun (The **most** I can give you is $100) and adverb (That cup of tea was **most** welcome) versions of this word.

Notes and examples

MOST OF (THE)

The majority of or much of a known group			
məʊst əv (ðə)	Majority of	Both	Both
Majority of known group	**Most of** us give money to charity.		
Much of a known mass	**Most of the** spilt milk went on the carpet.		

This superlative determiner is used to refer to either the majority of some previously known and countable people or things, represented by a plural <u>pronoun</u> (**Most of** <u>them</u>…) or if preceded by the definite article '**the**' it can be used to refer to the larger amount of an uncountable mass, represented by a noun (**Most of** <u>the</u> time…) or a larger number of a countable group (**Most of the** tourist buses tested were found to have defective brakes).

Notes and examples

<table>
<tr><td colspan="2" align="center"><h1>MUCH</h1></td></tr>
<tr><td colspan="2" align="center">A large amount or to a large degree but not a majority</td></tr>
<tr><td align="center">mʌtʃ</td><td>Large amount | Uncountable | Both</td></tr>
<tr><td>A large amount</td><td>I haven't had much success in fixing it.</td></tr>
<tr><td>To a large degree</td><td>I was much impressed with the speech.</td></tr>
<tr><td colspan="2">This determiner is usually used with uncountable nouns to indicate that there is a large amount of something or something has exceeded or surpassed an expected amount by a large degree. When used with the adverb too it indicates that there is more of something than expected or acceptable (He charged me too much money for my purchases) or more than enough (I have eaten too much food) – note, it is generally regarded as an adjective when used in this way.</td></tr>
</table>

Notes and examples

<table>
<tr><td colspan="2" align="center"><h1>MUCH OF (THE)</h1></td></tr>
<tr><td colspan="2" align="center">A comparatively larger number or amount of something that is known</td></tr>
<tr><td align="center">mʌtʃ əv (ðə)</td><td>Comparatively bigger | Both | Both</td></tr>
<tr><td>A large amount of</td><td>Much of the blame goes to the politicians</td></tr>
<tr><td>To a large degree</td><td>Much of it was complete nonsense.</td></tr>
<tr><td colspan="2">This determiner is used with either pronouns, where the object(s) have been introduced earlier (The corn got wet. Much of it was found to be unusable) – where it is not prefaced with the – or a noun, when it is usually a specific uncountable noun (Much of the money was donated to local charities) – where the abstraction is connected to something concrete like a specific amount; in this instance it would include the definite article the. If a countable noun is being prefaced then use many instead of much. The UK idiom 'much of a muchness' means below average, the same as or boring.</td></tr>
</table>

Notes and examples

MY

Of me *or* owned by me			
maɪ	Uncounted	Both	Both
Possessions	My car is very old but really reliable.		
Skills	My writing skills are debatable.		
Attributes	My eyes are blue and **my** hair is now white.		

This determiner is primarily used with nouns, either countable or uncountable, that are associated in some way, usually by possession (**my** car : countable – **my** money : uncountable – **my** charisma : abstract – **my** hand : concrete). It is not used with pronouns and it directly prefaces the noun phrase (**my** dog – prefacing noun, **my** big dog – prefacing an adjective inclusive noun phrase) and is not followed by any other article or determiner. It can be used to associate me with either a living thing (**my** mother) or a non-living thing (**my** pet rock).

Notes and examples

NEITHER

Not one or another			
ˈnaɪ.ðər	Not either	Countable	Both
Not either (abstract)	Neither idea appealed to me.		
Not either (concrete)	Neither hat suited her.		

This determiner is used to indicate that not one of the two options on offer is suitable or acceptable. It can be used with plain singular nouns (**Neither** car was fast enough) or noun phrases with <u>adjectives</u> (**Neither** blue dress fits her). It is not used with pronouns, previously identified nouns or with numerical determiners/adjectives in noun phrases (neither ~~two people~~ person knew the answer), use the determiner below in these instances; however, it can be used with ***noun representations*** of numerical representations (Neither ***couple*** wants to go on holiday with the other). Note, it would be followed by a third person singular verb

Notes and examples

NEITHER OF (THE)

Not one or the other of two known choices		
ˈnaɪ.ðər əv (ðə)	Not either | Countable | Both	
Not one (with pronoun)	**Neither of** <u>us</u> wanted to go to the party.	
Not one (with known noun)	**Neither of the** <u>men</u> admitted to the crime.	

This determiner can be used with a pronoun or to previously specified or identified nouns (with **the**). For example, if two people have been previously identified then this determiner is used to say that not one of the two individuals met a particular criteria. An example is: Two young men were interviewed for the job (the two individuals have now been identified); however, **neither of the** men was suitable. It can also be applied to noun phrases containing a numerical (cardinal) number; for instance, the above underlined clause can be rewritten as '**neither of the** two men was suitable'.

Notes and examples

NOT ALL

With some exceptions *or* not very		
nɒt ɔːl	With exceptions | Both | Both	
With some exceptions	**Not all** people agree with what he said.	
Not very (with adjective)	I was **not all** *that* bothered about the rash.	

This determiner is used to state that the entirety of the group identified by the noun is not being represented. It can only refer to a countable noun phrase (adjectives + noun) or noun clause – it cannot be followed by a pronoun (use '**not all of**' to do that – see below). The size of the group it refers to is not generally specified, possibly because the extent is unknown. It can be used with the indicative '*that*' to preface an adjective (In my opinion the painting was **not all** *that* beautiful) where it is used to say '**not very**' in the context of disagreeing with someone else. It can also be written as 'I'm **not** *at* **all** bothered by…' meaning I don't really care.

Notes and examples

NOT ALL OF (THE)

Exception within a specified group *or* not every part of a specific group	
nɒt ɔ:l əv (ðə)	**With exceptions | Both | Both**
Not every one of (*pronoun*)	**Not all of** *us* agreed to working with him.
Not every one of (*noun*)	**Not all of the** *people* wanted the new law.

This determiner is used to state that not all of a <u>known</u> specific group is included. It can be followed by a pronoun, where the noun has been previously presented or with a specified noun that has either been mentioned previously or is in reference to an inherently known, or believed to be known group (the people, the students, the faculty etc.). The group can either be countable (**not all of the** people in the office) or uncountable (**not all of the** people in the world) and can either be concrete (**not all of the** doughnuts) or abstract (**not all of the** ideas). It can be used in arguments against something to infer that a considerably sized (but uncounted) number of the group oppose it.

Notes and examples

NO

Not any	
nəʊ	**None | Both | Both**
Not any (uncountable)	**No** objections to it have been put forward.
Not any (countable)	**No** trees grow in the desert.

This determiner is used to indicate that either not one (with countable nouns) or not any (with uncountable nouns) things or people are in opposition to or are outside the group. It is often used with <u>gerunds</u> to indicate prohibited actions (**no** <u>smoking</u>, **no** <u>cheating</u>, etc.). It can be used with abstract nouns (**no** ideas were put forward to solve the problem) or concrete nouns (**no** letters have arrived for you this morning). It is not used with <u>pronouns</u> (use **none of** instead – **none of** <u>them</u> were late) or with previously specified <u>nouns</u>, prefaced with 'the' (use **none of the** instead – **none of the** <u>students</u> came today).

Notes and examples

NONE OF (THE)

Not one thing or person from a known group	
nʌn əv (ðə)	Not either | Countable | Both
Not one of (with pronoun)	**None of** us liked his plan.
Not one (with <u>plural noun</u>)	**None of** *the* <u>delegates</u> enjoyed the speech.

This determiner is used with <u>pronouns</u> or with *plural nouns* (prefaced with '**the**') to indicate that no single member, or thing, within the previously specified group is in opposition to (**None of** <u>them</u> disagreed) or the whole group reaction when referring to something from outside the group (**None of the** *group* has a clue what he is talking about). It was derived from 'not one', which can be used instead to add emphasis (**Not one** of us agrees!).

Notes and examples

NOT MANY

Only a few	
nɒt ˈmen.i	A few | Countable | Both
Only a few (concrete)	**Not many** people attended.
Some (abstract)	**Not many** dreams are remembered.

This determiner is used with countable nouns (use '**not much**' with uncountable nouns), to indicate a few from within a group represented by a group noun. It can be used with either concrete or abstract nouns to indicate that only a small number or amount of a particular unknown group is included in a result. This determiner is not used with pronouns or previously known or specified nouns from within a group. It is commonly used to indicate disappointment with the low number of people or things present or available. There is also an idiom in UK English to mean that it isn't as it seems or it is less than satisfactory (**Not many** it isn't).

Notes and examples

NOT MANY OF (THE)

Only a few of a known group			
nɒt ˈmen.i əv (ðə)	A few of	Countable	Both
A few of a group (*pronoun*)	Not many of <u>them</u> drink alcohol.		
A few of a group (*noun*)	Not many of *the* <u>students</u> passed the exam.		

This determiner is used with countable pronouns or previously introduced nouns (use '**not much**' with uncountable nouns), to indicate a few from within a group represented by a group or plural noun. It is used with pronouns (**Not many of** us…) or with plural nouns prefaced with 'the' (**Not many of the** group…) to indicate that no single member, or thing, within the previously specified group is in opposition to or is outside the group.

Notes and examples

NOT MUCH

Small amount *or* not a lot			
nɒt mʌtʃ	Not a lot	Uncountable	Both
Small amount (concrete)	**Not much** food was left after the party.		
Not a lot (abstract)	There is **not much** happening today.		

This determiner is used with uncountable nouns to indicate a small amount; it can be used with concrete (**not much** <u>glue</u> was needed) and abstract (It was **not much** <u>fun</u>) <u>nouns</u>. It is not used with pronouns or nouns within a previously specified group (use '**not much of**' for that). It is commonly used in idiomatic (and often ironic) speech to say that the result of something was almost the opposite of what was being enquired about. For example: Did you enjoy the movie? **Not much!** It can also be used to indicate that a minimal amount exists in which case the <u>noun</u> is implied, for example: Is there any fuel left in the car? **Not much.** It can also be used with abstract <u>nouns</u>, often to express a negative or hopeless outcome (There is **not much** <u>point</u> going now, as it has nearly finished).

Notes and examples

NOT MUCH OF (THE)

Not a lot of or a small amount of a known class		
nɒt mʌtʃ əv (ðə)	**Not a lot** | **Uncountable** | **Both**	
Not a lot (with *pronoun*)	**Not much of** *it* is left after the party.	
Not a lot (with *noun*)	**Not much of the** *snow* was left at noon.	

This determiner is mainly used with singular nouns to indicate that only a very small part of something is present, usually as a result of something happening earlier. With regards to pronouns it is generally used with the pronoun **it**, particularly when referring to pronouns representing concrete nouns (The <u>house</u> has been almost completely destroyed. **Not much of** *it* was left after the explosion – where the <u>house</u> is the noun and *it* is the associated pronoun). It can be used with possessive determiners, for example *his* or *their* (**not much of** *his* work has survived *or* **not much of** *their* money was left after their holiday). It can also be used, particularly in UK English, with the article **a** or **an** in an idiomatic (and often ironic) sense to indicate that something was not particularly good (It was **not much of a** buffet, was it? = The buffet was dreadful). This is an example of British understatement. Note the use of the tag question format to frame the statement.

Notes and examples

ONE

Indefinitely specified or unspecified individual, thing or item		
wʌn	**One** | **Countable** | **Both**	
Single item	There is **one** apple left.	
Indistinguishable member	He is **one** member and not our spokesman	

This determiner can used with countable nouns to indicate that an item, person or thing stands apart from others in some way or is the only example of its kind. It can also be used like 'a' or 'an' to show just one of many, in fact 'an' was derived from '**one**' originally. It is not used with previously specified nouns or pronouns. It can be used with both concrete (There is **one** *car* in the car park) and abstract (**One** *idea* I had was to…) *nouns.*

Notes and examples

ONE OF (THE)

Indefinitely specified or unspecified individual, thing from a known group

wʌn əv (ðə)	One	Countable	Both
A single item	Take **one of the** song sheets and join us.		
An outstanding thing	She is **one of the** best dancers I've seen.		

This determiner is used with <u>pronouns</u> (**one of** <u>them</u> is lying) or with plural <u>nouns</u> (**One of the** most relaxing <u>things</u> to do is to read books) to indicate that the thing or person being described is unique in some way and stands out from the rest of the group *or* is just a singular item in a group of similar items. It can also be used with the indefinite article '*a*' such as in the idiomatic phrase - He is **one of** *a* kind - meaning that he is totally unique.

Notes and examples

ONE OF (THESE/THOSE)

Specified individual, thing or item from an indicated group

wʌn əv (ðiːz/ðəʊz)	One	Countable	Both
One indicated item	You can have **one of these** prizes.		
One thing (abstract)	**One of these** ideas may work but which one?		

This determiner is used to highlight one particular individual thing from within an indicated group represented by a plural noun. It can be used with concrete (**One of these** <u>envelopes</u> contains cash) or abstract (**One of these** <u>concepts</u> will be chosen) <u>nouns</u>. It is not used with a pronoun. It can also be used with other indicative determiners such as **this** and **that**, where they preface group nouns (**One of this** group of students is a genius *or* **one of that** flock of sheep is the ram). It is also used, mostly in an idiomatic way, with **those**, for example "It has been **one of those** days" = Everything has gone wrong today *or* "It is **one of those** things" = there are some things we have no control over.

Notes and examples

ONLY

Not a lot of or a small amount of a known class

ˈəʊn.li	Limited number	Both	Both
Limited number	**Only** students with ID cards can enter.		
Singular (with <u>article</u>)	**Only** <u>an</u> idiot would believe him.		

This very flexible determiner indicates that a small or limited number of things are involved in something, which may or may not be part of a larger defined group, and to indicate that the number (countable) or amount (uncountable) is smaller than expected or required. It is commonly followed by another determiner, such as a possessive determiner (**Only** <u>her</u> boss stood in her way of the promotion), with **the**, to indicate that it is a select group (**Only** <u>the</u> bold succeed), <u>an</u> or <u>a</u>, to indicate someone/something outside a group or is of a particular type (**Only** <u>a</u> fool would even attempt it) or a collective group that is smaller than expected or desired (**Only** <u>a</u> few people came to the meeting because of the rain) or with an indicative, to indicate a single choice (**Only** <u>this</u> screwdriver will fit) or multiple choices within a limited range (**Only** <u>these</u> colours may be used). <u>Some</u> can be used to indicate a small group from a collective type (**Only** <u>some</u> plants grow in deserts). It can also be used with pronouns (Don't worry it's **only** <u>me</u> *or* **Only** <u>they</u> know the answer to that). When used with plural pronouns, it tends to be used as a *conjunction* (I nearly succeeded **only** <u>they</u> stood in my way). When it is used to indicate a single, outstanding individual or thing it is used in its *adjective* form (for example: following 'the' to indicate that the person or thing is unique - I was <u>the</u> **only** person in the room not wearing a tie – a/<u>an</u> – She is <u>an</u> **only** child – or a possessive determiner: i.e. <u>her/him</u> - It was <u>her</u> **only** chance of fame). It would not be used with an indicative determiner in this form. It is also an *adverb* (You must use this door **only**).

(THE) OTHER

Subsequent thing *or* additional thing *or* alternative thing(s)

(ðə) ˈʌð.ər	One	Countable	Both
Subsequent	His first idea was Ok, **the other** idea wasn't.		
Additional	One man led, **the other** man followed.		
Alternative	**Other** plans will be studied in due course.		

This determiner is primarily used to bring attention to thing(s) or person/people who are outside of, in addition to *or* aside from the first named group or individual. It is often used to draw attention to another in a group after the principal item(s) has been introduced and, in most cases it draws attention to the difference(s) between the featured remainder and the principal. It can also be prefaced with **the** to specify and name a subsequent person/thing that is generally of the same type (**The other** man is called Jeff – **The other** thing we need to think about is the cost).

OTHER THAN (THE)

Highlight an exception, apart from *or* except

ˈʌð.ər ðæn (ðə)	An exception | Both | Both
Singular exception	**Other than** her, we were in full agreement.
Plural Exception	**Other than** rats, people love furry animals.

This determiner differs from the previous one (other) in that it defines the exception first, putting the emphasis on it/them instead of the things or people that are, presumed to be, in the majority or take a more conventional stance. It can be defined as being **apart from** or **not considering**. It can also be used with <u>personal</u> pronouns (**Other than** <u>him</u> we are all going) and <u>indicative pronouns</u> (**Other than** <u>that</u> Mrs. Lincoln did you enjoy the play?). It can also be followed by **the** in order to draw attention to the fact that the exception is already known (**Other than the** car breaking down, how was your trip? – the exception must have already been known by the speaker or they wouldn't have mentioned it). It can also be used with the indefinite article **a/an** to indicate that the exception is not expected but possible (**Other than an** accident or **a** breakdown nothing will stop us).

Notes and examples

OUR

The possessions, skills or attributes possessed collectively by us

aʊər	None | Both | Both
Possessions	**Our** house is on a private estate.
Skills	**Our** skills were complementary.
Attributes	**Our** patience was tested by her behaviour.

This determiner is used to describe things that are held in common by all members of a group that contains the speaker. It is only used with abstract nouns (**Our** minds were made up) or concrete nouns (**Our** new car is bright blue), which can either be countable nouns (**Our** children are noisy) or uncountable nouns (**Our** water is contaminated). It is not used with pronouns.

Notes and examples

PLENTY OF (THE)

More than an adequate amount			
ˈplen.ti əv (ðə)	A large amount	Both	Both
More than adequate	Plenty of people signed the petition.		
A lot of	He has **plenty of** money in his account.		

This determiner is used to indicate that an adequate amount of something is available from within a group, usually in order to achieve something. It is generally used in positive terms – for example enough of whatever is needed is available to effect a positive result. It can be used with abstract nouns (**Plenty of** thought went into this plan) or concrete nouns (**Plenty of** people like living in Pattaya). It can also be used with <u>personal pronouns</u> (**Plenty of** <u>us</u> like eating cheese) and <u>indicative pronouns</u> (**Plenty of** <u>that</u> is involved – where it is mainly used in idiomatic terms – *indicative determiners* are used for specifying nouns – **plenty of** *these* books have been sold despite its misleading title). It could preface 'the' if the speaker is clarifying a (possibly contentious) viewpoint (**Plenty of the** people I know think that communism can be successful if done correctly).

Notes and examples

QUITE A BIT OF (THE)

An unspecified but not insignificant amount of		
kwaɪt ə bɪt əv (ðə)	A significant amount	Uncountable	Both
A significant amount	There was **quite a bit of** mess after they left.	
An unknown amount	**Quite a bit of** it went down the drain.	

This determiner is used with uncountable nouns (unlike **quite a few** – see below) to indicate a significant amount of something. It can be used with <u>pronouns</u> (I didn't see it all but I saw **quite a bit of** <u>it</u>) and specific nouns using **the** (**Quite a bit of the** opposition came from her).

Notes and examples

QUITE A FEW

An unspecified but not insignificant number of	
kwaɪt ə fjuː	Unspecified number | Countable | Both
Unspecified number	I think **quite a few** people want it.
Not insignificant number	**Quite a few** people didn't attend.

This determiner is used with countable plural nouns to indicate an unknown, but sizable, number of things or people. It differs from the determiner **plenty of** in that it can be used both in a negative sense to refer to either a sizeable number being against something (**Quite a few** people demonstrated against the new law) or in a positive sense to say that a sizeable number are for something (**Quite a few** people supported my campaign). It can be used with both <u>abstract nouns</u> (He has **quite a few** good <u>ideas</u>) or <u>concrete nouns</u> (There are **quite a few** homeless <u>people</u> in this city), but not with pronouns.

Notes and examples

QUITE A FEW OF (THE)

An unspecified but not insignificant number of a known group	
kwaɪt ə fjuː əv (ðə)	Unspecified number | Countable | Both
Unspecified number	I think **quite a few of** us like classical music.
Not insignificant number	**Quite a few of** the crowd started shouting.

This determiner can be used with <u>plural pronouns</u> (**Quite a few of** <u>them</u> cheered), and *possessive determiners* (**Quite a few of** *his* designs work well). It can also be used with *<u>the</u>* to specify the group being referred to (**Quite a few of** *<u>the</u>* stray dogs have fleas). This determiner is generally regarded as an idiom and does not quantify the number involved (although they could be counted). It is often used to imply that more people/things were involved than was the case, in order to add strength to an argument.

Notes and examples

SEVERAL

An unspecified number of different people or things	
ˈsev.ər.əl	**Unspecified amount	Countable	Both**
An unspecified number	**Several** people walked out during the show.
Some	**Several** pedestrians stopped to listen.

This determiner is used to say that an unspecified number of different people/things are involved in something. There is no actual numerical value specified but it is generally regarded as referring to a larger number than **few, some of** and **quite a few** and less than **more** or **many**. It can be used with <u>abstract</u> (**Several** <u>ideas</u> come to mind) and <u>concrete</u> (**several** <u>dogs</u> started barking when the jet flew over) nouns. It is not used with pronouns or with uncountable nouns; even though they wouldn't normally be counted.

Notes and examples

SEVERAL OF (THE)

Unspecified but not insignificant number of members of a known group	
ˈsev.ər.əl əv (ðə)	**Unspecified amount	Countable	Both**
An unspecified number	**Several of** them were sick during the trip.
An unknown amount	**Several of the** students watched the show.

This determiner can be used with <u>plural pronouns</u> (**Several of** <u>us</u> left the meeting early), and *possessive determiners* (**Several of** *her* ideas have been implemented already). It can also be used with <u>***the***</u> to specify the group being referred to – however it differs from the determiner **quite a few of** in that the <u>noun</u> commonly appears between the word '**several**' and the specifier '**of the**' that prefaces the *group noun* (**Several** <u>members</u> **of the** *crowd* cheered loudly). It can also be used with *indicative determiners* (**Several of** *these* apples are not ripe yet).

Notes and examples

SOME OF (THE)

Any unknown amount or number from a specified group			
sʌm əv (ðə)	Unknown amount	Both	Both
Unknown number	Some of them are coming back tomorrow.		
Unknown amount	Some of the paint went on the floor.		

This determiner is used to indicate that an unknown number of countable or uncountable people or things or an unknown amount of an uncountable substance has undertaken an action or is in a particular state. It can be used with <u>pronouns</u> (**Some of** <u>it</u> tasted ok, I'd like **some of** <u>that</u> *or* **some of** <u>us</u> come every week). When it is used with nouns it is always suffixed with **the**. It can be used with <u>abstract</u> (**Some of the** <u>concerns</u> were passed to the congressman) or <u>concrete</u> (**Some of the** <u>dishes</u> were cracked) nouns. It can either have the <u>noun</u> infixed (**Some** <u>members</u> **of the**...) or suffixed (**Some of the** <u>members</u>...); both methods are equally valid and can usually be used interchangeably with the infix focusing on the group the unknown nouns belong to, whereas with the suffix focuses on the members themselves - the definite article '**the**' usually indicates the focus. It can also be suffixed with <u>indicative determiners</u> such as <u>that</u> (I'll take **some of** <u>that</u> pie), <u>this</u> (I read **some of** <u>this</u> book before), <u>those</u> (I know **some of** <u>those</u> people) and <u>these</u> (I bought **some of** <u>these</u> cakes the last time I was here). '

SUCH

Of that type *or* to add emphasis			
sʌtʃ	Undefined	Both	Abstract
Of that type	Such bad attitudes have no place here.		
To add emphasis	He has such amazing charm.		

This determiner is most commonly used to draw attention to something being of a certain type and so it could be argued that it is exhibits adjective, rather than determiner, like behaviours. However, there are a number of reasons why it should be regarded as a determiner, for instance it always appears first in the noun phrase chain and it is never preceded by another determiner like an ordinary adjective would be (~~the~~ such behaviour will not be tolerated). It is mainly used with <u>abstract nouns</u> (**Such** <u>thoughts</u> will get you into trouble in the current British police state) and is not used with pronouns. It can precede <u>a</u> or <u>an</u> to emphasise a point (It was **such** <u>a</u> good movie). It is also used when referring to something without being exact (I was told it will start at **such** and **such a** time).

To determine whether it is being used as a determiner or a pronoun/noun you should look for the collocation word 'as', which if it follows 'such' indicates a pronoun; whereas, when '**such**' follows '**as**' it usually indicates a noun (Not **as such**).

THAT

An indicated thing that is out of reach *or* something mentioned earlier

ðæt	Single thing or group | Countable | Both
Indicated thing	I'd like to buy **that** hat on the shelf.
Mentioned earlier (clause)	I told you about **that** house we visited.

This indicative determiner is generally used to indicate the presence of a specific noun (hence *indicative determiner*). It can be used to indicate something out of reach – but normally within sight – or something mentioned earlier. It can also be used instead of **the** to indicate something specific and previously known; moreover, it is generally regarded as being more emphatic or specific than **the**, the specificity coming from adding extra details. For example; I'll meet you in **the** coffee shop *and* I'll meet you in **that** coffee shop <u>where they serve dragon-fruit lattes</u> – where the <u>adjective clause</u> makes the noun (coffee shop) more specific – even though it is assumed that both coffee shops are previously known to the listener. At one time 'the' was used as the definite article preceding consonants (like **a** is used) and **that** was used to precede vowels (like **an** is used) but this fell into disuse. It is also used as a pronoun - you can recognise it as such as it does not precede a noun - **That** is the most ludicrous idea I've ever heard – and as either a noun clause marker (I saw **that** girl you told me about) or an adjective clause marker (I saw the girl **that** you told me about).

(THE/A) MAJORITY OF (THE)

The largest amount or number of from a specified group

(ðə/æ) məˈdʒɒr.ə.ti əv (ðə)	The largest amount | Countable | Both
The largest amount of	**The majority of the** food was wasted.
The largest number of	**The majority of** us favour a referendum.

This determiner is sometimes prefaced with **a** rather than **the**. The difference between **the majority of** and **a majority of** is that the first refers to a group that are already known to the listener/reader; whereas, **a majority of** is used to introduce the group for the first time. For example – **The majority of** voters backed the party (the voters were already known) – **A majority of** new students sign up for the ethics class (the new students are not previously known). In the first instance, units from the known group can be emphasised by suffixing **<u>the</u>** (**A majority of <u>the</u>** members of the club voted against the new rule). Another difference in use between **a** and **the** is that **a majority of** tends, in common use, to be used with present tenses; whereas, **the majority of** tends to be used with past tense. It can be used with <u>group pronouns</u> (**The majority of** <u>them</u> are here). The word <u>**vast**</u> can be used in this determiner to emphasise the size of the group (**The <u>vast</u> majority of** people love it). The word **majority** is a noun and it is commonly used in unspecified group nouns such as moral **majority** and silent **majority**.

THESE

Plural people or things that are in reach or previously known		
ðiːz	Plural indicated things | Both | Both	
Available plural things	**These** socks are very good quality.	
Previously known	I told you **these** things when you last came.	

This indicative determiner is generally used to indicate plural things or people that are immediately available and, usually, within reach (How much are **these** apples?) or are previously known (**These** stories have been passed down through the generations). It can precede a concrete noun (**These** peaches are delicious) or an abstract noun (**These** figures indicate a problem in the company cash-flow). It is not usually used with another determiner (except plural numerical determiners - **These two** lovebirds look adorable) and is not used with pronouns. It can be used as a pronoun to refer to something plural within reach (**These** are the books I bought).

Notes and examples

THEIR

Property of or associated with a group		
ðeər	Unspecified number | Countable | Both	
Possessions	**Their** house has been sold.	
Skills	**Their** abilities exceeded our expectations.	
Attributes	**Their** design team is very innovative.	

This possessive determiner is generally used to associate singular or plural objects or people with a group. It is also used to avoid using gender based determiners to thing(s) associated with or owned by a single person (One student left **her** book behind = One student left **their** book behind). It can be used to refer to singular or plural objects. It can be used with abstract nouns (**Their** thoughts are focused on the upcoming exam) or concrete nouns (**Their** car broke down on the freeway). It is not used with pronouns (nor used as a pronoun) nor is it prefaced or suffixed by another determiner..

Notes and examples

THIS

ðis	Single indicated thing | Countable | Both
Person or thing that is in reach or is being indicated	
Available thing	Does **this** car you are selling run on petrol?
Indicated thing	Did you draw **this** cartoon by yourself?

This indicative determiner is used to indicate something that is immediately available or can be indicated - like a photograph (Do you have any paint in **this** colour?). It can refer to either <u>abstract nouns</u> (**This** <u>idea</u> may just work) or <u>concrete nouns</u> (You need to use **this** <u>key</u> to open the case). It is not used with pronouns or other determiners. It can be used as a pronoun when pointing to or holding something (How much is **this**?). It can be prefaced with 'by' to talk about an end or result (I thought you'd be finished **by this** time or I thought I'd achieve it **by this** method).

Notes and examples

THOSE

ðəuz	Unspecified amount | Countable | Both
People or things not being here *or* indicate multiple people or things	
Not here	**Those** people I mentioned are not coming.
Indicating plural things	Can I have a closer look at **those** gloves?

This indicative determiner is used to indicate or confirm people or things that are out of reach (**Those** boats *in the bay* look pretty) or people or things that are not present or are out of sight (**Those** dogs *next door* are barking again). The noun that it refers to is usually further defined using a *prepositional phrase* (see above) or an <u>adjective clause</u> (**Those** passengers <u>who have first class tickets</u> can board now). It can be used with <u>abstract nouns</u> (**Those** <u>thoughts</u> will get you into trouble if you put them into practise) or <u>concrete nouns</u> (**Those** <u>bananas</u> aren't ripe yet). It is not used with pronouns nor is it normally prefaced or suffixed by another determiner (except plural numerical determiners - I will take **those two** peaches); however, it can be used as a plural indicative pronoun (**Those** look nice).

Notes and examples

WHAT

To find further information about a specific noun *or* to give an opinion			
wɒt	Unknown	Both	Both
Find information	**What** movies do you enjoy?		
Give information	**What** a waste of time.		

This interrogative determiner is mainly used to clarify nouns. It is not used to obtain a name of something, the pronoun version is used for that purpose (This is a pronoun > **what** is your name?). Instead, it is used to find a particular subset of a set represented by the noun – for example to find out about a type of music, movie, food, drink etc. It is also used to make a statement in which an opinion is given, in a compound determiner form, suffixed with **a** (**What a** pity) or **an** (**What an** idiotic thing to do). It is commonly used in the idiom **"What the…"** (followed by a word like hell or heck) to express incredulity. It is also used in <u>noun clauses</u> (<u>**What** she said to me</u> is a secret) and as a pronoun to indicate something happening to unknown thing(s) or to repeat something said earlier (<u>**What** I said was…</u>).

Notes and examples

WHATEVER (THE)

Indicate all parts of a group or unspecified parts of a group or concept			
wɒt'ev.ər (ðə)	All parts	Both	Both
All parts	**Whatever** food is given to me I'll eat it.		
Unspecified parts	**Whatever the** problem he never worries.		

This determiner is not used to get an answer but to indicate anything or everything associated with the group represented by the noun. If it prefaces an uncountable noun it is not suffixed with **the**, but with countable nouns it can be. It can also preface a <u>pronoun</u> (**Whatever** <u>he</u> wants he gets). It is commonly used by teenagers as a form of disrespect when told to do something ("You will make your bed every day!" – "**Whatever**"). It can be used, suffixed with **the**, to say that irrespective of something else an action will still go ahead (The match will go on **whatever the** weather). It can also be used to say that something will not happen irrespective of something else (I will not work for him **whatever** he offers me) – note in the latter case it was not suffixed with **the**. It is also used in clauses, often to say that something won't affect the outcome (I'll buy it **whatever** it costs).

Notes and examples

WHICH

A specific choice from a limited and known set

wɪtʃ	One of a known set | Countable | Both
Advise on choice	Do you know **which** antivirus works best?
One of the indicated things	**Which** bag from these two should I buy?

This determiner is commonly used as a question with the speaker asking about the listener's advice on choices from a limited set, which can be described (for things that are not present) or indicated (for things that are both present and within view). It is commonly used in noun and adjective clauses. In noun clauses **which** is used to give more information about something previously described or known (**Which** train I catch doesn't matter) and in adjective clauses it is used to preface information that the speaker thinks might be interesting but is not important and can be omitted without affecting the main clause (These flowers, <u>**which** I bought on the way home,</u> are for my wife – the clause is <u>underlined</u> – without the clause the sentence would say 'These flowers are for my wife'). It can be prefaced with a <u>preposition</u> (<u>In</u> **which** town were you born?) as a question subject.

Notes and examples

WHICH (ONE) OF (THE)

Something not here *or* indicating multiple people or things

wɪtʃ (wʌn) əv (ðə)	One of known set | Countable | Concrete
What one	**Which one of** these dresses suits me best?
One of the indicated things	**Which of** the people in the photo is you?

This determiner is generally used to ask someone else to indicate something, for example by pointing. If it is suffixed with '**one**' then it generally indicates that the speaker is looking for a noun; whereas, without the '**one**' it generally indicates that the speaker would like the listener to indicate it directly (by pointing for example). Examples are: "**Which one of** these cars do you think I should buy?" (with the pronoun **one** – usually answered with a noun: "I recommend the Toyota") or "**Which of** these should I buy?" (without the pronoun **one** – usually answered with an indicative determiner "**that** car" or pronoun: "**That**" together with a physical indicator – such as a pointing finger). It it is followed by '**the**'. it indicates a specified and known, but not necessarily present, thing (**Which one of the** students won the prize?)

Notes and examples

WHICHEVER (OF)

Any one of a limited set or not an important choice	
wɪ'tʃev.ər (əv)	One of a set | Countable | Both
Any one of	**Whichever** cafe you choose is good for me.
Unimportant choice	I wear **whichever** socks are in the drawer.

Whichever differs from **which** in that it is commonly used to indicate that the choice doesn't matter; whereas, **which** is used to enquire or highlight something that does matter or is required. Like **which** it can be used in noun clauses (**Whichever** book I choose doesn't matter as I'll never read it) but not adjective or adverb clauses. It can also be prefaced with a <u>preposition</u> (You can travel <u>in</u> **whichever** car you want). It is interesting as its use is steadily increasing over time (doubling in use over the last century) both in noun clauses and, more commonly, as a determiner. It would not be used to directly preface a <u>*pronoun*</u>, instead you'd use **whichever of** (**Whichever of** us gets home first should turn the heating on) or **whatever** (**Whatever** *I* do I can't win) instead. If you need to indicate a specific choice using **'the'** as a suffix then use **'whatever'** instead (**Whatever the** outcome it was important we did it). It can be used as a pronoun (**Whichever** is good for you) but is not normally used with another determiner.

Notes and examples

WHOSE

To indicate or determine ownership	
huːz	Unspecified number | Countable | Both
Indicate ownership	I know **whose** car this is.
Determine ownership	**Whose** phone is this?

This determiner is mainly used to determine ownership by using it in questions and, to a lesser extent, to indicate that the ownership is known or is being stated. Note the difference between the determiner, which precedes a noun (**Whose** book is on my desk?) and the pronoun, used instead of the noun (**Whose** is this?). It is very commonly confused with the abbreviation **'who's'** (short for **who is**), which is used to ask for the name of an indicated person (**Who's** that girl?) rather than ownership. It is used in both noun clauses (I don't know **whose** it is) and adjective clauses (I am the father **whose** daughter you are dating). Another common use is to add extra information to something that has just been mentioned: 'Today I saw that man **whose** car you hit.'

Notes and examples

YOUR

Second person singular or plural's possessions, skills or attributes

jɔːr	One or more items	Both	Both
Possessions	Where is **your** house?		
Skills	**Your** artistic skills are very advanced.		
Attributes	**Your** feet are a bit smelly.		

This determiner is primarily used to confirm ownership. It differs from **whose** (see the previous determiner) in that the ownership is already known or assumed and **your** is used to confirm that ownership in a question (Is this **your** car?) or to attach or affirm conditions to the ownership in a statement (You have to tax **your** car). It is commonly confused with the abbreviation '**you're**' (**you are**), which relates to the <u>state</u> of the second person (You're very beautiful) rather than the <u>ownership</u> of something by the second person (Are you the owner of…?). It is also commonly misused as a possessive pronoun. For example, in the question 'Is this **your** pen?' **your** is a determiner; whereas, the pronoun use is 'Is this pen **yours**?

Notes and examples

ZERO

Not any *or* at the lowest point

ˈzɪə.rəʊ	None	Countable	Both
Not any	There is **zero** chance of us completing it.		
At the lowest point	Visibility is almost down to **zero** metres		

This determiner is usually used to emphasise that there is not a single item of the type described by the noun available. In that context it is viewed as being far stronger than 'no', and will be used to add emphasis to the fact that none are available, often inferring that the reason none exist is through negligence, incompetence, sloth or theft. 'No' is often used for concrete nouns (I have **no** fuel) and 'zero' would be used for abstract nouns (There is **zero** light in there) but writers often interchange the two. It is, unlike **no**, also emphasised in speech; for example, to convey a sense of anger or outrage. It is also used to say that something is moving down to a minimum, usually in order to add a sense of caution. Finally, It is often confused with the noun 'zero', which is a mathematical value represented by $1 - 1$.

Notes and examples

ENGLISH BOOK SHOP
WHERE YOU COME TO LEARN

The free companion website provides a number of useful tools. One of the most useful tools when working with verbs is the custom search facility. This tool allows you to type in, say, a verb structure, together with other keywords, and it then searches a number of high quality, international publications and newspapers to match your criteria. In the example below the verb structure "have been used" (note the "speech marks") together with the keyword "computers".

Phrase Search - enter a phrase in "commas" to see it in use

"have been used" + "computers"

Clicking the search button opened a pop up window on which the first entry was:

Are programs better than people at predicting reoffending ...
https://www.economist.com/.../are-programs-better-than-people-at-predicting -reoffending
Jan 17, 2018 ... IN AMERICA, computers have been used to assist bail and ...

Clicking on the link brought up the full article so the reference can be seen in the context in which it is used. The resulting paragraph looked like this:

IN AMERICA, computers have been used to assist bail and sentencing decisions for many years. Their proponents argue that the rigorous logic of an algorithm, trained with a vast amount of data, can make judgments about whether a convict will reoffend that are unclouded by human bias.

Source: The Economist - The full article can be found at:
https://www.economist.com/science-and-technology/2018/01/17/are-programs-better-than-people-at-predicting-reoffending

Using this tool and the dictionary on the site, you can search for any combination of tense structures and keywords to give you ideas on how you can structure your own sentences based on the results and the CORE colours. The website can be reached by using the QR code or the URL on the bottom of the page.

DETERMINER SELECTOR

A

DETERMINER SELECTOR

DETERMINER SELECTOR

DETERMINER SELECTOR

C

DETERMINER SELECTOR

D

DETERMINER SELECTOR

DETERMINER SELECTOR

DETERMINER SELECTOR

I

DETERMINER SELECTOR

L

M

DETERMINER SELECTOR

N

DETERMINER SELECTOR

O

P

DETERMINER SELECTOR

DETERMINER SELECTOR

DETERMINER SELECTOR

T

DETERMINER SELECTOR

U

V